mentoring in ACTION

2nd edition

a practical guide

david megginson, david clutterbuck, bob garvey, paul stokes & ruth garrett-harris

KOGAN PAGE

London and Philadelphia

Publisher's note

Every possible effort has been made to ensure that the information contained in this book is accurate at the time of going to press, and the publishers and authors cannot accept responsibility for any errors or omissions, however caused. No responsibility for loss or damage occasioned to any person acting, or refraining from action, as a result of the material in this publication can be accepted by the editor, the publisher or any of the authors.

First published in Great Britain in 1995 by Kogan Page Limited
Second edition, 2006

120 Pentonville Road
London N1 9JN
United Kingdom
www.kogan-page.co.uk

525 South 4th Street, #241
Philadelphia, PA 19147
USA

ISBN 0 7494 4496 7

British Library Cataloguing-in-Publication Data

A CIP record for this book is available from the British Library.

Library of Congress Cataloging-in-Publication Data

Mentoring in action : a practical guide for managers / David Megginson
...
[et al]. -- 2nd ed.
     p. cm.
  Rev. ed. of: Mentoring in action / David Megginson. 1995.
  Includes bibliographical references and index.
  ISBN 0–7494–4496–7
  1. Mentoring in business. I. Megginson, David, 1943- II. Megginson,
David, 1943- Mentoring in action.
HF5385.M43 2006
658.3'124--dc22

2005026147

Typeset by Saxon Graphic Ltd, Derby
Printed and bound in Great Britain by Creative Print and Design (Wales), Ebbw Vale

Contents

Acknowledgements

We are greatly indebted to our fellow mentoring enthusiasts who have provided the case studies that constitute Parts 2 and 3 of this book:

- Mike Allen is a founding director of Oakleigh Consulting Ltd, www.oakleigh.co.uk, and may be e-mailed at mikeallen@oakleigh.co.uk. Ray Hinchcliffe, CBE works for DfES in Sheffield and London.
- Peter Beck works with Clutterbuck Associates, South Africa and Leoni Van Wyk for Impala Platinum Ltd, South Africa.
- Liz Borredon is Chaire Managerial Competences, EDHEC Business School, Lille, France. Contact: liz.borredon@edhec.edu.
- Richard Field, OBE is an industrialist and consultant and can be contacted at richard@fieldenterprise.co.uk.
- Coral Gardiner is Learning Mentor Coordinator in Birmingham Education Service.
- Hilary Geber works at the Centre for Learning, Teaching and Development, University of the Witwatersrand, South Africa.
- Jonathan Gravells is an HR consultant who may be contacted at jonathan@fargoassociates.com.
- Zulfi Hussain works for BT and is a member of the Executive Board of the European Mentoring and Coaching Council. He is one of the 100 most influential people in Yorkshire and is also involved with Global Synergy Solutions, www.globalsynergysolutions.com. He can be contacted at zulfi@globalsynergysolutions.com.
- Colin Hawkins works for the East of England (Harlow) e-mentoring pilot project.

- Kate Kennett works as an associate consultant with the National Institute of Mental Health for England and as an independent consultant working in education, the NHS and the private sectors.

- John Lambert runs a mentoring and coaching consultancy, John Lambert Associates, and can be contacted at jlambert@baslow1.freeserve.co.uk.

- Kim Langridge works with the Greenwood Partnership; e-mail: Kim@greenwood-partnership.com; website: www.greenwood-partnership.com.

- Frank Lord is an entrepreneur and mentor.

- Lis Merrick runs a coaching and mentoring consultancy and may be contacted at lismerrick@coachmentoring.co.uk. She also works with Clutterbuck Associates and the Mentoring and Coaching Research Unit at Sheffield Hallam University. Rachel Tobbell is Mentoring Strategy Manager, UK Resource Centre for Women in Science, Engineering and Technology.

- Keith Metcalf lectures in the Faculty of Organisation and Management at Sheffield Hallam University. Eleanor Williams works as a solicitor for Capital Law in the area of unfair dismissal.

- Judy Morgan works for the Lantern Project.

- Kirsten M Poulsen is the founder of KMP & Partners, an international consulting network focused on leadership and talent development. Kirsten has a special interest in mentoring programmes and did a large research project in 2003–04 on the use of mentoring programmes in Scandinavia. See more at www.kmp-partners.com or contact Kirsten at kmp@kmp-partners.com.

- Tom Riddell was a member of the Executive and Organizational Development Team, HBOS.

- Chris Roebuck is Head of Strategic Mentoring and Coaching with UBS in Zurich, Switzerland.

- Jill Simpson works for the Youth Justice Board for England and Wales.

- Jonathan Wainwright lectures in the Faculty of Development and Society at Sheffield Hallam University.

- Imogen Wareing, The Growth Connection Pty Ltd, in Australia can be contacted via e-mail: iwareing@growconnect.com.au; website: www.growconnect.com.au.

David Megginson, d.f.megginson@shu.ac.uk
David Clutterbuck, david@clutterbuckassociates.co.uk
Bob Garvey, r.garvey@shu.ac.uk
Paul Stokes, p.k.stokes@shu.ac.uk
Ruth Garrett-Harris, r.garrett-harris@shu.ac.uk
Sheffield 2005

Part 1
The State of the Art

1

The Mentoring Framework

INTRODUCTION

Since the publication of our first edition in 1995 the world of mentoring has moved on. The same groups are still involved – everyone from those disadvantaged in seeking employment to professionals and directors. However, our knowledge and understanding of how to go about mentoring has deepened considerably.

We can now see that mentoring in an organization needs to be considered from a number of perspectives (see Figure 1.1). First we can think about how 'the mentoring way' (Garvey and Alred, 2000) impacts the *culture* of the organization. Then we can examine what needs to be done to make mentoring *schemes* work, and here our understanding of all the processes – recruitment, matching, training and so on, but particularly training for mentees and ongoing support and supervision for mentors – has deepened in the last 10 years. Next we can look at the individual mentoring *relationship* as it starts, blossoms and closes. Again the model we used in our first edition has been developed from four to five stages and each has been enriched as we have undertaken research on them. We have also become much more explicit about the frameworks that mentors and mentees can use for each of their sessions. Garvey's three-stage process, our elaboration of the GROW coaching model, and others offer guidance for new and experienced mentors in shaping their individual mentoring *episodes*. We have also enlarged the range of interventions that can be tried within the mentoring session and have collected and elaborated a significant range of *techniques* that participants in mentoring can try out. Finally, we are beginning to study and understand more about mentoring *moments* – about what it is that leads to transformation and change in the mentoring conversation or in the spaces between dialogues.

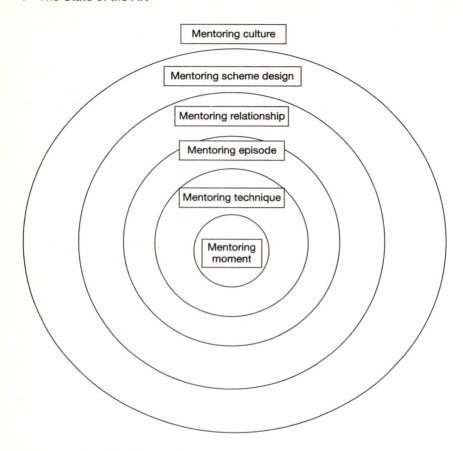

Figure 1.1   Levels of mentoring

These progressive layers of analysis offer the framework for the first part of this book and will be addressed after we turn our attention to the definition of mentoring.

We then conclude the chapter with a summary of the results of a recent survey that we have undertaken for Eastern England Development Agency (EEDA) on the benefits of mentoring and a piece on ethics and mentoring.

MENTORING DEFINED

We are still satisfied with our definition from the first edition of this book (Megginson and Clutterbuck, 1995: 13) that mentoring is 'off-line help by one person to another in making significant transitions in knowledge, work or thinking'. There is a lot in these few words, so we will highlight some of the features of our definition that point up the particular nature of the mentoring process.

First, we see mentoring as predominantly offline: that it is not normally the job of a line manager. A mentor is often more senior or experienced than the learner, but there are also cases of peer mentoring that work very successfully. A case in Part 3 of this book (Mike Allen and Ray Hinchcliffe, pp 190–195) highlights how these relationships between mentor and mentee shift over time in very long-term relationships. On occasion in formal schemes in work organizations (and more often in natural, spontaneous or informal mentoring relationships) the mentor is also the line manager. Where we find line managers successfully acting as mentors, they seem to have a highly developed capacity to separate out the two functions. The line responsibility is often about pressure for immediate results. The mentoring relationship tends more towards giving time and space for taking a wider view. Skilled mentors make these distinctions clear, even if they do not always formally say: 'This is now a mentoring session.' The message becomes clear as the meeting progresses.

There has been a long and largely sterile debate about the distinctions between mentoring and coaching. In a recent review of the literature (Clutterbuck and Megginson, 2005: 14–18) we noticed that both advocates of mentoring and advocates of coaching seem to value their own practice as being holistic and learner centred, while seeing the other as narrow and advice oriented. A healthier approach seems to us to be to specify the dimensions of the relationship, and where it stands on these. This approach was pioneered by Bob Garvey and is described in Part 3 of this book, pp 201–211).

One of the features of mentoring as we understand it is captured in our definition: it is about support in significant transitions. The mentor has a role to help the learner grasp the wider significance of whatever is happening, where at first sight it might appear trifling or insignificant.

A final feature of our definition is that mentoring is about one-to-one helping. There is an example in this book (Borredon, in Part 2, pp 85–93) of one-to-group helping. We leave it to our readers to decide whether this falls within the boundary of what they consider mentoring to be. The case is useful, because it is on the edge of the field and challenges us to consider our views on this matter.

MAKING A MENTORING CULTURE

There is virtually nothing written about making a mentoring culture. On the related topic of creating a coaching culture, we (Clutterbuck and Megginson, 2005) have recently written a book that builds on the small amount of largely impressionistic earlier literature and more particularly on the analysis of case studies of companies that are working towards this goal. In that book there are three case studies of organizations that emphasize mentoring rather than coaching, and the reader is referred to these for detailed cases of work in progress. The three cases in Chapter 9 of Clutterbuck and Megginson (2005) that are grounded in a mentoring approach are Janssen Pharmaceutica (J&J Europe), Scottish Executive and Walsall Council.

Lessons from these cases that offer a number of directions for making a mentoring culture are as follows:

- *Janssen Pharmaceutica (J&J Europe):*
  - link to business issues (cross-division cooperation, double number of executives in five years, organic growth);
  - match to meet these burning issues;
  - mentoring across sites;
  - develop those disadvantaged in employment, especially senior women;
  - long-term talent management focus (all relationships more than one year);
  - involve top management as project owners and mentors;
  - well-produced brochure to develop a common language;
  - mentees trained with mentors;
  - mentees in the driver's seat;
  - mentor is offline (balances short-term performance focus);
  - giving process feedback in mentor relationship develops this crucial skill for use elsewhere.
- *Scottish Executive:*
  - follows an open and evolving agenda;
  - focus on developmental mentoring;
  - focus on high priority of grades – others have access via web portal;
  - internet learning gateway – high-quality information;
  - grow the scheme organically with volunteers – Permanent Secretary sees it as part of being a good corporate citizen;
  - pace not forced – not compulsory or pushy;
  - robust process with clear scope and boundaries;
  - regular, light-touch supervision;
  - follow up central support by phone after matching;

- separate training for mentees;
- on top management's agenda;
- serves high-level culture change;
- no-fault call-off after first meeting – or later;
- transparent selection and matching (mentees decide degree of similarity or difference);
- mentees build 'change resilience' by getting hold of their own development;
- gives mentors thinking time;
- mentors build development skills and non-judgemental listening;
- trickle down to next grade for mentees who want to mentor;
- knowledge management helped by conversations across boundaries;
- senior leaders mentored externally;
- stories of successful relationships propagated.

- *Walsall Council:*
  - focused on change in climate from intimidation and bullying to trust and support;
  - burning issue was to build confidence and improve communications;
  - political leadership mentored by experienced politicians from other authorities;
  - senior management mentored first, then other managers;
  - mentoring aligned to new values and agreed vision;
  - after six months staff were more confident, relations were based on trust and integrity, and there was a clear vision for the future and high morale;
  - Walsall had become a safe place to work.

These schemes have the following high-level characteristics in common:

1. clear link to a business issue, where outcome is measured;
2. part of culture change process;
3. senior management involved as mentees and mentors;
4. link to long-term talent management established;
5. mentees in the driving seat;
6. light-touch development of individuals and scheme;
7. clear framework, publicized, with stories;
8. scheme design focused on business issues and change agenda.

These eight characteristics point to an agenda for those wishing to make a mentoring culture in their own organization. The bullet points above or the fuller stories in Clutterbuck and Megginson (2005) will fill in further details for those interested in implementing the shift to a mentoring culture.

PRINCIPLES OF SCHEME DESIGN

The broad perspective of mentoring culture is relatively new. Most writing about and practice of mentoring tends to focus on the mentoring scheme for a particular category of mentees. There are mentoring schemes in all sectors of society: public, private, small business, voluntary sector, education, retail, manufacturing, those disadvantaged in employment, people at risk of reoffending – the organization case studies in this book reflect this huge range. What becomes clear from our cases and elsewhere is that these schemes are extremely diverse in terms of purpose, scope, setting, activity and standards. However, there are certain issues that tend to present themselves in most schemes; these issues will form the bulk of the discussion in this section, which explores scheme purpose, evaluation, recruitment and selection, training and development, matching, supervision and standards.

Defining purpose

Mentoring schemes are developed in response to a need. As suggested above, these needs can vary hugely. For example, a large private sector business may have problems retaining key executives for longer than three months; alternatively, ex-offenders may find it difficult to gain employment or certain ethnic minorities within a public organization may find it difficult to get promoted beyond a certain level. All of these examples represent a need or gap that a mentoring scheme may be used to address. Given that mentoring schemes require resources (finance, effort, time, people), there needs to be a clear understanding of what is intended by the scheme. In other words, it is crucial that people involved understand from the outset what the scheme is there to do. If this is not the case, it has significant implications for evaluation (see 'Evaluation', below); after all, if it is not clear what is wanted, how is it possible to say whether the scheme is successful or not? One of the challenges raised by defining purpose is that the stakeholders (eg managers, employees, funders, community leaders, mentors and mentees) may not agree about what the purpose is. Indeed, lack of agreement/common understanding of purpose may make the scheme prone to failure in the eyes of many of the stakeholder groups due to the conflict and tensions that this may raise.

Evaluation

Whilst it may seem strange to deal with evaluation so early on in the discussion, it is important, given the exploration of purpose above, that all stakeholders have clear answers to the following questions at the start of the scheme:

1. How will I know whether the scheme has been successful or not?
2. What criteria will I use to make these judgements?
3. What measures will I use to assess the scheme against these criteria?

For example, if the stated scheme purpose is to get ex-offenders into employment, the scheme evaluator might need to know what sort of employment is deemed appropriate and what success percentages are hoped for/expected, as well as whether other qualitative factors, eg mentee self-confidence, might need to be taken into account. How these data are to be collected, analysed and presented needs to be factored into the scheme design from the outset. There are of course a number of methods of evaluation and which ones are used often depends on what assumptions key stakeholders (eg scheme funders) make about what is persuasive evidence; for some, this might be written accounts from mentees though, for others, only 'hard' statistical evidence of employment would be sufficient.

Recruitment and selection

Once key decisions about scheme purpose and evaluation have been made, other issues present themselves. Scheme organizers and designers then need to decide about who needs to be involved in the scheme. This might be broken down into several key issues:

- *Eligibility.* Who is eligible to be involved as a mentee? What are the criteria?
- *Credibility.* What characteristics, attributes, experience or knowledge does the mentor need to have, in order to be credible to the mentee?
- *Availability.* What is the likely availability for the scheme in terms of both mentors and mentees? Are there imbalances?
- *Motivation.* What is likely to motivate both mentors and mentees to be involved? What might be the other reasons (perhaps unhelpful) that might attract people to the scheme?

Once these questions about mentors and mentees have been addressed, the scheme organizer then needs to think about how the 'right people' might be recruited. Often the motivation question is crucial here; for example, in an inter-business scheme, how might those looking for financial gain be discouraged whilst those with the genuine desire to develop a mutually fulfilling mentoring relationship are encouraged?

In a situation where there is an oversupply of mentors and mentees, scheme organizers can be put in the difficult position of having to decide between people for entry to the scheme; this is another reason why clarity around purpose and the desired characteristics of mentors/mentees is so important. There may be several different stages to this selection process (screening via application, organization visit, police checks); there may be some selection activity at the mentoring training event itself.

Mentoring training and development

Mentoring training can fall into three broad categories (see Megginson and Stokes, 2004):

- a skills approach;
- developing the business case;
- conscious seeking out of each mentor's own way.

The skills approach focuses on specifically developing appropriate mentoring skills and behaviours within a mentoring conversation, eg asking appropriate open questions, checking out assumptions, and active listening.

The business case approach focuses on getting buy-in from the participants in terms of the values of the scheme and helping the participants to make sense of these values in the context of the organization or environment that they operate in. This raises key issues of power, culture and ownership in most interventions of this type.

The conscious seeking approach is learner centred and focuses on drawing out of all participants their existing skills and understanding of mentoring, and becoming more aware of these so as to be able to add to them.

Of course, it is likely that all schemes will contain elements of each, but it is important that conscious decisions are made with regards to the blend of these. It is also important to recognize that, although many mentoring schemes tend to focus on the mentor, the skills of the mentee are also very important. Skilled mentees are better able to draw what they want and need from mentors and are arguably better equipped to be able to cope with any weaknesses or deficiencies in mentors' skill sets.

Matching

One of the messiest and most difficult processes for a scheme organizer to manage is matching mentors and mentees. As the section 'Defining purpose' above revealed, what constitutes success for different stakeholders can vary considerably. There are a number of things to consider here:

- criteria for matching (stemming from purpose);
- mentor and mentee rapport;
- the balance between similarity and difference;
- choice;
- troubleshooting (see also 'Supervision', page 12).

The criteria for matching are critical and should arguably come from what the scheme is designed to achieve. For example, if a mentoring scheme is designed to connect farmers in remote locations with their counterparts in more populated locations, then clearly there is little benefit in connecting two farmers in remote locations within these parameters (though there may be other benefits in doing this). Also, the cultural background of the mentees may influence matching; for example, the parents of an Asian schoolgirl may prefer her to be matched with a same-sex mentor, possibly from a similar background (depending on scheme purpose).

However, set against these formal scheme requirements are other issues that may have a significant impact upon the success of a mentoring relationship and, therefore, a scheme. These include issues such as personal style and the chemistry between a mentor and mentee as well as issues around credibility. It may sometimes be important for the scheme organizer to compromise a little on the formal criteria to take account of these personal preferences. This raises the issues of choice and the balance between similarity and difference. One of the key principles of mentoring is that it is conducted within a spirit of voluntarism. In order to maximize participant engagement, the scheme organizer may wish to allow choice on both sides, ie mentors, as well as mentees, nominating whom they wish to work with. However, this raises significant challenges when these preferences do not fit with each other. For example, in an executive mentoring programme, most mentees may opt for the mentor who they believe gives them the most opportunity for career progression, eg the MD, and some may become disaffected when, due to time constraints, they need to be matched with someone else. In this case, the scheme organizer may wish to minimize the mentee's choice; this route may not be possible or may irrevocably damage relationships in a community mentoring programme (see Colley's (2003) work on mentoring for social inclusion for an interesting account of mentee agency).

Allowing choice and taking account of personal rapport may also raise some interesting challenges for effective development of the mentees on a scheme. If mentees and mentors are too similar, there may be relatively little added value for mentees in terms of their knowledge, awareness or capability due to the lack of 'stretch' in the relationship. On the other hand, as suggested above, if mentors and mentees are too far apart then there is a risk of scheme breakdown due to a perceived lack of empathy, credibility and motivation in both directions.

One of the dangers in mentoring schemes is that, when matching occurs, this can be regarded as an administrative function that can be entrusted to an administrator to perform. This can lead to problems if mentors and mentees then continue to approach the administrator as challenges occur, resulting in an unfortunate conflation of scheme organizer, administrator and supervisor roles that places immense pressure on someone who may not be best equipped to deal with that pressure. It is therefore important that supervision – rather like evaluation – is something that is set up to deal with these particular issues.

Supervision

Supervision is an area of mentoring that is experiencing significant growth and development (see Hawkins and Shohet (2002) and Merrick and Stokes (2003) for a more detailed account of these issues). However, just in terms of scheme design, it is an important issue. Inevitably, as in all personal relationships, problems and difficulties will occur. For example, an executive mentor may feel that her mentee is unresponsive and is not benefiting from the relationship and she (the mentor) may be considering ending the relationship. A mentoring supervision process, ie pairing a mentor with a supervisor, may enable the mentor to resolve some of these issues outside the mentoring relationship and, as a result, be more resourceful for the mentee. Supervision can also be a useful quality assurance process for organizations and community, although this does rather depend on how public and open (Megginson and Clutterbuck, 1995) the scheme is in terms of its orientation. Furthermore, mentoring can raise lots of issues, eg countertransference (see Lee (2003) for an exploration of this), for the mentor, and supervision has the potential to raise the mentor's awareness of these issues and, again, make mentors more resourceful from a scheme point of view.

Scheme organizers must make some key decisions about mentoring supervision, which include:

■ Who does the supervision and what skills and qualifications etc should they have?

■ When should supervision be introduced as a process?

■ Who should receive supervision?

Various occupational groups from the helping professions, eg counsellors, psychologists and psychotherapists, have periodically criticized non-therapist mentors for their lack of awareness of or training in psychological or therapeutic professional skills. It has been argued that there is the potential for damage as a result of not paying attention to issues such as transference, countertransference, parallel processing, projection etc. Therefore, there are arguments to support mentors being supervised by professionals trained in these areas. On the other hand, it can also be said that everybody needs a mentor (Clutterbuck, 1985), even the mentors in a particular scheme or initiative. Issues around recruitment and selection, matching and rapport apply to the supervisory relationship every bit as much as to a mentoring one. However, a very important question that is often neglected in schemes concerns whether mentees themselves need some sort of support or supervision. Whilst they are helpees, mentees may need some support in terms of how they conduct themselves in a mentoring relationship once the initial training period is over. There are of course other modes of support that both mentees and mentors might use as part of a scheme:

■ team mentoring;

■ action learning sets;

■ other mentoring relationships;

■ gatherings/scheme meetings.

In some schemes (eg Expert Patient Mentoring in the NHS), mentoring occurs as part of a group rather than within traditional dyadic mentoring relationships; hence this can enable mentors and mentees to draw support and strength from a range of perspectives to supplement their practice. Similarly, action learning sets have the potential to enable a similar sort of support in conjunction with mentoring schemes as well as other sorts of developmental relationships, eg peer mentoring, co-mentoring, coaching, counselling. Finally, on some schemes, participant meetings have been seen as an opportunity to offer support and encouragement to participants as they engage in their mentoring practice.

Standards

As suggested in the previous section, mentoring theory and practice have a number of stakeholders: clients, practitioners, professional bodies, academic institutions, consultancies, mentors and mentees. As a result, there are an increasing number of stakeholders attempting to define a set of standards for the area, which can then be used to compare schemes against. These include:

- professions and professional bodies, eg Chartered Institute of Personnel and Development, British Psychological Society;
- commercial standards, eg International Standards for Mentoring Programmes in Employment;
- specialist and network organizations, eg National Mentoring Network, European Mentoring and Coaching Council;
- university qualifications, eg Oxford Brookes University, Sheffield Hallam University, University of Hertfordshire.

Scheme organizers must make decisions about which, if any, standards their scheme will adhere to and how the accreditation will be funded and managed. As the issue of accrediting mentors becomes more prevalent, scheme participants may start to become more aware of how their skills are being accredited and perhaps more discerning about where they apply their efforts.

Conclusions

Mentoring schemes are extremely diverse. However, there is a range of issues – purpose, evaluation, recruitment and selection, training and development, matching, supervision and standards – that have to be addressed each time a mentoring scheme is established, whether that be in a school, a community, a private sector business or any other sort of organization or system. The better prepared the scheme organizer is placed to answer these questions, the more likely is the scheme to succeed in its own terms. The scheme examples in this book represent the very different ways various scheme organizers have chosen to answer those questions.

THE SHAPE OF A MENTORING RELATIONSHIP

The nature of the mentoring relationship is dynamic, in the sense that it:

- will be different according to the circumstances, purpose and personalities involved;
- evolves over time;
- may take and adjust its shape along a spectrum defined by two very different philosophies or models of mentoring.

The effect of circumstances

Some of the factors that influence circumstance include:

- The social environment in which the relationship occurs. For example, mentoring people in prison is likely to have a very different set of relationship dynamics from those in a programme supporting high-flyers in a multinational company.
- The level of formality. Is it an ad hoc, instinctive pairing of two people, or part of a structured (supported) programme?
- The gap in age, influence, experience, ability and so on of the participants.
- The expected and actual duration of the relationship, which may be from a few months to many years.
- The degree of rapport felt between the participants (which may change over time).
- The extent and nature of the support that the mentor may be able to provide and that the mentee is seeking.
- The motivation of both mentor and mentee to achieve change (in circumstance or self) through the mentoring relationship.

All of these factors are likely to have an impact on the expectations and behaviours of both mentor and mentee, and on the dynamic interaction between those expectations and behaviours. As in any other intense relationship, every interaction creates waves, which may be positive or negative. The oscillations of these waves can reinforce both positive and negative emotions or, in rare cases, cancel each other out to produce white noise. Managing expectations and equipping participants with the skills and knowledge to apply appropriate behaviours is therefore fundamental to the success of both relationships and programmes.

The success of the relationship may not depend on the organizational context, however. Current research by one of the authors (Clutterbuck) finds no significant correlation between how supportive the organization is towards mentoring and either positive or negative experiences of the mentors and mentees. As Ragins, Cotton and Miller (2000) have observed in research in the United States, the quality of the relationship – whether it is informal or part of a formal programme – is the critical factor in relationship success.

Evolution over time

The temporal dynamics of the relationship have been explored by a number of researchers and writers. Although they differ on the detail of the evolutionary stages of a relationship, these observers are generally agreed that there is a period in which the relationship gels and where rapport and its constituent elements – particularly trust – are established; another where the relationship assumes a greater sense of direction and purpose; and a period in which the relationship either comes to a close or metamorphoses into a supportive friendship. These phases are not necessarily neat and tidy; they may overlap and present no clear transition point. Yet the sense of gradual maturing of both the relationship and the individuals within it is essential to sustaining the relationship.

Contrasting models of mentoring

The emergence of two contrasting models of mentoring has been explored elsewhere by the authors (Gibb and Megginson, 1993; Clutterbuck, 2004). Often referred to as sponsorship mentoring versus developmental mentoring, these models are based on different assumptions, summarized in Table 1.1. The language used emphasizes these differences – for example, the use of 'protégé' in sponsorship mentoring and 'mentee' or 'mentoree' in developmental mentoring, although this may not be consistent.

In practice, both of these models can be much less clear cut than their idealized version would suggest. It may be difficult, for example, for a mentor completely to avoid using any influence on behalf of a mentee if he or she is asked for an opinion of the mentee's general abilities. Equally, sponsorship mentors sometimes do learn from their protégés, even if they do not see this as a substantive objective of the relationship. In a dynamic relationship, the boundaries of what is appropriate will vary according to factors such as national or religious culture, or how removed the participants are from each other's area of work. And multinational companies often find that they need to adapt their global mentoring programmes to account for national or regional cultural factors that predispose people to a mixture of elements of both models.

Maintaining relationship quality

Although the dynamic nature of the relationship creates opportunities for a great deal of variation in how people approach their roles, certain factors do seem to be generic in terms of relationship quality. These include:

■ *Goal clarity.* There needs to be a distinct sense of purpose to the relationship. Current research by one of us (Clutterbuck) indicates that relationship satisfaction and relationship quality, as perceived by both mentor and mentee, are closely correlated with the mentee having specific and/or individual learning goals, but that there is no such

Table 1.1   Sponsorship versus developmental mentoring

Sponsorship	*Developmental*
The mentor is more influential and hierarchically senior.	The mentor is more experienced in issues relevant to the mentee's learning needs (perhaps life in general).
'The mentor gives, the protégé receives and the organization benefits' (Scandura *et al*, 1996).	A process of mutual growth.
The mentor actively champions and promotes the cause of the protégé.	The mentor helps the mentee do things for him- or herself.
The mentor gives the protégé the benefit of his or her wisdom.	The mentor helps the mentee develop his or her own wisdom.
The mentor steers the protégé through the acquisition of experience and personal resources.	The mentor helps the mentee towards personal insights from which he or she can steer his or her own development.
The primary outcome or objective is career success.	The primary outcome or objective is personal development, from which career success may flow.
Good advice is central to the success of the relationship.	Good questions are central to the success of the relationship.
The social exchange emphasizes loyalty.	The social exchange emphasizes learning.

correlation with him or her adopting generic goals. Nor does there seem to be any significant correlation between organizational goals and relationship success. It is therefore an important part of the mentor's role to help mentees articulate what they want to achieve and how the relationship may help them do so.

▪ *The ability to create and manage rapport.* Hale (2000) and others have demonstrated the importance of a core alignment of values between mentor and mentee, both in terms of initial attraction or liking and in sustaining the relationship over time. However, relationships that have the greatest rapport may not be the most fertile opportunities for learning – the two partners may be too alike to provide the level of challenge and the difference of perspective that sparks insightful dialogue. Rapport building therefore encompasses the skills of accepting and valuing difference as a fundamental learning resource.

▪ *Understanding of the role and its boundaries.* All of the case studies in this book have engaged mentors and usually mentees in at least initial workshops to develop role clarity and basic skills in the role. Without this clarity, it is very easy for mentors to relapse into what they know best – a managerial, directive style. Not only does that reduce the benefit to the mentee; it also means that mentors will probably not achieve any learning for themselves. The better they understand the role, the more easily the mentor and mentee will be able to recognize and manage its boundaries. A sense of conscious incompetence about issues outside the boundaries (for example, needs for therapeutic counselling) is an essential prerequisite for the effective mentor.

▪ *Voluntarism.* It may seem obvious that the relationship will work best if the participants want to be there, but it is very easy to create situations where one or both participants are reluctant volunteers. This is a significant issue for some programmes involving senior managers (who feel obliged to demonstrate their people development credentials) and for programmes involving young people at risk, where a teenager may have given up on creating trusting relationships with any adult but sees the mentoring meeting as a 'least worst' solution compared to a session with a social worker! Colley (2003) has researched the issues relating to the reluctant or semi-reluctant participant, and provides some valuable insights.

▪ *Basic competencies on the part of mentor and mentee.* Both mentor and mentee need to bring some skills and attributes to the relationship. Ideally, they should also aim to improve those skills over time through the learning dialogue. The range of mentor and mentee competencies is discussed comprehensively in the book *The Situational Mentor* (Clutterbuck and Lane, 2004), which presents a variety of analyses and perspectives, dependent on different programme circumstances and models of mentoring. The common factors, however, include the communication skills to articulate problems and ideas, to listen and to challenge constructively; the ability to be honest with oneself and the other partner and to reflect upon what is said, both at the time and subsequently; and a capacity for empathy.

▪ *Proactive behaviours by mentee and developmental behaviours by the mentor.* David Clutterbuck's current research indicates that both the mentor and the mentee gain more from the relationship if the mentee takes the initiative and if he or she expects developmental behaviours from the mentor. At the same time, developmental behaviours by the mentor are closely correlated with relationship quality and satisfaction by both parties. The more passive the mentee and the more directive the mentor, the less successful the relationship – a conclusion supported by other researchers, such as Engstrom (1997).

■ *Measurement and review*. When mentor and mentee take the time and effort to review their relationship and what is going well and less well, they have an opportunity to enhance the openness of the continuing dialogue, assess how to make the relationship more valuable and reaffirm their commitment to the process. Many programmes now encourage participants to schedule such discussions at regular intervals. Measurement from outside the relationship can also have a positive effect – being asked to complete a short questionnaire for the programme coordinator, directly or via an independent survey resource, stimulates the mentor and mentee to re-examine what they are doing against what they have learned about good practice.

HOW MENTORING RELATIONSHIPS EVOLVE

Once they get started, mentoring relationships tend to follow a common pathway of evolution. How each stage – and the transition from one to the next – is managed may have a significant influence on the quality of the relationship.

Kram (1985) identified four stages for informal, sponsorship-oriented mentoring. Organizationally supported developmental mentoring tends to fit into a five-stage model, as follows (see Figure 1.2).

Stage 1 is the rapport-building stage. Here, mentor and mentee explore whether they are able to work together. The ability to establish rapport depends on a number of factors, including:

■ their perception of alignment of values, especially at a personal level;
■ the degree of mutual respect;
■ broad agreement on the purpose of the relationship;
■ alignment of expectations about roles and behaviours (for example, that both expect the mentee to be proactive in managing the relationship).

Achieving this level of rapport can only happen through dialogue – an open exchange that relaxes the typical barriers between (comparative) strangers. If rapport does not occur – and personality differences may prevent it – it is incumbent on both parties to explore the issue, rather than pretend it does not exist. The result may be a rematch or an understanding of the learning potential from someone who is different. Well managed, rematches often result in a continued dialogue between the individuals, which can sometimes lead at a later date to an informal resumption of the mentoring relationship as the mentee's needs change.

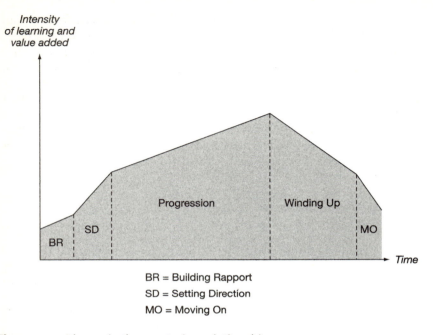

Figure 1.2   Phases in the mentoring relationship

Stage 2 addresses goal setting. Although the initiation of the relationship involves at least a sense of purpose, at this stage mentor and mentee clarify and refine what the relationship should achieve on both sides. They begin the process of linking the medium- to long-term goals with what happens on a day-to-day basis. The process of rapport building continues as they explore tactical responses to some of the issues raised.

Stage 3 is the core period. While rapport building and goal setting can often be accomplished in a few meetings, the progress-making stage typically lasts at least six months. Mentor and mentee become more relaxed about challenging each other's perceptions, explore issues more deeply and experience mutual learning. The mentee takes more and more of the lead in managing the relationship and the mentoring process.

Stage 4 – winding up – occurs when the mentee has achieved a large part of his or her goals or feels equipped with the confidence, plans and insights to continue the journey under his or her own steam. For either mentor or mentee to seek to hang on to the formal relationship is likely to result in an unhealthy dependency or counter-dependency. Planning for a good ending is critical if both parties are to emerge from the relationship with a positive perception of the experience. Winding up (reviewing and celebrating what has been achieved) is almost always more effective than winding down (drifting apart) (Clutterbuck and Megginson, 2001, 2004).

Stage 5 is about moving on and reformulating the relationship, typically into a friendship, in which both parties can use each other on an ad hoc basis as a sounding board and source of networking contacts.

Moving from one stage to another is not necessarily a clearly defined step. There is often a grey area between and they may overlap, particularly at the early stages (Bullis and Bach, 1989). Mentors and mentees need to be sensitive to the stage of relationship development and adapt their behaviours accordingly.

FRAMEWORKS FOR A MENTORING EPISODE

The mentoring process

The whole point of the mentoring process is to create a reflective environment in which the mentee can address issues of career, personal growth, the management of relationships and the management of situations, both current and predicted. It is a bubble of concentrated conversational energy in the soup of a working environment, which may often be over- or under-stimulating.

The role of the programme is to support the mentoring process, and that in turn demands effective programme processes. These are covered in some detail in the International Standards for Mentoring Programmes in Employment.

In practice, this means that there are four main components to the mentoring process:

- the formal, organizational structure, if there is any;
- the relationship agreement;
- the learning conversation;
- what mentor and mentee do as a result of the learning conversation.

Organization leaders and scheme organizers have a range of choices they can make about the purpose of the programme, how it will measure success and how it will support participants. It can adopt a highly interventionist or a laissez-faire approach, and a centralist or decentralizing structure. A critical question here is the extent to which the relationship is enhanced by the degree of support given and, in spite of a considerable weight of academic literature on formality and informality, there are no clear answers. It is to be expected that different programme purposes may require different levels of support and that the characteristics of each learning dyad will also be relevant.

The relationship agreement (sometimes referred to as a contract) is the result of mentor and mentee discussions about how the relationship will be conducted. This may cover, for example, frequency, duration and location of meetings, expectations about contact between meetings, issues of confidentiality, boundaries, expected behaviours and ethical factors. How formal this agreement should be is a matter of organizational and / or individual preference. A critical question appears to be: 'Do mentor and mentee find it helpful in managing their relationship?'

The learning conversation in turn can be seen as having five component parts:

- *Reaffirmation.* Mentor and mentee spend time at the beginning re-establishing the personal connectedness, before getting down to business. This is often more than the usual social niceties. In a well-established mentoring relationship, there is a reaffirmation of mutual respect, a recognition of emotional state and a demonstration of interest in the other person as a person that go beyond client–helper interaction.

- *Identifying the issue.* Mentor and mentee spend energy articulating what the issue for discussion is, why it is important (and why now) and what outcome the mentee is looking for from the dialogue to come. This is also an opportunity for the mentee to indicate any preferences for *how* he or she would like the mentor to help.

- *Building mutual understanding.* The mentor encourages the mentee to explore the issue in depth, by asking questions that stimulate insight. The aim of the questions is for both of them to understand more clearly what is involved, how the problem comes about, what its dynamics are and so on. The mentor is careful at this stage to avoid either entering solution mode or making close analogies with his or her own experience. When both parties feel they have bottomed out the issues, the mentor may summarize both to think out loud and to check that they have achieved mutual understanding.

- *Exploring alternative solutions.* The mentor and mentee allow themselves to be creative about possible ways forward, developing a range of options from which the mentee eventually chooses or decides which to take away for reflection. In the former case, the mentor may help the mentee set deadlines and consider how they will know when the mentee has achieved what he or she is now setting out to do.

- *Final check.* The mentor encourages the mentee to review what he or she is going to do and why, and what the mentee has learned about both the situation in question and about him- or herself. This provides a check on the level of mutual understanding and places the responsibility for what happens next firmly on the mentee's shoulders.

Between mentoring sessions, the mentee in particular needs to reflect on what has been said and to relate individual, day-to-day issues with the broad developmental themes that overlie the learning conversations. The mentor, too, may find it useful to reflect upon his or her own practice in the role. This is especially important as the relationship reaches the point where it is time for the mentee to move on. Preparation for a good ending is as important as preparation for a good beginning (Clutterbuck and Megginson, 2004).

The three-stage process

One of the classic models for the mentoring conversation is the three-stage process, derived from Egan's work (1994) and applied to mentoring in Alred, Garvey and Smith (1998). It is a process that gives shape to a mentoring session. It is very simple to remember, but there are a few challenges in its operation.

The process is:

The idea is that, through appropriate exploration, new understanding is gained and then actions can be considered in relation to the understanding.

In the first stage, the mentor may have a range of strategies:

- Take the lead to open the discussion.
- Pay attention to the relationship and develop it.
- Clarify aims and objectives and discuss ground rules.
- Support and counsel.

The methods used include:

- questioning;
- listening;
- negotiating an agenda.

In the second stage, the mentor may have other strategies including:

- Support and counsel.
- Offer feedback.
- Coach and demonstrate skills.

The methods employed include:

- listening and challenging;
- using both open and closed questions;
- helping to establish priorities;
- summary;
- helping identify learning and development needs;
- giving information and advice;
- sharing experience and story telling.

In the third stage, the mentor may use the following strategies:

- Examine options and consequences.
- Attend to the relationship.
- Negotiate and develop an action plan.

The methods may include:

- encouraging new ideas and creativity;
- helping in decisions and problem solving;
- agreeing action plans;
- monitoring and reviewing.

The process rarely moves in a straight line from stage one to stage three. More often, in use, the conversation moves about between all the stages. There can be a temptation to get to the action as quickly as possible, but often the quality and the commitment to the action are dependent on the thoroughness of stages one and two. Summarizing regularly can help to establish the boundaries between each stage and move the conversation either on or back into the previous stage.

The three-stage process can be viewed as a map of mentoring. A map shows the way and helps us to plan a route and it helps us to find where we are when we get lost. The three-stage process fits within the five phases outlined in Figure 1.2 and can be used to address each of those phases. It will be used several times over during the progression phase.

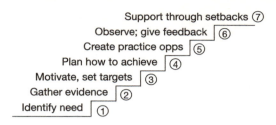

Figure 1.3   The seven steps of mentoring

It is helpful to share the process within the relationship so that both the mentor and the mentee understand what is happening. Doing this also gives the mentoring pair a language or a shorthand to talk about their conversation. Perhaps the most interesting thing about the three-stage process is that, with practice, it becomes very natural and does not seem like an intrusive technique.

An alternative process that can be used is the seven-stage model outlined in Figure 1.3. Readers familiar with the coaching literature will notice, embedded in this model, the GROW model of goals, reality, options and will (Whitmore, 2003). Whether the process has three stages or four or seven, the important issue for mentors is to have a model that they are happy with and can use as a 'container' for the anxiety that both mentors and mentees can feel in dealing with the ambiguities of work and life. This holding of the reflective space is discussed more fully in Clutterbuck and Megginson (1999: 8–10). Suffice it to say here that, if the mentee is assured that the mentor has a 'way of going on' that will enable the pair to make progress, then the mentee need not worry about the shape of the discussion, and this can sink beneath the level of his or her consciousness. The mentor, liberated from concerns about where to go next in the broad flow of the conversation, can concentrate on what the mentee is saying now, and help him or her to use that to contribute to a chosen direction for future action.

TECHNIQUES IN MENTORING

Techniques can be related to other terms in an approximate hierarchy:

Techniques are similar to models, but in addition have a process for using the model attached to them. So a model may be embedded within a technique.

Techniques fall within processes but, whereas processes are relatively content free and may cover a framework for a whole mentoring session, techniques describe the context in which they may be used and the purposes that they might serve.

We have argued that, in training mentors, it is best for each mentor to develop his or her own process (Clutterbuck and Megginson, 1999: 149–50). And in mentoring it seems crucial that we have 'a way of going on' that extends before the use of one technique and beyond the end of it. The three-stage process and others discussed above fit this bill.

What is a technique?

We adopt Megginson and Clutterbuck's (2005) definition of a technique as 'a process to assist a mentee to address a specific purpose within a particular context as part of an ongoing development relationship'.

Arguments against techniques

The use of techniques may not seem to be in the spirit of mentoring. Some will see them as:

- helping-by-numbers, where the user does not have the knowledge or skill to use the technique appropriately;
- having a premeditated quality that goes against the spirit of mentoring where the best tools are those that are invented on the spur of the moment;
- devices to be used to shape the mentees' understanding and action, where the key role of the mentor is to help mentees make these decisions for themselves;
- based on an atomistic model of learning. They can be seen to work by breaking a complex task into simple components. There is no guarantee that such a procedure enables one to reconstruct the whole from the parts.

Arguments for techniques

On the other hand, techniques are seen to be helpful in enabling mentors to be:

- more helpful than they otherwise would, in a wider range of situations than before;

- more able to address intractable situations or reluctant learners, knowing that they have a way of going on in these situations;
- less anxious and more at peace in making their intervention, thus enabling the learner the better to benefit from it.

How to use techniques well

For mentors to realize these benefits they can:

- use techniques that they have practised in training or with sympathetic friends;
- have lots of techniques rather than only a few;
- make a habit of being explicit both to themselves and to those they help about the technique and its intended outcomes. This in itself can lead to a freer, more equal negotiation of what to do and how to do it in the relationship.

Where to use techniques

In Megginson and Clutterbuck (2005), techniques are outlined addressing the following issues:

1. establishing and managing the coaching or mentoring relationship;
2. setting goals;
3. clarifying and understanding situations;
4. building self-knowledge;
5. understanding other people's behaviour;
6. dealing with road blocks;
7. stimulating creative thinking;
8. deciding what to do;
9. committing to action;
10. managing the learner's own behaviours;
11. building wider networks of support, influence and learning;
12. reviewing and ending the coaching or mentoring relationship;
13. building your own techniques.

It is good practice to enable mentors through initial training and continuing support to build a portfolio of techniques to address each of these areas. They may come from texts and training manuals, but they can also come from mentors reviewing their own work with their mentees.

EMERGING UNDERSTANDING OF MENTORING MOMENTS

Mentoring is about transition, change and transformation. Many of the cases described in this book touch on these issues. Transition, change and transformation can happen gradually but, at other times, may happen in moments of time. We could call these 'eureka' moments. In Kim Langridge's case in Part 3 (pages 220–224), he refers to the moment as a 'click'.

We are successful as a species because, as Emler and Heather (1980) suggest, 'we cheat; we tell each other the answers'. Mentoring conversations are about exploring problems, issues and answers. These are natural conversations that we are used to participating in almost from birth. We are social beings and learn through conversation in a social context.

Time is an inescapable dimension of human experience. Any satisfactory account of how we are and how we behave must attend to the ways in which our lives are constructed in time and recognize that our lives are changing constantly.

The way we live our lives could be viewed in relation to our pasts. Our 'pasts' are in our 'presents' but we are not often aware of this – we simply get on with our lives. There are times when the 'past' confronts our 'present' and this tends to happen in 'moments' of awareness or significance. To explore this perspective we suggest three propositions:

- *Proposition 1.* We could live in the past by falling back on to traditionalism. We could view our lives as something fixed in time and this may have the effect of making us resistant to change. In this state, our basic reference point for action in the present is our tradition. Here, it is often the case that the tacit assumptions that frame everything we do in an uncritical celebration of the past act as a guide to how we are in the present and the future – trusted paths dominate.

- *Proposition 2.* We may reject our past or rewrite our histories. We could devalue our past, making it worthless. We could apportion blame, attach guilt or have a 'rose-tinted' perspective on our histories. This attitude often prevents us from learning from the past or encourages us to suppress its continuing influence on present actions.

- *Proposition 3.* Thirdly, we may attempt to build on our past by understanding it profoundly. We could do this through reflection and through critical awareness and dialogue. To do this requires openness and a willingness to be critical, to learn and to change. It invites us to take risks. For some of us, it will be a painful realization that cherished beliefs are misplaced and that current attitudes have been unhelpful.

Moments

We believe that Proposition 3 offers us the most potential to respond appropriately to a moment. Moments happen. We cannot control the moments, only our responses to them. We respond to these moments by referencing our past. As we cannot predict from where or when these moments happen, we can only prepare for our response by understanding our past. Mentoring can be viewed as a moment in time when our pasts confront our presents, and mentoring can prepare us for dealing with the moments.

We cannot realize our futures without having a firm and critical understanding of our pasts. The writer Salman Rushdie (1998) expresses this point when he says, 'Those who do not have the power of the story that dominates their lives – power to retell it, rethink it, deconstruct it, joke about it, and change it as times change – truly are powerless because they cannot think new thoughts.'

Mentoring can help us to explore our story, think new thoughts and realize a new future. Mentoring gives us the opportunity not to be condemned to repeat our pasts.

Research into mentoring conversations

The European Mentoring and Coaching Council Research Committee is supporting a collaborative project, involving 10 academics from three countries with many different research strategies, which seeks to understand transformations that occur in one-to-one development conversations.

The researchers are recognizing that it is often impossible to specify when the moment of transformation occurs, and indeed it may not be in the conversation itself, but on reflection in the space between meetings. One important way in which learning does occur during dialogue is in the negotiated understandings that emerge. Learning can be said to occur by the act of changing a customary way of viewing the world or people in it and, in the safe environment of the mentoring conversation, trying out a new view. For this process to occur and to embed it is useful that:

- Mentors negotiate their way through the conversation, bringing into awareness what is going on.
- Both parties seek to influence the direction of the conversation, and do this overtly.
- Both mentor and mentee reflect upon the conversation and seek to make sense of it and to share their sense making. Mentors can do the sense making in supervision sessions.

- They make sense of the conversation using models, theories and frameworks that may be implicit, but this reflective practice offers an opportunity to make them explicit. The theories can be formal ones learned from study, or informal ones derived from life's experiences.
- They review the sense that they made of previous sessions at the beginning of each new meeting.

This research is continuing at the time of writing and will be reported more fully at European Mentoring and Coaching Council annual conferences.

BENEFITS OF MENTORING

In a recent commissioned study (Garvey and Garrett-Harris, 2005), researchers in the Mentoring and Coaching Research Unit at Sheffield Hallam University looked at the benefits of mentoring across all sectors – public, private, large, small, voluntary and not-for-profit. The study looked at over 100 research papers from the United States and Europe. The researchers classified the benefits into four broad categories:

- business performance and policy implementation;
- motivational benefits;
- knowledge and skills development;
- managing change and succession.

'Business performance' is widely interpreted and includes 'performance' in any sector.

The study showed that the majority of cited benefits relate to the mentee but with the 'business' (broadly defined) and the mentor benefits not too far behind:

- benefits for the mentee – 40 per cent;
- benefits for the 'business' – 33 per cent;
- benefits for the mentor – 27 per cent.

It is not surprising that the category with the most reported benefits is the mentee – after all, mentees are seen as the intended beneficiaries. What is surprising is the closeness of the percentage number of citations for the 'business' and the mentor. This suggests that mentoring activity is beneficial for all stakeholders.

The categories of benefit break down in percentage number of citations as follows:

- motivational benefits – percentage of total citations 33 per cent;
- business performance and policy implementation benefits – percentage of total citations 30 per cent;
- knowledge and skills development benefits – percentage of total citations 24 per cent;
- managing change and succession benefits – percentage of total citations 13 per cent.

Again, it is not surprising that the motivational benefits are in the majority. However, the closeness of the citations in the business performance and policy implementation category is interesting and provides evidence for decision makers in all sectors that mentoring is good for the individuals and good for the host organization in terms of performance and the achievement of business policy imperatives.

When ranking the benefits for all three stakeholders they break down as follows:

- *Mentee:*
  - improved performance and productivity;
  - career opportunity and advancement;
  - improved knowledge and skills;
  - greater confidence and well-being.
- *Mentor:*
  - improved performance;
  - greater satisfaction, loyalty and self-awareness;
  - new knowledge and skills;
  - leadership development.
- *Business:*
  - staff retention and improved communication;
  - improved morale, motivation and relationships;
  - improved business learning.

Problems with mentoring

The researchers also point out that a few writers mention some potential problems with mentoring. These problems include:

■ fostering elitism;

■ excluding the socially different;

■ replicating management behaviour rather than changing it;

■ maintaining the 'status quo' based on 'accumulation of advantage';

■ replicating and sustaining exploitative hierarchical systems;

■ manipulation.

Some research suggests that these problems manifest themselves under certain conditions and in certain types of organization. For example, in 'fast tracking, career oriented schemes' in large organizations, some of these negative effects are more likely. These effects are less likely in 'developmental mentoring' environments.

The variable conditions the researchers identified are:

■ the social context (culture, climate, type of business, values etc);

■ the purpose of the mentoring;

■ the skills of the mentor and mentee;

■ attitudes and values of the mentor and mentee;

■ training and support for the mentor and mentee;

■ formal schemes vs informal, natural mentoring;

■ amount of time given to mentoring and length of relationship;

■ scheme design;

■ human 'chemistry';

■ stakeholders' understanding of the mentoring process;

■ recognition within the 'business' of the legitimacy of mentoring;

■ recognition that learning is important;

■ evaluation/research methodology.

It is therefore important to consider the combinations of elements that contribute to effective mentoring in any research or evaluation.

Conditions for success in mentoring

The researchers state that there is broad agreement in the literature as to the conditions needed to realize the benefits of mentoring. The literature (and indeed the evidence of the case studies in this book) suggests a range of issues that need to be considered as follows:

■ *Voluntarism.* Mentoring is essentially a voluntary activity. The degree of voluntarism will depend on the situation and the circumstances. In some cases, putting people together and asking them to contract for a specific number of meetings (eg three) before they review the relationship can be helpful. It can also assist the process if both parties agree on a 'no-fault divorce clause' as a safeguard.

■ *Training.* Both the mentor and the mentee will need some orientation towards the scheme. This may involve a skills training programme for both mentors and mentees. Sometimes this can be done with them together in the same programme.

■ *Ongoing support.* Mentors often need support. This may take the form of a mentor support group or one-to-one mentoring supervision – a mentor to the mentor. There is also benefit in mentors from different sectors coming together to share practice and experiences. The purpose of bringing mentors together is to discuss mentoring process issues, debrief mentors, develop skills and improve understanding.

■ *Matching.* It is important to have a clear matching process to which the participants subscribe. It is also important to establish a 'no-fault divorce clause' after, say, the first three meetings.

■ *Establishing reviewable ground rules.* It is important to clarify the boundaries of the relationship at the start. Garvey's (1994) 'Dimensions Framework' is helpful here.

■ *Ongoing review.* Recent research from the United States (Neilson and Eisenbach, 2003) concludes that the most important factor in successful outcomes to mentoring is regular feedback and review within the relationship about the relationship. Establishing ground rules at the start can facilitate this process.

■ *Whose agenda?* Mentoring is for the mentee. The research suggests that attempts to impose the agenda within mentoring on the mentee result in manipulation and social engineering. The benefits of mentoring to all stakeholders result from broadly following the mentee's agenda.

■ *Evaluation and monitoring.* Ongoing evaluation of the scheme is important also. There is little point in evaluating the scheme after, say, two years to unearth problems that could have been resolved at the time.

THE ETHICS OF MENTORING

Having a clear understanding of the ethics of mentoring – both in general and in how they apply to the specific mentoring relationship – is important for several reasons:

■ It protects both mentor and mentee by providing clarity about what is and is not acceptable practice.

- It gives both mentor and mentee greater confidence in opening up about sensitive issues, where they might otherwise feel vulnerable.
- It establishes and clarifies boundaries, so that you know when to stop and question what you or the other party in the relationship is doing.

The ethical framework requires both an external and internal reference:

- The external reference is usually provided by a knowledgeable professional body. These guidelines are generic and provide a broad benchmark for thinking about the ethical issues.
- The internal reference is provided by the mentor (and, in many cases, by the mentee, too) and tends to be more situationally specific. The more aware both are of potential ethical conflict, the easier it will be to head off difficult situations. A key question is 'What do my own values tell me about this issue?'

Ideally mentors, in particular, should reflect as a matter of course on their own ethical approach. The following checklist indicates some of the areas that reflection might usefully cover:

- To whom do I have responsibilities and in what priority order?
- How will I sort out any conflicts in priorities, especially with regard to confidentiality?
- What boundaries should I make sure we stay within?
- What level of personal intimacy is appropriate?
- When should I withdraw from a relationship?
- When should I let the mentee fail?
- When should I push mentees towards what I know they need, rather than what they say they want?
- When should I withhold information from the mentee?

REFERENCES

Alred, G, Garvey, B and Smith, R (1998) *The Mentoring Pocket Book*, Management Pocket Books, Alresford, Hants

Bullis, C and Bach, BW (1989) Are mentoring relationships helping organizations? An exploration of developing mentee–mentor–organizational identification using turning point analysis, *Communication Quarterly*, **37**, pp 199–213

Clutterbuck, D (1985) *Everyone Needs a Mentor: How to foster talent within the organization*, Institute of Personnel Management, London

Clutterbuck, D (2004) *Everyone Needs a Mentor: How to foster talent within the organization*, 4th edn, CIPD, London

Clutterbuck, D and Lane, G (eds) (2004) *The Situational Mentor: An international review of competences and capabilities in mentoring*, Gower, Aldershot

Clutterbuck, D and Megginson, D (1999) *Mentoring Executives and Directors*, Butterworth-Heinemann, Oxford

Clutterbuck, D and Megginson, D (2001) Winding up or winding down? Proceedings of the 8th European Mentoring Centre Conference, Cambridge (UK), November

Clutterbuck, D and Megginson, D (2004) All good things must come to an end: winding up and winding down a mentoring relationship, Chapter 15 in *The Situational Mentor: An international review of competences and capabilities in mentoring*, ed D Clutterbuck and G Lane, pp 178–93, Gower, Aldershot

Clutterbuck, D and Megginson, D (2005) *Making Coaching Work: Creating a coaching culture*, CIPD, London

Colley, H (2003) *Mentoring for Social Inclusion: A critical approach to nurturing mentor relationships*, RoutledgeFalmer, London

Egan, G (1994) *The Skilled Helper: A problem management approach to helping*, Brooks & Cole, Pacific Grove, CA

Emler, N and Heather, N (1980) Intelligence: an ideological bias of conventional psychology, in *Coming to Know*, ed P Salmon, Routledge and Kegan Paul, London

Engstrom, T (1997) Personality factors' impact on success in the mentor–protégé relationship, MSc thesis to Norwegian School of Hotel Management

Garvey, B (1994) A dose of mentoring, *Education and Training*, 36 (4), pp 18–26

Garvey, B and Alred, G (2000) Developing mentors, *Career Development International*, 5 (4/5), pp 216–22

Garvey, B and Garrett-Harris, R (2005) *The Benefits of Mentoring: A literature review*, Report for East Mentors Forum, Mentoring and Coaching Research Unit, Sheffield Hallam University, Sheffield

Gibb, S and Megginson, D (1993) Inside corporate mentoring schemes: a new agenda of concerns, *Personnel Review*, 22 (1), pp 40–54

Hale, R (2000) To match or mismatch? The dynamics of mentoring as a route to personal and organizational learning, *Career Development International*, 5 (4/5), pp 223–34

Hawkins, P and Shohet, R (2002) *Supervision in the Helping Professions*, Open University Press, Buckingham

Kram, KE (1985) *Mentoring at Work: Developmental relationships in organisational life*, Scott, Foresman, Glenview, IL

Lee, G (2003) *Leadership Coaching: From personal insight to organisational performance*, CIPD, London

Megginson, D and Clutterbuck, D (1995) *Mentoring in Action*, 1st edn, Kogan Page, London

Megginson, D and Clutterbuck, D (2005) *Techniques for Coaching and Mentoring*, Elsevier Butterworth-Heinemann, Oxford

Megginson, D and Stokes, P (2004) Development and supervision for mentors, Chapter 8 in *The Situational Mentor: An international review of competences and capabilities in mentoring*, ed D Clutterbuck and G Lane, pp 94–107, Gower, Aldershot

Merrick, L and Stokes, P (2003) Mentor development and supervision: a passionate joint enquiry, *International Journal of Mentoring and Coaching*, **1** (1) (electronic journal of the European Mentoring and Coaching Council, www.emccouncil.org)

Neilson, T and Eisenbach, R (2003) Not all relationships are created equal: critical factors of high-quality mentoring relationships, *International Journal of Mentoring and Coaching*, **1** (1) (electronic journal of the European Mentoring and Coaching Council, www.emccouncil.org)

Ragins, BR, Cotton, JL and Miller, JS (2000) Marginal mentoring: the effects of type of mentor, quality of relationship and program design on work and career attitudes, *Academy of Management Journal*, **43** (6), pp 1117–94

Rushdie, S (1998) in B Williamson, *Lifeworlds and Learning: Essays in the theory, philosophy and practice of lifelong learning*, National Institute of Adult and Continuing Education (NIACE), Leicester

Scandura, TA *et al* (1996) Perspectives on mentoring, *Leadership and Organization Development Journal*, **17** (3), pp 50–56

Whitmore, J (2003) *Coaching for Performance: GROWing people, performance and purpose*, 3rd edn, Nicholas Brealey, London

Part 2
Organization Cases

2

Case Studies

INTRODUCTION

The following cases introduce a wide spectrum of approaches to the development of mentoring schemes in a massive range of organizations. We have obligatory and voluntary schemes; schemes for the disadvantaged and for the privileged; wide-ranging goals and focused goals; face-to-face and electronically mediated schemes. Finally, in contrast with our first edition of 10 years ago, we have schemes from a considerable number of countries: Australia, Denmark, France, South Africa, Switzerland and the United Kingdom. There are many that are Europe-wide or worldwide.

In reading these cases, you may well be struck, as we were, by common threads such as the need to develop mentors and mentees, the importance of the art of matching, and many more that we bring together in Part 4 where we analyse the themes that we spotted. As in 1995, we are still persuaded by this evidence that at some time in their lives it is still the case that *everyone needs a mentor*.

Case Study 1

MENTORING WITHIN THE YOUTH JUSTICE BOARD FOR ENGLAND AND WALES: THE SIGNIFICANCE OF TRUST

Jill Simpson

INTRODUCTION

This section explores the reasons of the Youth Justice Board for England and Wales (YJB) for implementing mentoring programmes attached to youth offending teams (YOT) and looks at the effectiveness in general of mentoring disaffected young people. It also explores the significance of trust and its relationship to a young person's motivation to change his or her behaviour.

It aims to give the reader some understanding of:

- the reasons why the Youth Justice Board decided upon a countrywide mentoring programme;
- how the programme was funded, set up and run;
- young offenders;
- the complex nature and effectiveness of mentoring disaffected young people within this scheme.

METHODOLOGY

The chapter is based on informal discussions with personnel within the youth justice system (YJS) and in education, by phone and in person. I also use specialist literature and internet sites such as the Youth Justice Board and Crime Concern and more general sites regarding mentoring young people in the UK and United States.

Further, I draw on my own personal experience of working within the Hertfordshire youth offending team and an Enfield comprehensive school of 1,400 pupils.

YOUTH JUSTICE BOARD FOR ENGLAND AND WALES MENTORING PROGRAMME

In the late 1990s, government research confirmed that the UK had an unacceptably low level of literacy and numeracy skills. Detail showed that, within certain ethnic groupings, the prison population and young offenders' levels were even lower. A government initiative offering free basic skills courses to over-16s at further education colleges expanded to fund probation offices to set up basic skills courses locally and / or within their own premises.

Youth offending teams had for a long time prioritized education but needed to find ways of getting more young offenders back into education.

Crime Concern said that mentoring could be an effective way to help raise academic, personal or job-related achievements of mentees.

In July 1999, Crime Concern was commissioned by the YJB to provide an implementation support service to 40 mentoring projects. The YJB provided funds, and bids were requested from YOTs nationally. The two main criteria were 'disaffected minority ethnic young offenders' (Mentoring Plus) and 'mentoring help with literacy and numeracy'.

Crime Concern also produced a source guidance document to help providers design and deliver effective schemes.

YOUTH OFFENDING TEAMS – BRIEF OVERVIEW

The Crime and Disorder Act 1998 establishes that 'preventing offending by children and young persons' will be the overarching aim of the YJS. Youth offending teams fulfil the YJS's remit to help prevent reoffending throughout the young offender's life whilst protecting communities. YOTs are multi-agency organizations, working with young offenders on all aspects of education, health, housing, activities, drugs and reparation projects, courts and the police, with their own specialists under one roof.

Eighty-four schemes were set up. All but a few are currently undergoing evaluation.

YOUNG OFFENDERS

Research into offending behaviour suggests that many young people offend once or twice. The multiple risk factors that pose a much higher chance of more serious or persistent offending are:

- troubled home life, poor parenting, criminal family member, violence or abuse;
- peer group pressure;
- poor attainment at school, truancy and exclusion;
- out of employment or training;
- personal issues such as drug or alcohol misuse or mental illness;
- deprivation – poor housing or homelessness.

MENTORING WITHIN YOUTH OFFENDING TEAMS AND 'ORDERS'

Mentoring within the YJS works within the remit of the Crime and Disorder Act 1998. Young people found guilty of offences can be subject to a variety of orders: final warning; referral; community punishment and rehabilitation; action plan; supervision and detention and training orders. These can be combined with other services attached, eg reparation. Mentoring can play a part within these, but participating in a mentoring scheme is voluntary and not part of the young person's order.

YJB principles state that:

1. Mentoring is a natural part of child development.
2. The main purpose of mentoring is to benefit the young person, ie the *young person's* agenda is the priority.
3. The relationship should be supportive, yet challenging.
4. Involvement (permission) of the parents or carers is important.
5. In a youth justice context, mentoring requires workable structures, and processes for supervision, monitoring and evaluation.
6. Action planning and goal setting (ie forms, approach, review and paperwork) should take into account culture, age, literacy level, gender and such things as attention deficit hyperactivity disorder.

EFFECTIVENESS OF MENTORING WITHIN YJB PROGRAMMES

Essential components of a scheme to maximize effectiveness are:

- voluntary involvement;
- high levels of contact between mentor and mentee and regular meetings with up to three or four meetings a month being ideal (Tierney and Grossman with Resch, 1995);
- good matching of mentee and mentor;
- perception of being independent of the YOT;
- effective support of the mentor.

My experience suggests that to gain any success the young person's motivation needs to change and his or her engagement with the project must be in place. Of paramount importance is the development of trust. This is primarily trust of the mentor by the scheme organizer and trust by the mentor of the mentee, and both must work to overcome the young person's mistrust of 'the system'.

THE SIGNIFICANCE OF TRUST

It is generally recognized that supporting vulnerable young people is an effective way to prevent young people from becoming involved in crime and anti-social behaviour. It is equally important to engage and support young offenders to enhance their life and prevent reoffending.

As mentors, if we are to engage them, we need to be trusted. Without trust, a young person, within a mentoring programme, will not voluntarily engage, cooperate or be motivated to change and learn.

Garvey (1994) illustrates this point in his dimensions model of open and closed mentor/mentee relationships. His research shows that when the relationship is an open one (ie one of trust) the mentoring tends to be successful for both parties. Of course, this can be said of many types of relationships.

Maddern (1994) suggests that research confirms that learning begins in the limbic system of the brain and that this part of the brain is also where our emotions are controlled. So, an emotional content to our learning is inevitable.

If openness, trust, motivation, engagement and learning are all linked to the limbic system of the brain, emotions will inevitably be involved. As trust and openness are needed for a mentoring relationship to be successful, both parties need to be emotionally engaged for the mentoring to be effective.

Goleman (1995) states that socio-biologists say that our emotions guide us when facing danger, tackling difficult goals and facing change. Emotions offer a readiness to act. Some emotions like 'angry aggression', commonly found in young offenders, need to be overridden and channelled into determination. An effective mentor is often 'emotionally intelligent' (Goleman, 1995) and is able to support the young person to make this emotional change through empathizing with him or her.

Consequently, I believe that mentors can guide their young mentees to find and use their emotions to motivate themselves towards life-changing actions.

EVIDENCE OF EFFECTIVENESS

Evidence has shown (Tierney and Grossman with Resch, 1995) that after approximately 12 hours of work over a month with a volunteer mentor:

1. The onset of drug use was significantly lower than in a non-mentored control group.
2. The onset of alcohol use was 27 per cent less.
3. There was 32 per cent less frequency of hitting.
4. There was slightly improved educational attainment.
5. There was significantly reduced truancy.
6. There were improved relationships with family.
7. There were slightly improved friendships with peers.

The Dalston Youth Project (DYP) in Hackney (Benioff, 1997) highlights the effectiveness of mentoring with young offenders. It pioneered the Mentoring Plus model of a 9- to 12-month comprehensive, structured programme rooted in the local community (in Hackney 90 per cent of DYP's mentors are Afro-Caribbean). In brief, it begins with a three-day residential group course for 10- to 17-year-olds. Once the young person has been matched with a mentor for nine months, a minimum two-month course runs alongside the mentoring, focusing on interpersonal skills, literacy, numeracy and motivation.

Nearly three-quarters of those who left the project moved into full-time education, training or employment, and reoffending reduced by 60 per cent.

UPS AND DOWNS

Shiner *et al* (2004) published an evaluation of Mentoring Plus. They stated that the majority of participant mentees moved from disengagement to engagement. This helped them with education and work, and Shiner *et al* concluded that the achievements of Mentoring Plus were particularly impressive when taking into account this inherently difficult target group. They also noted that the positive work with young people could be undermined by restricted financial commitments.

YJB says that no further funds from the YJB are available and that some schemes have mainstreamed and secured local funds.

US research by Jekielek *et al* (2002) supports these findings. They asked the question 'Do mentoring programmes work?' Their work shows that mentoring programmes can be effective in enhancing:

- the positive development of youth;
- reducing truancy;
- improving attitudes;
- fewer incidents of hitting;
- less drug and alcohol abuse;
- improved relationships with parents.

However, it also suggests that mentoring relationships of short duration may be harmful.

ACCURATE MONITORING TOOL – ASSET

The Asset computerized assessment profile used within YOTs provides a good basis for monitoring every aspect of success by the young people. Assessments can be made at predetermined intervals, with no break of confidentiality by the mentor.

Asset is completed after an informal interview and covers: ethnicity; care and criminal history; accommodation; family and personal relationships including attitude and behaviour; education including truancy and relationships with teachers and peers; employment; neighbourhood; lifestyle; substance use – type and amount; attitude; health; perception of self and others; thinking and behaviour – easily led, aggressive etc; attitudes to offending; motivation to change; positive factors; indicators of vulnerability; and potential to harm others or self.

It is a comprehensive point-scoring assessment that should highlight any changes during the period of mentoring.

COSTS

The YJB's Disaffected Minority Ethnic Project, using Mentoring Plus, was assumed to cost £3,000 per young person per annum, offering 30 mentees a place at £90,000 per annum.

The YJB's mentoring help with literacy and numeracy was estimated to cost £1,000 per place, with an average of 30 places on each project at £30,000 per annum.

CONCLUSIONS – YOUTH JUSTICE BOARD MENTORING PROGRAMME

I have shown that some YOT mentoring schemes can be effective and can help the government raise basic skills of young offenders and improve their attitudes and behaviour with the support of multi-agency and Mentoring Plus strategies.

Eventually Thomas Coram Research Unit's evaluation will confirm the actual costs of the schemes and whether stand-alone mentoring programmes are as effective as Mentoring Plus.

There is general concern regarding funding, which is only available for a fixed term. This could have detrimental effects on young people and mentors and undermine the value of running the scheme at all. More long-term future funding sources should be identified.

REFERENCES

Benioff, S (1997) *A Second Chance*, Belmont Press, London

Garvey, B (1994) A dose of mentoring, *Education and Training*, **36** (4), pp 18–26

Goleman, D (1995) *Emotional Intelligence: Why it can matter more than IQ*, Bantam, New York

Jekielek, M *et al* (eds) (2002) *Child Trends, Research Brief*, Washington, DC, http://wwwchildtrends.org

Shiner, M *et al* (2004) *Mentoring Disaffected Young People: An evaluation of 'Mentoring Plus'*, Joseph Rowntree Foundation, York

Tierney, JP and Grossman, JB with Resch, NL (1995) *Making a Difference: An impact study of big brothers/big sisters*, Public/Private Ventures, Philadelphia, PA

OTHER SOURCES

Centre for Criminology, London School of Economics

Crime Concern, http://www.crimeconcern.org.uk (accessed May 2005)

Youth Justice Board, http://www.youth-justice-board.gov.uk/PractitionersPortal/PreventionAndInterventions (accessed May 2005)

Case Study 2

MENTORING SUPPORT FOR VICTIMS OF DOMESTIC ABUSE

Judy Morgan, The Lantern Project

INTRODUCTION

The Lantern Project trains volunteer mentors to provide long-term one-to-one support for women who are and have been affected by domestic abuse (DA).

The mentors are women of any age, status, creed or colour with a wide range of experiences, skills and backgrounds. Some are survivors of DA. Their training covers domestic violence issues, mentoring, police procedures, crown prosecution service procedures, child protection, confidentiality, risk assessment and safety planning, working with other agencies, alcohol dependency and civil law options. In future it may also include advocacy skills.

Victims are referred to the project by the police, health services, social services, education and schools, housing services, neighbourhood offices and other voluntary sector organizations. They can also be referred by friends and family or they may ask for help themselves.

The mentoring gives victims and families practical and emotional support to help them take more control of their lives and to:

- break out of the cycle of violence they have been subjected to;
- make *lasting* changes to their lives, to improve their prospects and those of their children;
- deal with the highly complex practicalities of making those changes;
- recover from the emotional damage caused and move on to a brighter future.

Additional benefits include reduction in the damage to children who witness DA and/or are subjected to abuse, better coordination of services for victims and more cost-effective use of the resources of other DA support agencies, and the potential to reach victims at an early stage to reduce the time that they and their children live with DA.

BACKGROUND

The Lantern Project was inspired by trying (and failing) to find help for someone whose life was being blighted by the aftermath of growing up in a violent and abusive home followed by extremely violent adult relationships. The 'baggage' left by her past controlled her to such a degree that she was unable to deal with the normal stresses of life and she began to disintegrate both emotionally and mentally.

It became clear that victims of abuse might benefit from support to find ways to control the 'baggage' rather than it controlling them, and it seemed that mentoring could provide a useful approach to such support. In some cases it might be the sole form of support; in more severe cases mentors could help find and then supplement the work of counsellors and therapists by providing additional emotional support to help mentees implement the advice and guidance given to them.

VALIDATION OF THE IDEA

The current project manager wrote up the ideas in some detail and informally but extensively researched them by talking to a wide range of people providing DA support services, survivors of DA, experienced practitioners, organizers of mentoring projects and others with wide voluntary sector experience.

Every single person approached greeted the idea with enthusiasm. One DA worker even said that she would 'snatch the hand off' anyone who could provide mentors to help her support the women she was working with.

WHAT IS MEANT BY MENTORING

Within the context of the Lantern Project, the specific role of mentoring is to enable victims of DA to:

- reduce the length of time they would otherwise spend in the violent relationship;
- take more control of their lives through increased confidence and self-esteem;

- evaluate all their options to make well-informed decisions and plans for the future;
- find and deal with all the other services and agencies that could assist them;
- handle the practical and emotional issues they will face if they have to leave home;
- support and protect any children in their care;
- be more certain that they can manage on their own if they need to;
- go through any police, court and other legal proceedings they are involved in;
- rebuild their support networks (family and friends);
- find help to deal with issues such as alcohol and drug dependency etc;
- take up education and training and find work;
- feel more confident in making decisions and evaluating risks without being discouraged if the outcomes of those decisions are less than perfect;
- use the strength that they have shown in coping with DA to help them cope with any other adversities that life may bring;
- deal with any 'emotional baggage' that is affecting their emotional well-being;
- rebuild their lives and make long-term positive changes.

Because of the nature of DA and its effects on victims, mentors may initially have to take action (eg phone calls to agencies) on behalf of their mentees. All decision making remains with the mentee, who is expected to direct the mentor. Obviously the mentor's ultimate aim is to make sure that the mentee is able to take such actions for herself in the future.

To focus its activities more effectively, the project uses the five-stage model of DA that has been developed from observations made over years of working with victims of DA. It provides a useful framework upon which to base the goals set with women and the immediate aims of the mentoring activity.

THE FIVE-STAGE MODEL AND HOW MENTORING CAN HELP AT EACH STAGE

At all stages mentors must be prepared to listen without probing and to help the victim and those around her understand that she is not to blame. Considerable work is usually needed to repair the victim's self-esteem and to show her that she has the right to live without fear. In brief the five-stage model consists of:

1. *Denial*. This happens early on in the relationship when the perpetrator's violence may be relatively infrequent but he will have started to blame her for his actions. He will always be very sorry, promise not to do it again and be extra charming to show his contrition. The victim will not realize or want to admit that she is going through DA and it may be very difficult to reach victims at this stage. However, family and friends may ask for help to deal with the situation, and mentoring could:
   - provide emotional support for family and friends who are distressed by the victim's situation;
   - explain to family and friends what the victim may be going through, why she may find it difficult to leave and that she may be forced to break contact with them;
   - help family and friends to support the victim, including encouraging the victim to seek direct help when the time seems right;
   - encourage family and friends to maintain some level of contact with the victim and reassure her that they will still be there for her in the future.

2. *Acceptance*. The victim now realizes that she is being abused but believes that if she works hard enough she will be able to stop it happening. She now firmly believes his constant assertions that she is to blame, that she could not manage without him and that she is useless. She will typically be seen by the different health agencies. She is unlikely even to consider leaving at this stage. She will not ask for help directly but may be open to help if approached carefully, and if so a mentor could:
   - gently work with her to enable her to accept that there is nothing she can do to change his behaviour;
   - discuss how the situation may be affecting her children and look at ways in which she communicates with them about what is going on;
   - support her through situations that may arise with agencies such as social services if action needs to be taken regarding her children;
   - help her maintain or re-establish her relationships with family and friends;
   - assist her in dealing with any practical issues arising from her situation.

3. *Realization*. The victim begins to realize that nothing she can do will make any difference to his behaviour, and she may start to call the police because she wants them to make him stop! Even if she gives a statement she may retract it and do so repeatedly. She may still not be ready to leave but may be starting to consider taking action and it may now be easier to persuade her to accept help. A mentor could:

- gently work with her to enable her to accept that it may be difficult if not impossible for anyone else to be able to make him stop and that she may have to move on;
- encourage her to research her options without forcing her into any decisions;
- motivate her towards making changes in her situation;
- help her maintain or re-establish her relationships with family and friends;
- assist her in dealing with any practical issues arising from her situation, including dealing with other agencies, solicitors etc;
- support her in making important decisions through helping her to analyse her options.

4. *Flight.* This is the point at which the victim decides that she must get away. This can often prove very difficult for a number of practical reasons, which can also make it hard for her to stay away. Support at this stage is extremely important to help her sustain the changes she makes. At this stage a mentor could:
   - help her to make effective escape plans;
   - provide emotional support through all the changes and reassure her that she can cope on her own;
   - help her deal with agencies such as housing, social services, police and the benefits agency etc;
   - attend criminal and civil court proceedings with her;
   - help her find and deal with solicitors;
   - support her in making important decisions through helping her identify and analyse her options;
   - assist her to find support for her children, if needed.

5. *Recovery.* Even after a woman has physically left her violent partner there may be emotional damage that can affect her future and she may still need to leave him emotionally. She can find it very hard to shake off his influence on her and this can affect what she expects from any new relationship she may form and from life in general. There is very little support for women at this stage, and a mentor could:
   - help her settle in to her new life;
   - assist her to put what has happened to her into perspective;
   - support her through any ongoing court procedures;
   - help her resist persuasion by the perpetrator to return to him;
   - assist her to find counselling and other help to deal with any emotional damage and support her in acting on the counsellor's advice;

- help her plan her future development;
- signpost her to training and employment support where necessary;
- assist her to find support for her children, if needed.

EXPERIENCE WITH THE PROJECT

The project started in April 2003 but ran into governance problems (it was then being managed by West Midlands police). The first year was spent in setting the project up and establishing a new organization – The Jan Foundation – to take over as the managing body. At the end of February 2004 the project had five volunteer mentors who were ready to start work with victims of DA.

Mentors

The project has not had to work very hard to recruit mentors, as women tend to come forward whenever they hear about the Lantern Project. If the project had not been beset by the governance problems that affected the funding strategy it would have been possible to recruit and train at least 20 mentors.

Mentees

The project received 35 referrals in the first year, of which 23 came from the police. Others included three self-referrals, four from a contact in occupational health for the local hospital, two from a safe house and one each from a family member, a ward support officer and the drugs referral worker at the police station. Requests for its services have exceeded the current capacity to deliver.

Women referred to the project have an initial meeting with the project manager who explains the service to them and carries out an initial assessment. They are also told about the limits of confidentiality within the project. This first meeting can be a long one, as victims often need to talk at length about what has been happening to them. It allows them to gain confidence that they will be listened to and believed and gives them insights into the possible causes of the behaviour to which they have been subjected.

They are then matched up with a mentor who does a more detailed assessment of needs and risks and works with them to decide how they want to move forward. Not surprisingly, the pace at which women move forward varies greatly.

This process has proved to be highly effective, and very few women with long-term needs have refused further help at this stage. The support given to people living with DA has included:

- Helping an elderly victim of DA with health problems obtain a care plan and access day care centre facilities to reduce her social isolation.
- Lengthy support to enable women to overcome their fears in order to give evidence in criminal court proceedings. This has also involved supporting them after adjournments and over several days of a trial.
- Supporting victims who wanted to make use of the civil court system to obtain occupancy and non-molestation orders and deal with access to children, including accompanying them on visits to solicitors and to county court.
- Emotional support to help with decisions that mentees have to make and with the recovery process once they have extricated themselves from the influence of the abuser.
- Finding advice on a benefits issue that a perpetrator had been using to 'blackmail' his partner.
- Helping women repair relationships with family and friends. In some cases the fact that the victim has received support from the Lantern Project has brought previously slightly hostile friends and relatives rallying round.

All of the women said that they found the support valuable. Some have said that they feel that they would not have managed to make the changes that they have without it and that they might have made moves much more quickly if they had been able to access such support sooner.

Monitoring

A spreadsheet was established to allow monitoring of the work with the mentees. It includes recording of ethnicity, disability and health issues, and sexuality. The monitoring and evaluation process will be developed further, and the paperwork used to track clients' progress is under review.

Referral mechanism with West Midlands police

The referral process with West Midlands police has worked very successfully. Victims are asked if they would like their contact details to be passed to the Lantern Project or they are given the numbers to ring. If calls come in to the DA officers (DAOs) they will occasionally arrange for the project manager to talk to the victim then and there. Nothing is done without the full consent of the victim.

A formal procedure, based on practice, has been written out and agreed with the DAOs and the relevant sergeant in the community safety bureau at the local police station.

Referral arrangements to other agencies

A procedure with appropriate forms is written up and discussed with the mentors on an ongoing basis when the need to refer to other agencies arises. To date, the project has facilitated referrals to or contacts with housing support services, solicitors, witness support and benefits advisers. All of this has been done with the full knowledge, consent and partici-pation of the victims concerned.

OVERVIEW OF THE FIRST YEAR OF MENTORING

A great deal has been learned from running the project to date. It has been possible to refine the referral process between the project and the police and for all concerned to gain very useful experience and knowledge. Some informal links with women's groups have indicated that having access to such groups could support the work being done by the mentors.

The project has run very well in 2004–05 with no major problems, other than funding. Some of the positive and negative experiences are summarized below.

What has worked well

- *Mentoring work.* This was highly successful and valued by the women themselves. The support given through both criminal and civil court proceedings has been especially effective.
- *The mentors.* They have worked very well both individually and as a group. They have supported each other well and have been able to bring considerable experience and expertise to the project. They have retained their enthusiasm and are keen to carry on as mentors and for the project to continue.
- *Training package.* This has taken shape very well and mentors have found that it has given them the right foundation to help them with the work they are doing.

- *Work with the police.* A very good working relationship has been developed with both the DAOs and all of the field officers who have had direct contact with the Lantern Project.

What has not worked so well

- *Fund raising.* A great deal of effort has been put into this with some success, but the time available to do it was drastically reduced as the project gained momentum. Ideally this activity should have started from the very beginning but it was critically hindered by the governance problems alluded to above. This situation was unforeseen and unfortunate.
- *The number of mentors.* These were much lower than was initially hoped because of the funding issues mentioned above.
- *The number of mentees.* These were obviously lower than hoped for because funds were not available for training new mentors. The numbers supported by the current group of mentors have met and slightly exceeded those required by the current funders.
- *Development of the project.* Funding issues have again affected this activity.

CONCLUSION

Experience to date has shown that the support given by the Lantern Project is very effective and that there is considerable demand for it from both victims of DA and agencies.

THEMES

- *Listen without probing.* A striking warning against thinking that penetrating questioning always works.
- *Explain and persuade.* This is part of the role for this kind of mentoring.
- *Who to help.* Notice that different people are mentored at different stages: first stage – family and friends; second and following stages – mentee herself.

Case Study 3

THE LEARNING MENTOR

Coral Gardiner

BACKGROUND

There are in the region of 15,000 learning mentors in schools across the UK. The term 'learning mentor' originates from a conversation between a senior civil servant and Sir Michael Barber in 1999 and refers to people who help pupils to achieve their learning potential. David Blunkett, then the UK's Secretary of State for Education and Employment, set the agenda in the paper *The Learning Age* (DfEE, 1998), in which he said:

> Learning is the key to prosperity – for each of us as individuals, as well as for the nation as a whole. Investment in human capital will be the foundation of success in the knowledge-based global economy of the twenty first century. Our first policy paper addressed school standards [DfEE, 1997]. This Green Paper sets out for consultation how learning throughout life will build human capital by encouraging the acquisition of knowledge and skills and emphasising creativity and imagination. The fostering of an enquiring mind and the love of learning are essential to our future success.

Learning mentors in secondary schools were one of six strands in an initiative called 'Excellence in Cities' (EiC). Blunkett (DfEE, 1999) described EiC as a plan of implementation to raise standards of education for students in the inner cities. It specified that the programme be introduced across six cities: London, Leeds, Birmingham, Manchester, Liverpool and Sheffield. The 'action plan' included providing a 'learning mentor' for every young person who needed one to help tackle barriers to learning.

The paper painted a background of urgent need:

> To ensure that barriers to learning are overcome, the Government is determined that every child in the designated areas will have the personal attention they need in order to succeed. For many families the support they are meant to get has no coherence. It demands so much energy to access it that many simply give up, and for others it delivers too little too late. From September 1999, each secondary school pupil will have access to Learning Mentors, based

in schools and professionally trained for their role and responsible for making sure that any barriers to an individual's learning – in school or outside the school – are removed. Learning Mentors will build on successful models of multi-agency behaviour support teams, which the Government is promoting in order to reduce truancy and exclusion.

Learning Mentors will be available to all who need them and will devote the majority of their time to those individuals needing extra support in order to realise their full potential. They will liaise with Primary schools to identify children about to enter secondary school who need help.

In addition, the Laming report on the death of little Victoria Climbié has propelled the role of learning mentor into mainstream educational provision. Today, learning mentors are employed in nurseries, primary schools and secondary schools. They are well placed to play the role of 'key worker' in response to 'every child matters' (Children's Act 2004).

ONE CITY

As the Learning Mentor Coordinator, I joined Birmingham education service in 1999 from National Probation, West Midlands (Gardiner, 1998, 1999). I was tasked with developing learning mentoring in 92 secondary schools. I worked in partnership with headteachers and education service and voluntary sector agencies. Because this was such a new concept to education, I found a lack of understanding and clarity about the role. Everywhere I turned I was immediately asked, 'What is mentoring?' Having developed the BEAT Project for National Probation, I was well placed to address this question. I therefore transferred my criminal justice mentoring model into the educational setting.

Getting started

Initial analysis of the role, using SWOT, showed that the role of a learning mentor is complex and multifaceted. Owing to the newness of the role there was also the risk that learning mentors could become used as 'all things to all people'. In addition, I identified a number of other pitfalls. These create barriers to effectiveness and professional development. For example:

- *time* – lack of it at appropriate levels for the task(s);
- *access to mentees* – lack of agreement to suspend the curriculum for short regular periods for mentoring;
- *relationships* – the role being dependent on developing positive relationships with all parties, ie parents, teachers etc;
- *a space for privacy* – the relationship requires relative privacy to develop confidence, mutual respect and trust;

- *curriculum knowledge* – knowing something about the learner's experience in school enhances mentoring intervention;
- *training* – learning mentors need to be supported with appropriate CPD and training;
- *expectations* – all stakeholders had high expectations of the role;
- *communication* – at all levels with all those in and outside of education to develop common understanding and greater clarity;
- *resources* – appropriate to the needs of the role;
- *appropriate support* – need for supervision and support for learning mentors due to isolation and because they are not the same as other members of staff who have different needs;
- *understanding* – of the role and what it involves.

Analysing these issues helped inform the policy direction.

WHAT ARE LEARNING MENTORS?

Learning mentors are essentially educational practitioners. They come from all walks of life and are paid. They work with school staff, children and young people. In some cases they work with those waiting to return or returning to school after a period of absence due to a range of reasons.

Learning mentors work with individual pupils, providing one-to-one mentoring, as well as working with groups. Their aim is to raise standards by removing barriers to learning for individual students and their families. They act as a bridge between home and school. This is to improve children's life chances, educational attendance and attainment, and reduce rates of truancy and exclusion rates.

In addition, they aim to resolve barriers to learning by increasing self-esteem, confidence and self-directed success. The DfEE indicate that 'The Learning Mentor will personally target efforts on those disproportionately at risk of underachieving, who would not be catered for by the SENCO or the gifted and talented co-ordinator' (DfEE, 1999).

Learning mentors are tasked with:

- developing one-to-one mentoring relationships with children;
- working closely with local community and business mentors;
- taking an active role in coordinating and supporting the work of voluntary mentors working with pupils both in and out of school, so that the mentor's efforts meet the needs of the young person in a focused and integrated way.

In addition, they are required to network with other learning mentors to share best practice. In Walsall, they are recruited from a range of backgrounds including teaching, counselling, youth work, estates management, social care, education welfare and bank management.

'MENTORING' ASPECT OF THEIR ROLE

The definition below was agreed with Birmingham headteachers in 2001. It helped clarify their role and shares a common professional understanding of what they actually do: 'The Learning Mentor lifts barriers to learning by extending the potential of the learner.'

GOALS OF LEARNING MENTORS

'The key challenges will be to champion the learning needs of the child and to overcome any barriers to effective learning. Learning Mentors will work closely with the pastoral and other staff of the school with the individual achievement of the pupil as the common focus' (DfEE, 1999).

This 'champion' of the child, the learning mentor, therefore brings a shift of focus to the cultural perspective of school. The learning mentor involves the learner in drawing up and implementing his or her own individual 'action plan', which is monitored and evaluated. The learning mentor has regular one-to-one contact with the pupil/learner and as needed with his or her family.

What learning mentors are not!

It was also helpful to explain to schools what learning mentors are not. They are not:

- corridor monitors;
- surrogate parents;
- teachers' assistants;
- cover supervisors;
- attendance officers.

However, these are all potential tasks in the life of a learning mentor but are not the main or only one.

What do they do?

The core of the learning mentor role in Walsall is one-to-one mentoring, which is directed at helping pupils manage their school life and to assist individuals and groups with practical solutions to often complex problems.

This may involve the learning mentor observing a child in the classroom, visiting parents at home, helping teachers improve lesson organization, running breakfast club or after-school activities and advising pupils on managing their learning.

Planning the action

Robust criteria are used in schools to prioritize which children are offered mentoring. The student has an individual action plan negotiated and drawn up specifying his or her learning targets and goals with a timeline and reviewing procedures.

School policies and development plans include protocols and criteria for entry and exit as well as the rigorous programming of evaluation processes. Further evaluation takes place at school level to measure the overall impact of work. In addition, qualitative and quantitative data are collected, collated and analysed by the strand coordinator on behalf of the LEA. This is peer evaluated, assessed and sent on to the Department of Education and Skills.

Freeing teachers to teach, helping children to cope and liaising with outside agencies and families are all in a day's work for learning mentors. Their role in Walsall is fluid and flexible, and Ofsted (the inspection agency for schools) (2003: 46) said of them:

> Learning Mentors are making a significant effect on attendance, behaviour, self-esteem and progress of the pupils they support... the most successful and highly valued strand of the EiC programme... In 95% of the survey schools, inspectors judged that the mentoring programme made a positive contribution to the mainstream provision of the school as a whole, and had a beneficial effect on the behaviour of individual pupils and on their ability to learn and make progress.

A headteacher of a Walsall Excellence Cluster school says of their learning mentor: 'It is actually very difficult to think back to what our school was like before she arrived!'

A teacher in a Walsall school with a learning mentor said, 'Our learning mentor is highly valued by both pupils and staff! His smartness, sense of etiquette, calmness and wisdom make him an exemplary adult for many – a positive role model.'

A parent of a child in a cluster school says: 'The programme has given S a lot of confidence. Stopped all her worrying at school and it has improved her literacy and numeracy skills. All the mentoring helped S through the worry of the SATS.'

A student of a learning mentor says: 'They really help you and talk about my problems. Every problem I have had, C has sorted!'

SOME LESSONS LEARNED

1. In the spirit of mentoring, the style and approach of the learning mentors are as diverse as with any other group of mentors.

2. There are operational differences between the educational phases that relate to child and adolescent development. In general, the younger the mentee, the more directive the mentor seems to need to be.

3. A learning mentor needs the freedom within the role to be flexible and adapt to the needs of the child in the context of his or her school and family.

As the role is the most successful of the EiC initiative, it has mainstreamed mentoring into the UK's educational system and reinforced government belief in mentoring as a strategy for success.

For more information on learning mentors contact this website address: www.standards.dfes.gov.uk/sie/eic/eiclearningmentors/.

REFERENCES

DfEE (1997) *Excellence in Schools*, White Paper, DfEE, London

DfEE (1998) *The Learning Age*, Green Paper, DfEE, London

DfEE (1999) *Learning to Succeed*, White Paper, DfEE, London

DfEE (1999) *Planning Guidance for LEAs on Learning Mentors*, CircularEiC (G) 0/99–8/99, DfEE, London

Gardiner, C (1998) Mentoring: towards a professional friendship, *Mentoring and Tutoring Journal*, **6** (1/2), Summer, Trentham Books, Stoke-on-Trent

Gardiner, C (1999) Community justice mentoring: a congruent mentoring network, Unpublished, Presented to the 6th European Mentoring Conference, Robinson College, Cambridge

Ofsted (2003) *Excellence in Cities and Education Action Zones: Management and impact*, Ofsted, London

EAST OF ENGLAND (HARLOW) E-MENTORING PILOT PROJECT

Colin Hawkins, Hub Manager, Harlow Open Road e-mentoring project

THE SCHEME

The East of England e-mentoring project is funded by Aim Higher Healthcare Strand. It is focused on raising aspirations towards higher education of youngsters living in the Harlow and West Essex area. This area is in the top 10 per cent of social deprivation in the East of England, and the current rate of students attending university is around 16 per cent.

The mentoring forms part of the Open Road project. This comprises several aspects of healthcare work-related learning including:

- work experience;
- work shadowing;
- interactive workshops;
- half-term activities;
- specific coursework support;
- meet-the-expert sessions.

The mentors are recruited from Princess Alexandra Hospital Trust along with Harlow and Epping Forest Primary Care Trusts.

The 47 students mostly came from either the main Aim Higher group or were those who had identified the healthcare sector as a possible career choice. Other recruits to the programme were students who had the potential to be in the main Aim Higher cohort but fell short of having the predicted five or more GCSE A–C passes.

The group consisted of 18 Year 9 students, 22 Year 10 students and 7 post-16 students studying science or business.

Following a recruitment campaign, 28 mentors volunteered to take part in the scheme. They were from the following areas of healthcare:

- senior surgical consultant;
- director of workforce development;
- head of training;
- head of emergency care;
- senior nurse practitioners;
- head of occupational care;
- senior educational manager;
- recently qualified biomedical scientists;
- management graduates.

The mentors attended a one-day training session held within the trust. The content of the day included:

- information about the overall project;
- what is mentoring?
- matching procedure;
- child protection;
- what mentoring is and is not;
- how the technology works;
- listening and questioning skills;
- effective e-mails.

The mentors all decided to take a City and Guilds award in mentoring. This mainly consists of keeping a detailed reflective mentoring log. The assessor supports the mentors individually during this process and this should enable the mentor to plan and structure the mentoring process.

During the training day, it was clear that all the participants had a good idea of what mentoring was about and could give real examples of their own experiences of mentoring.

Most of the sessions were structured as either discussion or small group work and it was explained that mentors were not teachers or parents but were there to support and guide. The mentors agreed that a mentor is:

- a sounding board;
- someone who wants to put something back;
- someone with experience of learning and the world of work;
- a good role model.

The mentors took part in a matching exercise and some of the responses from the matching questions were as in Table 2.4.1.

The mentors created an action plan during the training. This focused on what was going to happen next. Participants also agreed that they would be happy if they were not anonymous but identified by their first names and job roles.

It was agreed that the coordinator would act as a mentor for the group and towards the end of the scheme the mentors and mentees would meet in a structured celebration event. The group felt that this would be interesting because when people meet for the first time they often subconsciously make value judgements based on first impressions. The event would be the first face-to-face meeting after they had established a relationship on e-mail.

The evaluation of the training was very positive.

Table 2.4.1   Questions and responses from the matching process

Question	Some responses
What their interests were	'Spending time with my children.'
Why they want to become mentors	'I want to put something back.' 'Personal development.' 'To support and guide.' 'To use my experience and knowledge.' 'To give directional guidance in order to help someone develop.' 'To help with future recruitment.' 'I have benefited from having a mentor myself in the past which has helped me grow into my current role.' 'I want to be less shy.'
The skills they believe they can bring to mentoring	'An ability to point someone in the right direction.' 'Communication skills.' 'Understanding of young people.' 'Good listening skills.'
Can they think of examples of being mentored?	'I was mentored throughout my nursing career.' 'I was mentored whilst studying at university.' 'I have never had a mentor.' 'Since becoming a very senior manager having started as a clinician I would benefit from some mentoring from the business world.'

SAFETY

The issues of child protection and Criminal Records Bureau checks were also covered in the training. The Firefox system used on this scheme is as close to being totally secure as possible. The system operates in what is known as a trust zone, and when the users log in via the internet they have a standard-looking e-mail account that monitors the following:

- adult swear words;
- racist and homophobic language;
- text language;
- vulgar references;
- words within words, eg Middlesex, Essex.

Words and phrases used are monitored according to guidelines from child protection experts. No personal details are able to be included in e-mails, including personal phone numbers and e-mail addresses. No pictures are allowed to be included on e-mails; the same applies for attachments.

MENTEE TRAINING

The mentees were trained either in schools or at the trust. The training was jointly facilitated with Essex Education Business Link.

The sessions were similar to the mentors' training and included what mentoring is and is not. The students were shown the same presentation on how the computer system works and how their safety is a very high priority.

There was a lot of discussion around the reasons why people want to be mentors and the qualities they possess. The students worked in small groups and represented their finding in picture form. Although they were mostly shy at feeding back, they soon got over this and gained confidence whilst presenting.

The students seemed to enjoy the session on where mentoring fits into their current support networks. This was represented in the form of a drawing of a tree and the main trunk of the tree being mostly family and the branches being other sources of support like teachers, tutors and Connexions advisers. It was interesting that mentoring seemed to fit naturally into the young people's support networks. This session helped them discover the mentoring that already exists in their lives along with how mentoring can benefit them in the future.

The young people were very confident with the technology but were anxious about what they were going to talk about in their first e-mail session. As a group, they developed some suggested questions and introductions that they felt would be good in their first e-mails.

YOUNG PEOPLE'S THOUGHTS ON MENTORING: WHAT IS MENTORING?

- ▓ 'Creating and building aims.'
- ▓ 'Raising awareness.'
- ▓ 'Exploring ideas.'
- ▓ 'Building confidence.'
- ▓ 'Supporting me and you.'
- ▓ 'Encouragement.'
- ▓ 'Advice from more experienced people.'
- ▓ 'Confidence building in life.'
- ▓ 'Problem solving.'
- ▓ 'Inspiration.'

Some thoughts on why the young people want to take part in the scheme included:

- ▓ 'To gain information to help me in the future and find out what it is like in the NHS.'
- ▓ 'To give me guidance and help me to understand things better about nursing.'
- ▓ 'To give me more of an idea of what I have to do to get to my goal in life.'
- ▓ 'Help me achieve my ambitions.'
- ▓ 'To know where to go for advice and help me through some difficult times.'
- ▓ 'To get information and help about my future and how hard or easy it is in the NHS.'

The relationships have started and the scheme will be evaluated as it goes along. This will be done partly by monitoring the amount of e-mail exchanges and also by using pop-up forms that both the mentees and mentors will complete. These ask questions such as 'How are you getting on with your mentor?'

The evaluation will also consider if the young person feels more confident and has become a more self-directed learner.

There will be an event in the new school year where all members of the scheme will meet to discuss progress and how it can be developed. It is hoped that this can also take the form of workshops on CV preparation, interview skills and information on careers.

The link person in each school will support the mentees, and the project coordinator will mentor each group to help them become active members of the scheme.

BENEFITS OF E-MENTORING

The benefits of this type of mentoring (as opposed to more traditional forms of mentoring) are:

- It is less time consuming in terms of time off work for the mentors and travel.
- It is less disruptive for the mentees as they can also access the system from home, libraries or anywhere where they can access the internet.
- It can help to equalize the power differential between mentor and mentee.
- It removes 'first impression prejudice'.
- It gives more time for reflection and learning.

Also, within the healthcare environment staff tend to move around to other jobs in other areas of the country. This system means that the relationship can continue from anywhere.

Another major benefit is the security of the system and how easy it is to evaluate and monitor progress in the relationship.

THE CHALLENGES OF E-MENTORING

Relying on technology means that opportunities are not always equal for all. Some people may have a greater access to technology than others. For example, one school was not considered for the scheme despite having a very strong health and social care department. This meant we had to rethink the structure of the group.

There is not much doubt that e-mailing cannot replace face-to-face mentoring, and it would be pointless to try. However, it is clearly better than no mentoring and does at least embrace technology, which can add value to current learning.

The scheme has made a bit of a slow start, but the amount of e-mails has started to grow steadily. When holidays approach, the scheme will need to be supported closely in case holidays mean momentum is lost.

Currently, the main source of support is login details. These are quite complicated combinations and, consequently, the school coordinator is key to the success of the project.

Case Study 5

MENTORING IN INITIAL TEACHER TRAINING – A JOURNEY OF DISCOVERY

Jonathan Wainwright, Sheffield Hallam University

INTRODUCTION

As a recent returner to the world of education from a large commercial organization, I wanted to use this case to explore some of the differences that I perceived existed between mentoring in a business environment and mentoring in an educational context.

In the organization where I have spent the last five years it was easy to take a positivist stance on life and to come up with very clear definitions of how we, as an organization, saw coaching and mentoring. In fact, I wrote the company manual. These were my definitions of coaching and mentoring:

> Coaching is an intervention delivered by an external, professional coach.
>
> The assignment is designed to focus on a specific area of the development of an executive's performance. It takes place over a fixed timescale (usually six or twelve months) and will have a clearly defined outcome.
>
> Mentoring is a longer term, informal relationship designed to support an executive in their personal and career development. Mentors will usually be at a more senior level and are likely to be from a different part of the organisation.
> (Bank guide to executive development, 2004)

It is easy, after only a short time in my new role as a lecturer in a university, to look back and think that my interpretations lacked flexibility or even any consideration that there could be any deviation from this norm. My learning that the educational context is one that has more scope for diversity of view and greater collegiality has been quickly assimilated.

One of my first actions in coming to grips with this new use of terminology was to attend a Department for Education and Skills (DfES) conference on mentoring. This conference was part of a DfES-sponsored research into defining a national framework for mentoring and coaching. I came away more confused than when I started. Under the title of 'mentoring and coaching' – now seemingly inseparable concepts – were things like peer mentoring, classroom observation, strategic improvement partnerships and consultant headships.

This conference identified three types of mentoring and differentiated these from coaching as follows:

- *Mentoring for induction* is practical assistance offered to professional learners on joining a new school by a mentor or mentors knowledgeable about the culture and day-to-day running of the organization. For newly qualified teachers this will also include induction into the profession as a whole.

- *Mentoring for progression* is support offered to professional learners developing their understanding of the rights, responsibilities and values of their new role at the same time as developing their emerging teaching and learning or leadership practice. This may translate quickly into coaching.

- *Mentoring for challenge* is support offered to professional learners that enables them to address significant issues that may be impeding their own or their pupils' progress.

- *Coaching* is support requested by or offered to professional learners who own the responsibility for their learning development and wish to review and refine established practice in the light of their interest and concern about their students' learning, their school's development priorities and/or the introduction of alternative possibilities for teaching and learning. It is also used to develop, across a department or school, a professional culture in which it is natural to share the development of and thinking about practice.

None of these fit either of my definitions made at the start of this case and I am glad to see that I am not alone. 'As a result of rapid rise in the utilisation of the mentoring process, we believe that its meaning has become confused' (Megginson and Garvey, 2004).

This 'confusion' was recognized by the DfES in their final project report:

Whilst definitions and a framework would be widely welcomed by providers and facilitators of Continuing Professional Development, many practitioners worry that definitions will inhibit their interest in just getting on with things. There is also anxiety about imposing prescriptions or overly rigid definitions. The framework and definitions need to enable colleagues to define and refine skills and practices with increasing specificity rather than reframing every aspect of current practice. The latter would risk stalling extensive, but not yet fully developed, investment in deeper and more extended models of CPD.

There is comfort at hand when a simplified definition is offered:

> Mentoring is a relationship between two people with learning and development as its purpose. Central to mentoring is 'the mentee's dream' (Caruso, 1996), mentoring is primarily for the mentee. The process is therefore fundamentally associated with a desire to progress, to learn and understand and to achieve. This core knowledge about mentoring offers both opportunity and challenge. Mentoring has the potential to be equally constructive as destructive. This is the nature of the human condition.
>
> (Megginson and Garvey, 2004)

Subsequent DfES work offers the conclusion that 'mentoring and coaching are widely recognised as potentially powerful forms of CPD; there is a new wave of enthusiastic attempts to harness them but practice is not always well understood or appropriately resourced'.

In my journey, and as seen in much educational literature, the only time that the word 'mentoring' is used other than in the expressions 'mentoring and coaching' or 'coaching and mentoring' is in the mentoring of a student undergoing initial teacher training. Students who are training to be teachers undertake a course that includes three teaching practices, ie periods of time with a class where they are to a greater or lesser extent left to their own devices.

This analysis focuses on two students who are taking part in their final teaching practice. In this practice they take over a class from the current class teacher. The teacher may or may not be present while the student is teaching.

The mentoring process here forms the description of a very clear journey where there is a determined timescale – seven weeks; a defined destination – the teacher's success (or failure); and clear staging posts – five meetings.

Seven weeks, five mentoring meetings and one result.

THE STUDY

The semi-structured interviews I conducted were in two primary schools, both accustomed to welcoming students on their final teaching practice. I spoke with a mentor/student pair in each school. Let's call them Fieldhouse and Bracken.

At Bracken, and at her request, I first interviewed Karen, the mentor. Richard (the student) joined us later. Richard was quite happy with this arrangement. At Fieldhouse, Emma, the deputy head, is the mentor. Her student is Sara. It was my original intention to interview them together. However, this did not happen so I had to carry out two separate interviews. There are some interesting side issues here. Sara is a late entrant to teaching, having previously worked as a classroom assistant in the same school. Her sister is also a mentor at the school.

I wanted to explore four areas of interest:

1. the meaning of mentoring;
2. the history and development of the relationship over the timescale;
3. a description of a typical mentoring conversation;
4. learning from the process.

I was also interested in the idea of power in the relationship. Habermas (1979) has the idea that the differences in power and status between people can distort the communication between them (Garvey and Williamson, 2002).

My own concern was that I thought that the mentor ultimately has control over whether, or not, the student has a future as a teacher.

AREAS OF COMMONALITY

In both schools, mentoring conversations follow a lesson observation. Specific targets are set to be observed during the lesson, and briefing on what these targets are is given at the previous feedback session. A key part of the mentoring relationship is then about the mentor providing the student with feedback on his or her performance.

BRACKEN

Karen's definition of mentoring was about 'finding the fine line between offering support but not telling how to do things. I think the hard part is allowing them to make mistakes. If they were handed everything then the mentoring would not be successful… Ultimately I want to get him to look forward to becoming a classroom teacher.'

This gives an indication that mentoring is seen as a process designed both to support the student in becoming a teacher and to add an air of excitement and anticipation.

Over the course of the mentoring relationship, Karen describes the conversation changing from 'guiding', in the initial meeting, to asking 'What did you think?' in the final meeting, and eventually the idea that 'Richard should take on the responsibility of mentoring himself'. There is here the possibility of a new concept of 'self-mentoring', which may well be worthy of further exploration elsewhere.

The conversation itself seems to follow the structure of the lesson starting with a discussion on how the targets have been met, looking at areas for improvement and setting targets for the next session. There is always an outcome expected from the conversation and this is around action based on the feedback and to embed change in practice.

Richard was difficult to engage in conversation. He saw mentoring as 'guidance and support to improve practice' and conceded that without mentoring he would not have progressed. I tried to pursue issues around power in the relationship. Richard offered the view that he had felt daunted when, at a previous teaching practice, his mentor had been the deputy headteacher. Karen's earlier comment was that she was surprised by the 'huge confidence with which people enter the profession... I don't understand this. Maybe it does look a bit easy... until they try to plan their first lessons.'

I was reminded of Furlong and Maynard's (1995) view that 'Systematic enquiry into one's own practice can be a highly potent form of professional development for the experienced practitioner; but students, in the earliest stages of their professional development, have neither the time nor the breadth of experience to do more than experiment with such an approach.'

FIELDHOUSE

Sara saw a mentor as 'someone who is there to support and is there to listen; to point out good and negative things; to tell me the things to work on and then to give a really good example... examples of things to do better drawing on her range of experience. That's the stage that I'd like to get to.'

Once again the emphasis is on the support side of the relationship and there continues to be a perception that the mentor is there to provide guidance.

Sara sees the relationship as being formal – 'I'm the student, Emma's the mentor' – but also one that is helpful, where she is 'open to all the advice Emma gives'.

The concept of power was interesting. Sara was adamant that 'it's not about what she says goes' but that 'she has the experience... I was apprehensive at first but I was completely put at ease'.

However, Sara also describes a residential course for the children that she attended with Emma. 'It felt as though I was being watched all the time – a 48-hour interview.'

Emma saw this quite differently. 'I felt that Sara made a valuable contribution. She really took responsibility for making sure that the children had a good time.'

Emma is the most experienced teacher in this small group. She saw mentoring as 'making sure that the student gets the best chance at getting the best from the course – supporting in whatever we can do to help a non-teacher to become a teacher'.

She describes an approach almost identical to Karen's, which again follows the structure of the lesson and again expects that there will be outcomes and targets set for next time. 'There is a degree of formality because there is so much riding on this and so little time.' She leaves a meeting 'hopeful that what's been spoken about will happen, hopeful of change, hopeful that the student is not destroyed and that they feel good about the good bits of feedback. There has to be some challenge – if we were both just happy there would be no point us being there.'

There is much in this, the ideas that a mentor knows and tells whether something has been good or bad practice (though the word 'bad' is not used by teachers), that the mentor does have the power to destroy the future of the student (but does not use it) and equally has the ability to bestow blessing.

Emma did talk about power in terms of her 'sneaky deputy head side'. At Fieldhouse, one of the recent drives has been to have children face the front of the class, in rows, when they are engaged in individual work. The class teacher whose class was being taken by Sara had not adopted this practice. Emma has been able to use her role as a mentor to get Sara to put this into practice.

She also saw the mentoring of the students as an opportunity to bring in new tools and techniques that she felt should be the most up-to-date information. 'If it's my class they are teaching it also gives me the opportunity to look at my class when they are being taught by someone else.' However, it is unlikely that the usual class teacher will be the student's mentor.

Emma later, on reflection, e-mailed me this statement:

I've been thinking about summing up mentoring in a sentence. – Here goes – A mentor is an agent of the university to develop the existing skills of students in the profession of teaching as it exists at that time. Mentors also have the duty to challenge and support the student in their initial training.

I didn't feel comfortable with the term power and have thought that actually the power lies with the joint work between the University/Mentor/Senior Management team at the school.

The difference between feedback to teachers and students is that with an existing teacher it is about developing their skills within the context of the school and the teaching profession and this responsibility lies with the school. With a student, the responsibility is a joint venture and is about meeting the standards set out by the Teacher Training Agency.

CONCLUSIONS

Mentoring in initial teacher training seems to mean support and guidance. It is the formal part played by someone I would describe as a school-based tutor in converting a student into a teacher. It involves assessment and control over the admission or refusal of entry into the profession and it involves passing on practical knowledge, tips and hints to a student. While learning and development are the purpose of the conversation, that learning seems to belong to the student to the extent that the 'mentor' role becomes redundant.

In these mentoring conversations it seems that the overwhelming amount of time in the conversation is spent with the student listening and the mentor talking. In our conversation, Emma thought that by the final meeting she was down from 95 per cent to 60 per cent of the time. This would make interesting further study.

The fixed nature of intervention was not seen as something to be challenged. It was five sessions over seven weeks with forms to be completed and submitted and files to be maintained. It follows the lesson plan, starting at the beginning and finishing with actions and targets for next time. I wonder whether the rigour of the lesson structure is transferred into the way that the mentoring conversation is conducted.

Learning from the conversation is about improving performance. Perhaps the short nature of the relationship prevents the discussion of anything further or deeper. It is tempting to wonder whether this means that teachers only get the opportunity to talk about the immediacy of doing a better job in the classroom rather than becoming a teacher.

There is undeniable power in the relationship though this is rarely consciously used. The students do not seem overly concerned by this though hierarchy has more of an impact than the mentor's role.

Teachers seem to enjoy the opportunity to welcome and support others into the profession and to help and guide them on that journey.

REFLECTIONS

Does this process really give students enough to reach their maximum potential? Or is it just enough for now because they do not know what their potential is or could be or they just do not have the time to think about it?

I feel strongly that the relationships described here are not mentoring relationships. At best they are performance coaching. I prefer the term 'tutor'.

From a practical point of view, neither of the mentors I spoke to had received, or asked for, feedback on her mentoring style. Again, is this a capability that needs to be developed in the student?

None of the relationships had established ground rules on how the mentoring would work. The student therefore has no choice but to see this as another hurdle on the way to being a teacher.

THE END OF THE JOURNEY... AND THE START OF A NEW ONE

So where does this leave me in my own journey? I feel slightly saddened for the present but full of excitement for the future.

As a result of this peep into my new world, I am concerned that assessment, and ways of getting things done, however pleasantly managed, form part of this particular mentoring process. I am saddened by the inflexibility of the 'five sessions, seven weeks, one result' approach to mentoring in initial teacher training. I see it as a wasted opportunity that students undertaking initial teacher training are not given access to real mentors – mentors who will take time to challenge, support and offer much more of themselves and their experience. The mentors I spoke to have extremely well-developed mentoring skills, though are the last to admit it. Teachers seem to be a more modest group than their students. Perhaps they could blow their own trumpets more tunefully.

One of the reasons for me leaving the commercial world was my becoming increasingly dismayed with the pressure to conform and the fear of not conforming. My resentment of the expectation that I would demonstrate a set of competences by doing what I was told to do, and in a particular way, was becoming unbearable.

Where was the ambiguity with its inherent excitement and adventure?

I was on a journey of self-destruction. I indeed was one of the people responsible for creating the very definitions and labelling the processes that I found so harmful.

I am now excited that, amongst the teachers that I meet, there is an overwhelming desire to help students enjoy their new world and to become as good as they can possibly be. There is not a hint of parochialism in sight, simply a generosity of spirit. This I suspect is based on a deep desire for learning that pervades the profession. I find it so refreshing to talk about learning without sounding like an evangelist.

'The impact that any individual has on our lives cannot easily be measured. But the benefits of having a mentor... someone who has given freely of his or her own time, can last a lifetime' (Ivan Lewis, Parliamentary Under-Secretary of State for Young People and Adult Skills, May 2002).

For the onward journey I am enthused that coaching and mentoring will form such a large part of the continuing professional development agenda that will affect all those who work in schools.

I am delighted that there will be no delay as a result of an etymological struggle, however fascinating that would be. I am pleased that definitions of coaching and mentoring are ambiguous and are likely to remain that way. I am glad that there is a profession where ambiguity around learning does not cause discomfort. I am optimistic that energy and time will be invested in really using dialogue to support learning. I have made the right move.

Mentoring in education is at its beginning.

REFERENCES

Furlong, J and Maynard, T (1995) *Mentoring Student Teachers*, Routledge, London

Garvey, B and Williamson, B (2002) *Beyond Knowledge Management: Dialogue, creativity and the corporate curriculum*, Pearson Education, Harlow

Habermas, J (1979) *Communication and the Evolution of Society*, trans T McCarthy, Heinemann, London

Megginson, D and Garvey, B (2004) Odysseus, Telemachus and Mentor: stumbling into, searching for and signposting the road to desire, *International Journal of Mentoring and Coaching*, **2** (1) (online journal, www.emccouncil.org)

OTHER SOURCE

www.teachernet.gov.uk

JIVE: TACKLING GENDER STEREOTYPING IN ENGINEERING, CONSTRUCTION AND TECHNOLOGY

Lis Merrick, Coach Mentoring Ltd and Rachel Tobbell, Mentoring Strategy Manager, UK Resource Centre for Women in Science, Engineering and Technology

AIMS OF JIVE

JIVE (Joint Interventions) Partners is a partnership of 10 organizations in England and Wales working together from May 2002 until May 2005. The two lead partners are based at Bradford College and Sheffield Hallam University and it includes organizations such as the Open University and the Equal Opportunities Commission. JIVE provides models and strategies for breaking down barriers and tackling gender stereotyping in the engineering, construction and technology sectors, addressing current skill shortages and aiming to reduce the gender pay gap.

THE AIMS OF JIVE MENTORING

The JIVE mentoring programmes aim to achieve the objectives by:

- providing motivation;
- increasing confidence;
- providing role models;
- encouraging networking;
- increasing retention within both learning and employment;
- inspiring women and girls to work and study in non-traditional fields;
- increasing recruitment levels in both employment and education;

■ tackling issues such as managing the transition into a non-traditional role;

■ providing support through professional examinations and career breaks and helping women to break through the 'glass ceiling'.

JIVE MENTORING

This case study considers who has been involved in the mentoring programmes, how the programmes originated, the range of mentoring offered, the implementation model utilized and some personal reflective experience of one mentoring pair.

Since May 2002, over 400 women and schoolgirls have been trained and matched nationally as part of the JIVE national mentoring programmes. These include:

■ schoolgirls interested in a career in science, engineering, construction and technology, or who wish to find out more about non-traditional careers;

■ women students studying craft and technician-level courses;

■ women studying on degree courses in engineering, construction and technology;

■ women who are working in engineering, construction or technology and have completed their education and training.

JIVE mentoring has established a national network of women working and studying in the engineering, construction and technology industries, and within the engineering construction industry. The regular networking meetings offer an opportunity for women to meet other women studying or working in a similar field to their own.

JIVE mentoring evolved from an original mentoring scheme called 'Let's TWIST', which began in March 2001 and which included schoolgirls, undergraduates, further education students and alumni from the University of Bradford.

As JIVE Partners' mentoring experience has grown and with the gathering of formative evaluation material, the mentoring programmes have been further developed to meet the varying needs of the mentees. This has been part of a conscious development framework for the programme. As a result, JIVE now offers a range of mentoring programmes to women in non-traditional areas of study and work.

The JIVE approach is to invite women to mentor other women in their industries, as they have experienced directly the benefits and difficulties of studying and working in these fields. In role model mentoring, a partnership approach is encouraged with mentor and mentee working together and learning from one another. Both parties are found to benefit from this two-way learning relationship, and growth in self-confidence, self-esteem, self-awareness and personal focus has been acknowledged as an output of the programmes. The mentoring is entirely voluntary and is based on learning and encouraging individual responsibility towards the management of self-development.

JIVE MENTORING TOOLBOX

JIVE has developed its mentoring programmes with consideration for women's learning needs, and Figure 2.6.1 demonstrates the range of mentoring products offered. These vary from an informal mentoring programme, which offers women 'friendship' and support in their first few days in a new environment, through to programmes where women are highly motivated to learn with the ongoing support of a role model mentor.

Generally, role model and peer mentoring have been utilized most widely within the programmes. However, with groups of further education and craft students and women in the trades, the Pal scheme, group mentoring and COCO programmes have been set up.

Pal scheme (partner in active learning)

- A short-term supporting relationship where a woman who has knowledge of an environment is introduced to a new entrant, to show her around, take her for coffee, introduce her to other people etc.

- May meet once, or as many times as is needed by the new entrant.

- The Pal supporter receives minimal preparation training.

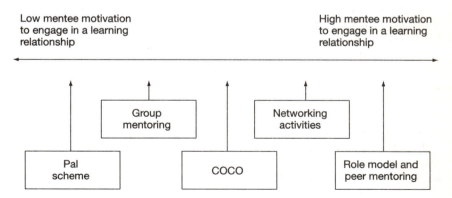

Figure 2.6.1 JIVE mentoring toolbox

Group mentoring

■ Group mentoring is generally aimed at further education students, crafts- and tradeswomen, and schoolgirls, or those more comfortable working with a small group of friends or peers.

■ One or two mentors or a JIVE mentoring coordinator plan regular sessions, perhaps once a month, which may include inviting a role model guest speaker.

■ Mentees can discuss issues and experiences with the whole group, with the mentor being present to facilitate the session and to provide extra support.

COCO (coaching for confidence)

■ A very informal one-to-one coaching relationship for a woman who does not wish to form a formal, structured learning relationship with another woman.

■ The learner is assigned a woman role model and there is no need to set objectives, unless the learner is comfortable to do so. The learner will simply articulate what she wants to get out of the relationship. Minimal training is given to the learner, mainly to set out expectations of the relationship.

■ The COCO supporter is fully trained and only makes herself available to the learner when she needs guidance or support through a particular issue, so the relationship is entirely learner driven.

Networking activities

■ All participants in the JIVE mentoring programmes are invited to regular networking events.

■ Events may consist of further mentoring skills training and providing participants with support in their relationships.

■ These sessions also allow women to meet other women in similar areas of work or study, and to form informal networks amongst themselves.

Role model and peer mentoring

■ A structured one-to-one mentoring relationship where the mentee is responsible for her own learning and maintaining contact with her mentor.

- Both mentor and mentee attend the same training to provide them with a good understanding of what mentoring is, the skills required and the benefits of a good relationship. They can also explore their own expectations of a relationship.

- Mentors and mentees are matched, usually with support from the mentoring coordinator, and a contract is agreed to clarify boundaries, expectations and objectives.

- Relationships are initially started up for one year, but may finish before this time if objectives are completed, or extended further if both mentor and mentee agree.

- Contact is maintained on a regular basis, either by meeting face to face, by e-mail, by telephone or by a mixture of these forms.

Company in-house/association programmes

- An application of role model and peer mentoring programmes that are being run in-house for women in large organizations or for members of women-only professional associations, eg at the Institution of Civil Engineers (ICE) and within the Simon Group and Lend Lease.

- Some company programmes have internal mentoring coordinators trained by JIVE Partners, so that the mentoring programme can be maintained even after the end of the project, which is an excellent method of effectively mainstreaming the programme.

- Each programme is designed, in consultation with the host organization, to focus on the most relevant and appropriate of the JIVE objectives. For example, key objectives of the ICE programme are to support newly established civil engineers through their professional examinations and to build networking contacts with women in other companies, whilst one of the programmes Lend Lease wanted to focus on involved supporting high-potential female employees.

STEP MODEL

Figure 2.6.2 is the JIVE mentoring implementation step model, which acts as a framework for the successful implementation and running of each programme.

This model was designed to support the regional mentoring coordinators of JIVE to roll out their programmes regionally with minimal support from the centre. In addition, organizations with their own mentoring coordinator could follow this model with support.

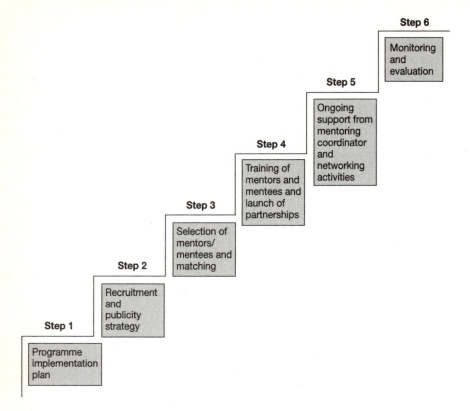

Figure 2.6.2   JIVE step model

A MENTORING PAIR – BARBARA AND PAULA

Barbara Entwistle and Paula Bleanch have been in a mentoring relationship since February 2004. Paula is a design coordinator in construction
and has worked for one company since graduating. Their experience of
mentoring demonstrates how role model mentoring can be used to
support and inspire women working in male-dominated industries. A
female mentor can provide empathy and advice, which is invaluable to a
young woman who, in this case, is still in the process of establishing her
career. For the individuals concerned, the outcomes of this relationship
included increased confidence, networking, career planning, enjoyment of
the relationship and skills development.

This is Paula's view:

I like working at the front end of the construction industry, being based on site and seeing buildings being built. My role involves managing the designers and design information on projects, acting as a bridge between the consultants and the construction team.

At the outset of the mentoring relationship, I hoped to have someone to discuss problems with and give some perspective on work situations as another woman. I don't know any other women working in construction in the North-East and I needed someone to talk to.

I originally had a woolly idea that I lacked confidence, but through the relationship Barbara has helped me to identify more accurately what the problem was and how to start to deal with it. It has also helped me to look at the boundaries that I have in my work life and because of that I decided to leave my current position, and I will be starting a new job soon.

It's great to have support from another woman in the industry, who knows what it's like to be out there working in construction. It's not really something you can explain to friends and family. It's reassuring to know that someone can understand and is there to give you a hand.

Just being involved in the mentoring programme has been a positive for me. Meeting other women working in my field has given me a big boost.

On average, we are in touch once every two weeks, but sometimes less, and use e-mail and telephone. Telephone works well as we have both been really busy recently. We have met face to face as luckily Barbara came up to Newcastle with work. Now it's my turn to visit her in Manchester.

Barbara is the area manager for VELUX roof windows. This is her view:

I originally wanted to be a nurse, but other circumstances meant that I couldn't fulfil this dream. I fell into the construction industry and have been in it for the last 15 years, starting with the building chemicals industry, then the lead manufacturing industry, which gave me the opportunity to work on many listed buildings such as cathedrals, castles and stately homes.

Through my work at VELUX, I visited Bolton Institute, which is now a university, and started studying with them. After graduating in building and construction, I was offered a place to study for a Master's degree in construction management, and I am in the last year of a three-year course, with only a 20,000-word dissertation to be submitted. I will then apply to become a full member of the Chartered Institute of Building.

Paula and I have met but mainly communicate by e-mail and telephone, as we live quite a distance apart. We haven't experienced any difficulties in our relationship, and I know that Paula feels that she is getting something from it. I do think my listening skills have improved since becoming a mentor, as I have to listen carefully to Paula in order to evaluate the problem before offering suitable advice, which hopefully helps her to resolve the issue.

Time is precious to us all and our mentoring does not take up a great deal of time, but the benefits are very satisfying. I believe that giving someone some support as a role model can have profound results. Hopefully, the relationship I have with Paula will be a long-term one, and in turn she may become a mentor herself, offering advice on her experiences to another woman in the industry who needs it.

I joined this mentoring programme to 'put something back', as I don't come across many women in the industry.

SUMMARY

The JIVE mentoring programmes have been made sustainable by training women in companies and associations to be mentoring coordinators so that they can implement women's mentoring programmes with minimal support from JIVE. Good practice in mentoring women has also been disseminated by attending and presenting at many workshops, conferences and seminars.

Evaluation has been carried out throughout the project, mainly using questionnaires and focus group techniques, and the schemes have been found to have multiple benefits for the women and the organizations taking part. In particular, reported benefits for both mentors and mentees have included:

- an increase in confidence;
- development of skills, such as listening, objective setting and learning through reflection;
- enjoyment;
- an increase in motivation;
- greater knowledge of the organization or industry;
- active career planning.

One of the main challenges facing the programme initially was using role model mentoring with women who felt a one-to-one mentoring relationship was too challenging and personal. It was at this point during 2003 that the toolbox approach to mentoring was developed to allow the flexibility of having mentoring products that suited every participant in the programme. JIVE has found this more flexible approach utilizing a range of mentoring products has been extremely successful.

Case Study 7

PLUMBERS, POETS AND LEARNING FOR EDHEC BUSINESS SCHOOL STUDENTS

Liz Borredon, EDHEC Business School, Lille, France

In the first edition of *Mentoring in Action* (Megginson and Clutterbuck, 1995), we discussed how a leading French business school launched a pilot mentoring scheme. We took a sequential approach to describing stages in setting up a mentoring programme and how finally the project was shelved. We evoked the need for cultural consideration in setting up formative relations such as mentoring. Cultural issues are often tacit initially, but they can hinder or distort a process as they reveal themselves in action. Other points were raised. The first considered the importance of role clarification, whether for the mentor or the learner; the second concerned managing the mentoring process and providing support for both mentor and learner and, in conclusion, we focused on disappointment as a potential catalyst: a catalyst if we are able to rethink our programmes and regroup to innovate.

Unlike the sequential approach we adopted 10 years ago, this section is about the complex interaction between several learning contexts and the building of formative relations. We have not focused on mentoring as the sole means to an end but have taken mentoring as a pivotal element within a learning process. As such, we could question how valid the term 'mentoring' is within the context described. We leave the reader to determine the usefulness of this terminology and the degree to which the EDHEC Business School experience is transferable to other contexts.

Apart from being placed in the league of the first five business schools in France recognized for academic excellence that underpins preparation for management, EDHEC Business School has long been dedicated to the personal development of its students. While such development was visible and valued in 1995, the seminars and projects associated with personal development did not permit the learner to see this as a continuous and integrated learning process. The pilot mentoring scheme was not fully integrated into the syllabus either. Thus, when the school redefined its programme recently, the more traditional 'expert'-oriented

teaching was partnered with an inductive programme that lays foundations for lifelong personal development and learning. Named the
Managerial Competency Programme, this new orientation has now
become the Managerial Competences and Leadership Chair.

What follows is the values that guide our work within the Chair, how
mentoring contributes to developing aspects of leadership and, in
conclusion, where the Chair stands in 2005 with its projects and aspirations for collaboration and further development.

THE MANAGERIAL COMPETENCES AND LEADERSHIP CHAIR

Foundations and values

Initially, we were asked to teach leadership. However, those of us engaged
in responding to this suggestion believed that, while leadership could not
be taught, it could be developed. Central to leadership development is the
creation of contexts that are favourable to learning. Thus we needed to
identify our own approach to leadership development and what type of
context we could create that would enable this development to take place.

James March of Stanford University talks about leadership in terms of
being both *plumber* and *poet* (March and Weil, 2003):

- *Plumber* because of the capacities needed for ensuring efficiency:
  complementary skills that ensure maintenance of functions, delegation
  permitting initiative, quality control and attaining standards of
  achievement, with a discreet coordination permitting the continual
  attuning of the engines that power the system.
- *Poet:* when sense is given to actions undertaken, the mundane is trans-
  formed into the exceptional, meaning is discovered and life is rendered
  purposeful. Words forge vision, and inspiration is transferred through
  personal and collective fulfilment rather than through power and
  coercion. Humble, able to anticipate, open minded, with personal
  values and self-esteem, sensitive to interpersonal relations, risk taker,
  the *poet* crosses boundaries and overcomes intimidating limitations.

So, to build on James March's positioning of leadership, we sought to
awaken the individual who accesses the *plumber* and the *poet* within themselves. We could say that 'plumbing' is dealt with in some traditional
seminars or training programmes. 'Poetry' is less clearly integrated and, as
the hypothetico-deductive scientific basis is absent, many would shy away
from this. Our concern, of course, is not to create poets in the literal sense
of the word. It is to focus on the individual who chooses his or her own
focus of development.

Also inspired by the work done at Case Western Reserve University (Boyatzis *et al*, 1995) and encouraged by our own collaboration with corporations that choose to recruit EDHEC alumni, we identified a human competence approach as a road into leadership, and identified seven areas that were to guide our pedagogy and our innovation:

1. ethical and cultural awareness;
2. initiative and entrepreneurship;
3. collaborative thinking and team spirit;
4. self-mastery and interpersonal skill;
5. leadership and team facilitation;
6. managerial communication;
7. creativity in decision making and problem solving.

So what contexts would permit development? We based our design on David Kolb's learning cycle (Kolb, 1984). Figure 2.7.1 shows the type of context we put in place. We have not explained how we have developed the experiential and action learning components in this section. While we refer to lectures and formal input under 'Theory, concepts' at the base of the model, we have described this in relation to deeper levels of learning in the next section where we also explain how development within the learning team draws on mentoring for this purpose. We suggest that all aspects illustrated in our figure contribute to the emergence of both

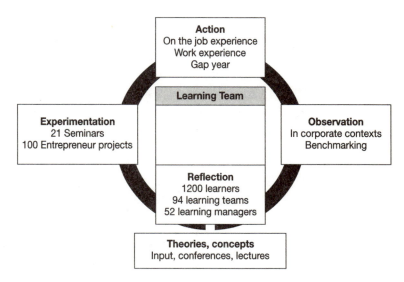

Figure 2.7.1   Learning contexts in 2005

plumber and *poet*; however, specific focus is on the impact of the learning team in this respect.

The learning team and the learning manager

In most institutions, whether they be academic, business or other, creating space in which knowledge is created is seldom considered. And yet, human intelligence, insight, understanding or creativity is lost or untapped, to the detriment of the institution and, above all, to the detriment of human fulfilment and actualization of personal potential. At EDHEC Business School we found that opportunity for building on the other areas of learning was not maximized and certainly learning through dialogic exchange was almost non-existent. The learning team is a context that encourages learning through reflection and through conversation. The learning manager is similar to a mentor, coach or facilitator (Rosinski, 2003) who adopts a maieutic approach (Socratic-type questioning) to guiding learners.

The learning team is made up of 12 students who remain together throughout their study at the school. They meet regularly, they have a number of specific challenges, and each learner records observations in a log book. Thus there is an ongoing, formalized personal record of incidents that influence learning.

The learning manager is usually but not always a permanent faculty member. All participate in an initial training programme, and learning managers review together regularly. The reviews permit stepping back, understanding the process and building improvements. They learn through doing, reflecting and experimenting and through conversation between themselves, quite apart from learning when with students.

LEARNING CONVERSATIONS: CENTRAL TO MENTORING WITHIN THE LEARNING TEAM

Although conversation is our daily practice, learning conversation is of a very different order. By learning conversation (Baker, Jensen and Kolb, 2002), we mean the process by which interpersonal understanding is attained through the equally valued contribution of each of its members. In this sense, such conversations are learning dialogues concerned with the surfacing of the political, social and even emotional reactions that might be blocking operating effectiveness (Raelin, 2000). This is not easy! Even if the institutions we mentioned earlier aspire to this degree of transparency, our natural human tendency is to rely on routines that ensure normal functions of business development, without modification of frameworks. This is referred to as single loop learning, level one learning or maintenance learning (Argyris, 1993).

And yet, if we aspire to drawing on the excellence of the *plumber*, we need to be able collectively to sustain enquiry into the process, assumptions and certainties that compose everyday experience. If we aspire to accessing the *poet*, we need to encourage expression, lucidity, listening to others, drawing out meaning and making explicit that which is tacit, intangible and difficult to verbalize. This is associated with aspects of mentoring, and the role of the learning manager gradually to permit the creation of a space that allows for such dialogue.

In Figure 2.7.2, we see how Isaacs (1999) positions the fundamental choice that leads to the type of conversation he terms generative dialogue and the stages that lead up to making this possible. The underpinning values are very different to those that ground debate, a form of conversation sometimes accompanied by *unproductive defensiveness*, allowing little space for the authentic questioning and collaborative understanding that we suggested leadership would include. When we talk of double loop

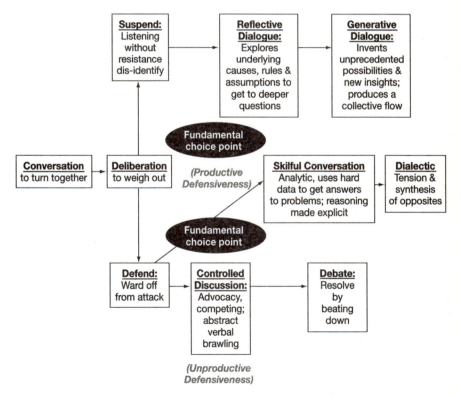

Figure 2.7.2   Conversational learning as turning together (Isaacs, 1999:41)

learning, or deeper learning, we mean that we have the courage to examine the theories in which our actions are grounded. In so doing, reflective dialogue modifies and evolves our so-called 'theories'. Thus, as David Kolb suggests, action informs theory, and theory informs action. This does not happen automatically. It is an intentional act that involves reflection and most often needs others with whom to reflect and develop.

In Adair's book on leadership (1983), Schweitzer is quoted as saying: 'I do not believe that we can put into anyone ideas which are not in [them] anyway. As a rule, there are in everyone some good ideas, like tinder. But much of this tinder catches fire only when it meets some flame or spark from outside; that is from some other person.'

For us, Schweitzer's 'ideas' are the individual and collective inherent wisdom and potential that seeks actualization. The tinder is sparked through relationship; it is part of the chemistry between individuals as experienced between 'seeker' and 'guide' or in the relationship between 'mentor' and 'learner'. Progressively, we have found members of the learning team themselves become catalysts in the development and deepening of learning.

It would, however, be an illusion to claim that all students integrate this approach at the same pace and with the same degree of interest and personal engagement. We see that each one works at his or her own pace and that, in spite of negativity, misunderstanding or withdrawal in the first year of the learning team, there are quite considerable transitions made when the learning team enters its second year. By transitions, we mean a shift from silence to *skilful conversation* and even a shift from *skilful conversation* to *reflective dialogue* (see Figure 2.7.2). It is also interesting to see how the team moves between *choices* and how awareness of these choices develops. As with all learning programmes, student evaluations provide us with feedback at the close of each academic year. In 2004, the end of the first academic year in which learning teams and Managerial Competence Development were formalized, 68 per cent of respondents were either satisfied or highly satisfied with the learning team experience.

ORIENTATIONS AND ASPIRATIONS IN JUNE 2005

We have not explained the content of the 21 seminars that nourish reflection and sense making within the 94 learning teams with 54 learning managers from all disciplines. These are, however, an integral part of the learning process. Without all facets of learning we believe that the learning team would not provide sufficiently fertile ground for the development we aspire to.

The Managerial Competences Chair is represented in Figure 2.7.3. Mentoring and the learning team are situated within innovation and learning and are seen as transversal. This means that all disciplines within the business school contribute to the development of competences. The

Figure 2.7.3 The Managerial Competences and Leadership Chair

angle from which a competence is addressed will differ, as will the context created for developing awareness, theory or experience in a given domain. When we speak of theory as provided, we often experience this as a deductive approach to programme design. There is also another theory-building approach that is inductive. Most of our seminars allow learners to build theory and compare this with research in a given area. The learning team, however, provides yet another space for examining theory and enriching it through reflection based on experience.

At present we have two corporate sponsors. With them we develop a number of collaborative projects; they contribute to research as well as to creating and developing learning situations. We await another two sponsors before forming our steering committee.

We are conducting two major research projects. These converge in their focal investigation, which is inquiry into leadership learning. One project questions the nature of leadership and the degree to which recognized leaders adopt strategies for developing their leadership. Thus, it considers what type of learning impacts practice and developmental strategies at executive level. The other project researches the nature of engagement in learning, with a specific focus on the structured conversation in which there is a mentor role, whether this is within the business school or within corporate situations. EDHEC Business School is conducting the project in collaboration with five other institutions within three different countries. The European Mentoring and Coaching

Council supports the project, and the Academy of Management Mentoring Committee (USA) is a member of our network.

CONSIDERATIONS FOR LEARNING FROM THE EXPERIENCE TO DATE

In this section we have outlined a project that could appear heavy in logistics and ambitious in its vision. We have an admirable support team; board-level confidence was remarkable at the outset when there was little to prove that faculty would readily integrate the project. Having two corporate members is immensely valuable and we are continually rewarded by the enthusiasm and the breakthrough in understanding that comes unexpectedly.

In conclusion to this section, we share some lessons learned and questions that we have asked and are continually asking:

- The learning teams function over a period of between three or four years. Learning maturity increases. It takes time before there are noticeable transitions. Transformation in terms of personal development appears to be slow. We have noticed, after the transition has been made, that much happened in silence, without revealing itself. It is difficult for those who manage mentoring projects to identify given stages in development especially where groups are involved. Paradoxically, there is both a timeless alchemy to learning and a linear time span. Change manifests itself at a moment in time while the process is ongoing. The log book and learning summaries contribute to learners monitoring awareness of their own progress. But progress is seen after it has taken place. Some learning managers want to avoid a 'no man's land' syndrome where students do not see the point. They think it best to structure and explain. Others see 'chaos' as an inevitable part of the process. How do we integrate both approaches?

- Managing such projects involves passion, conviction and patience. Trusting the process is critical. Leaders or pioneers of such projects need their own developmental process firmly in place. Even if there are no answers, questions need to be deepened. How do you encourage your mentors' personal development?

- It is easier to convince on the need for *plumbers* than for *poets*. The language we use has to be understood. Critical to any such programme is having the equivalent of board involvement, even if the board is absent on a daily basis. What happens if conviction is apparent at middle management level but not at senior level? Conversely, if board approval is given, how do you engage potential collaborators in such a project?

REFERENCES

Adair, J (1983) *Effective Leadership*, Pan, London

Argyris, C (1993) *Knowledge for Action: A guide to overcoming barriers to organizational change*, Jossey-Bass, San Francisco, CA

Baker, A, Jensen, PJ and Kolb, DA (2002) *Conversational Learning: An experiential approach to knowledge creation*, Greenwood, Westport, CT

Boyatzis, RE *et al* (1995) *Innovation in Professional Education: Steps in a journey from teaching to learning*, Jossey-Bass, San Francisco, CA

Isaacs, W (1999) *Dialogue and the Art of Thinking Together*, Doubleday, New York

Kolb, D (1984) *Experiential Learning: Experiencing as the source of learning and development*, Prentice Hall, New Jersey

March, JG and Weil, T (2003) *Le Leadership dans les Organisations* (Un cours de James March, rédigé et annoté par T Weil), Les Presses de l'École des Mines, Paris

Megginson, D and Clutterbuck, D (1995) *Mentoring in Action*, 1st edn, Kogan Page, London

Raelin, J (2000) *Work Based Learning: The new frontiers of management development*, Prentice Hall, New Jersey

Rosinski, P (2003) *Coaching across Cultures: New tools for leveraging national, corporate and professional differences*, Nicholas Brealey, London

Case Study 8

MENTORING BLACK JUNIOR ACADEMICS AT THE UNIVERSITY OF THE WITWATERSRAND

Hilary Geber, Centre for Learning, Teaching and Development, University of the Witwatersrand, South Africa

The careers of young academics at South African universities are situated within the context of the last two decades of rapid change in the global and national environment. There were extremely low numbers of black academics employed at traditionally white universities in South Africa during the apartheid era. Racial segregation was enforced and black students were excluded after 1959 when universities specifically for African and Indian students were established. In post-apartheid terminology these are referred to as historically disadvantaged universities (HDUs). Historically advantaged universities (HAUs) are those that were almost exclusively white and that remained so until the end of the apartheid era. The integration of black *academics* into historically white universities has been a national priority since 1994, although the process has been slow compared with the rapid increase in black *student* enrolments at HAUs.

The University of the Witwatersrand (Wits) attempted to redress the under-representation of black academics on its staff by establishing various equal opportunity programmes from 1987 onwards. The success rate in retaining black academics was very poor, attributed to a lack of long-term employment opportunities and career progression and a general failure to provide mentorship and guidance to participants in such schemes.

The Wits transformation process is not informed merely by increasing the numbers of black academics: excellence and added value are also desired. As part of this transformation process, the Dr TW Kambule Growing Our Own Timber (GOOT) mentoring programme was established with donor funding to enable aspiring black academics to pursue the completion of their studies as well as introducing them to the academic workplace. A mentor is appointed to nurture and guide participants to become fully fledged professionals in their own right.

The Growing Our Own Timber mentoring programme aimed to recruit, develop and retain a more diverse academic staff from 2000 to 2005 through the creation of 30 three-year contract associate/junior lectureship posts (10 per year in 2000, 2001 and 2002) for black postgraduates wanting to become academics. In addition to the salaries of these mentees, the programme provided funds for mentoring, visits to overseas institutions and conference attendance.

The university community was informed through a call for applications sent by the Office of Transformation and Employment Equity. The vice-chancellor championed the programme, and deans and heads of schools were keen to endorse applications from pairs partly because promising young academics who could not afford to pay for tuition could be enrolled and have their salaries paid as supernumerary members of staff. Junior members of staff doubling as higher degree candidates were appointed to the school at no cost. The terms of the grant allowed extra research funding to be given to the mentor as well.

No programme of this nature for mentoring of early-career academic staff had ever been launched before in South Africa, so a full-time coordinator and part-time administrative secretary reporting to the Director of Transformation and Employment Equity were appointed to manage the programme.

Two cohorts of mentors and mentees were appointed in the first two years, 10 pairs in each cohort. The pairs set their own objectives, mostly to do with higher degree studies, as all mentors were also the mentees' higher degree supervisors, and the programme coordinator spent time on routine administrative tasks and disbursing the grants but did not address the training needs of mentors and mentees in the first two years. As most mentors in higher education in South Africa have not had any formal training, they tend not to be aware of the scope of academic mentoring for junior colleagues. An important facet of the training would be to distinguish the differences between higher degree supervision and mentoring of junior colleagues. It would have been desirable to build a core group of competent, committed mentors to mainstream the process for all newcomers. One senior mentor admitted that:

> Even when the programme started it never occurred to one that mentoring was significantly different from supervision… and what supervision and mentoring as we understand it currently has on expectations. I think the most exacting thing in mentoring… is that you are forced to reflect fairly critically about what you are likely to achieve… I think the most challenging thing is having to live up to the expectations, that the mentee will have gotten something out of you, both in terms of his academic research production and also perhaps, more importantly, and because this is not something which we always take into account when we are doing supervision, and that is the teaching.

An external evaluator was employed by the programme to evaluate the progress of the programme at the end of the first year. The evaluator made many recommendations that were not implemented and were reiterated in the second and third evaluations undertaken during the second year of the programme.

The programme was transferred to the Centre for Learning, Teaching and Development at the beginning of the third year after the resignation of the coordinator. As the Centre for Learning, Teaching and Development is a staff development unit in the university it was felt that the expertise needed for the ongoing support of the participants would be better addressed by a coordinator who had such expertise. A third cohort was appointed and trained in the third year. In the final year of the programme the coordination was transferred to a new equity development training unit that deals with all equity programmes funded by external donors, but which does not have any specialist knowledge of mentoring.

The culture of Wits and other HAUs has long been perceived as indifferent and unfriendly to aspiring black academics, so when it became clear in the third year of the programme that some mentees were having to deal with exclusion and covert racism in their departments a workshop on diversity called 'Acknowledging and working with difference' was organized. But it was used by both mentors and mentees to discuss structural issues and did not address real concerns about diversity. The facilitators of the workshop expressed the opinion that there is a silencing of issues of difference and discrimination in these types of descriptions, but the workshop seemed to have suggested that this is enabled by the overwhelming attempt on the part of both mentors and mentees to assimilate into an ideal type of what is perceived to be an academic identity.

They noted that the implication here is serious in that the assimilation into a HAU or Wits academic identity has the potential to silence the actual identities people may have, their situated knowledges and experiences, their histories, their pasts and presents and their ways of knowing and experiencing their worlds. The point here is that the construction of the HAU academic identity seems to be based predominantly on assimilation rather than working with and acknowledging difference.

It is clear that the whole environment in which they work is highly racially charged as well, as one mentee described:

> There is a lot of antagonism because of the programme. The other PhD students not on the staff kept saying: 'How did she get on to the programme?' Perhaps the programme is not sufficiently communicated or advertised and the other peers registered for PhD were antagonistic; this is reverse racial discrimination. But we don't get enough guidance from the head of department.

The GOOT programme has been partially successful in meeting its aims. Lack of training in the first two cohorts contributed to problems for the first three years of the programme. There was a lack of clarity about the roles of academic mentors. The role of *mentor* was divided up into the component parts of the work done by academics. Mentees were asked if their mentors fulfilled the roles of *collaborative teacher*, *publisher* and *co-enquirer* for research. Between a third and a half of all mentees in this programme did not benefit from these roles.

There is a very small incidence of the *collaborative publisher* mentor role for early-career academics, and only a quarter of mentees saw their mentors in this role. It may be difficult for early-career academics to begin to publish their work without sufficient mentoring in the writing and publishing process. Yet only about one in four mentors in this programme systematically helped to shape the writing and publishing skills of their mentees by collaborating with them in producing written work for publication. As confirmation and tenure rest heavily on an academic's publications, this is one of the most vital functions for mentors to perform and yet, clearly, very few of them are doing it or, if they do, they do not begin it soon enough with their mentees. Almost three-quarters of the mentees have to brave the world of writing for internal or journal publication on their own with the attendant risk of rejection for any number of reasons. Mentees feel the lack of this kind of mentoring but few of them broach the subject with mentors, nor do they find other sources of support such as a research writing group that can provide peer support and mentoring.

Different emphases in mentoring are reported by men and women, reflecting the ways in which the relationships are constructed. Three-quarters of the men are in same-gender relationships with their mentors and report receiving more sponsorship, critical friendship, help and guidance during the transition and education than women mentees. Women have fewer same-gender relationships and most have male mentors. The tendency is for them to receive more coaching, collaborative teaching, consultation, encouragement and role modelling than men. Very few black women have black women mentors as role models and they may be doubly in difficult relationships because many have mentors who are white men. Even women in same-gender relationships report difficulty with mentors who belong to different cultural groupings.

Mentors are not being seen as role models but, although mentees emphasize how important the function is, mentors tend to downplay this, perhaps out of modesty. However, the fact that mentees expect their mentors to behave like role models cannot be ignored. This is a matter for concern in formal mentoring programmes. One of the women said her mentor should behave as a role model:

He must maintain himself as a role model – he must stay on his pedestal. The criticism he gives must be constructive and discreet and given in private. He must treat me the same as everybody else so as not to increase antagonism against me with other junior lecturers and PhD students in the department. He must be there for me when I need to talk.

When the mentor does not acknowledge the mentee or give credit for challenging work done independently, the mentee eventually realizes that the relationship is abusive and dysfunctional. A woman mentee commented on the hurt inflicted on her when she said: 'My mentor went behind my back about modules for the programme. He didn't respect me and the work I had done. He takes credit for my work. I kept that programme alive while he was sick.'

Manipulative credit taking is not something that mentees can easily counteract, as it is insidious and the mentee may only discover the credit taking long after it has happened. The length of time between the mentor's taking credit for the mentee's work and the mentee's discovery of it may be sufficiently long for others to regard the mentee's silence on the matter as condoning what the mentor has done. The mentor's behaviour may further manipulate the mentee into resentful and disempowered silence and outrage. This is a reflection of similar situations found at all levels in all academic institutions and not just in this programme.

Power issues and the denigration of women exist in some mentoring relationships. It is clear that sexism and racial discrimination can be eliminated if the person with the greatest position of power takes a strong stand against it. At least then, overt displays of it will be curtailed and women and black mentees would be able to establish relationships that do not rely on their being inferior or subordinate.

A great deal still needs to be accomplished in mentoring, although for the GOOT programme itself both time and funding have run out. The need for more systematic mentoring and coaching has been recognized by the university. The mentoring workshops being requested by both mentors and coaches have grown substantially even in schools where there is a GOOT mentoring pair.

DISCUSSION

There are a number of lessons that might be useful to other higher education organizations:

1. It was definitely not in the mentees' best interests to conflate the roles of higher degree supervisor and mentor, as supervision was seen as the primary task of the mentor. The range of mentoring roles beyond

supervision was restricted and limited by the double duty being performed by the senior academic in the relationship. The mentor as supervisor perpetuates the notion that good mentoring is the same as good supervision. The element of assessment of the mentees' work and its impact on the openness and trust in the hierarchical power relationship is often ignored by the supervisor-mentor. Mentees are certainly aware of it but are not in any position to challenge the dynamic or to have it set aside.

2. Given the pressures of time, mainly for the mentors, it would be useful if mentoring responsibilities are shared in collaborative ways with other mentors to provide wider access to academic expertise and specializations.

3. The managers, coordinators and administrators of mentoring programmes need to be knowledgeable about mentoring in higher education contexts and need to use resources expeditiously, structure programmes carefully and provide adequate support for all participants. Equity development is not the same as mentoring and it should not be assumed that mentoring will automatically take place in equity development programmes. Mentors in equity development programmes need to be trained and have their awareness of diversity issues expanded. They may also need support, particularly if they find themselves in cross-cultural mentoring relationships.

4. Selection criteria for mentees (in the sciences in particular, where a PhD is required as an entry-level qualification for a permanent post) need to be tightened to make sure that mentees taken into the programme are able to complete their studies within the period of their contracts.

5. Central to the motivation of the programme is the retention of mentees on the staff once the use of 'supernumerary post' contracts has ended. This suggestion took into account the point that no guarantee for retention of mentees was ever made in the GOOT programme. One mentee explained how her head of school handled the situation: 'Certainly it was made clear to me by my mentor, it depends on the circumstances of the school at the time the contracts end. My head of school did say to the other GOOT mentee and me from the start, and it was mentioned in meetings in the groups, that retention was not guaranteed. They would work towards it, so I had no expectations of being retained. I did not bank on it. Personally I had no expectations of being retained. I'm not saying it didn't upset me not having a job at the end but I did not bank on it.'

6. The retention rate of 50 per cent is better than the retention rate of any other programme at Wits in place from 1996 to 2005. Several factors contributed to the loss of those completing the programme: posts were not available in the departments in which they were mentored; some

departments were too small to accommodate additional staff; too
many GOOT mentees were placed in the same department and found
themselves competing with their GOOT colleagues for the only
available permanent post. Two mentees affected by the confusion
expressed it in this way: 'We had the insecurity about our jobs. It was
very stressful and it was ongoing. It was the inhumane way it was
handled, not taking our feelings into consideration. We needed closure
and it just dragged on and on. It was very stressful, wondering
whether we should focus on our PhDs or go out job hunting.'

7. Restructuring and some downsizing at the university contributed to a
    sense of insecurity and unease for many permanent members of staff
    who felt threatened by the presence of GOOT mentees. Other univer-
    sities in South Africa have appointed some GOOT mentees to the
    academic staff and have benefited from the inability of Wits to offer them
    permanent employment. One mentee commented: 'I turned down job
    offers at other universities based in the belief that I would be retained.'

The conclusions drawn by the external evaluator in the final evaluation
report of the first cohort, at the end of the fourth year, indicated that interventions like GOOT are essential in overcoming employment barriers for
black academic staff so that, when senior positions become available, there
are qualified and competent black intellectuals from within the university
to fill these positions, particularly as many resources have been ploughed
into this programme. Senior managers at Wits had well-meaning intentions to transform the racial composition of academic staff by securing
sufficient resources and formulating policy to support the establishment
and implementation of the GOOT programme. However, in their haste to
respond to the national transformation agenda, they did not pay sufficient
attention to the conditions necessary for the timber to grow.

Insufficient planning prior to the appointment of the first cohort created
unrealistic expectations and raised the spectre of the moral obligation of
the university to retain them although the university is under enormous
financial pressure, particularly around proposed salary cuts. Further
equity staff development programmes need to confront issues of institutional resistance to the challenges of academic staff transformation in a
transparent and inclusive way before they are implemented.

Nevertheless, those in the first two cohorts completing the programme
have been full of praise for the programme as they were offered opportunities to teach, publish, study abroad, attend conferences and get exposure
that other postgraduates do not get. Mentors themselves realized that the
mentoring programme had stimulated and stretched them, especially if it
was their first experience of mentoring in a higher education context, and
have been keen to disseminate their experiences to other potential mentors

at the university and at other universities in South Africa. The pairs in the third cohort have benefited from the changes made to the programme through ongoing training and support, and more regular contact. There has been a much faster completion of studies, better utilization of the study-abroad periods, better mentoring for teaching and publishing, and greater commitment on the part of the mentors to act more like mentors than simply as higher degree supervisors.

DIVERSITY MENTORING IN BT

Zulfi Hussain

BT'S ETHNIC MINORITY NETWORK (EMN) MENTORING PROGRAMME

The BT EMN mentoring programme has been running for the last 10 years. It has become an extremely successful diversity mentoring programme over the years from its very humble beginnings. It is a good example of how a mentoring programme can be developed to benefit a diverse range of people across the world by providing a local touch with global reach.

BACKGROUND

The BT EMN is a proactive, employee-based, self-help group, which is run by a small group of dedicated people over and above their very busy 'day jobs'. The EMN has grown into one of the largest company-sponsored networks of its kind in the world since its inception 10 years ago, with thousands of members worldwide.

The EMN was established to encourage greater diversity throughout BT and to help bring significant commercial benefits to BT, by helping its people and the community at large. The network has a key role to play in persuading, advising and guiding individuals in the effective promotion of racial equality. The network contributes to the creation of a level playing field for all BT's people and influences decisions in the areas of recruitment policy, personal development and training.

KEY ACHIEVEMENTS

The EMN has grown to become the leading employee development organization since its inception. It has helped BT to provide opportunities at all levels for its people and has become a role model for the business world. It has achieved successes at all levels both internally to BT and externally on a global scale.

Internal successes include:

- winning support from the BT board and aligning the network's objectives with BT's global aspirations;
- establishing strong links with the Race for Opportunity (RFO) campaign and presenting to RFO member companies regularly on employment and community initiatives;
- developing customized employee development programmes for its members;
- producing a quality magazine called *Aequalis* (Latin for 'equal'), which is read by well over 5,000 BT people including the BT board and key members of a number of external organizations;
- introducing divisional diversity awards;
- launching a highly successful mentoring programme.

Externally:

- The network has received numerous prestigious external awards and has, notably, been British Diversity Award winner for several years.
- It continues to help other organizations launch similar ethnic minority networks and has provided professional advice and consultancy to various government departments including the Home Office, Metropolitan Police, Cabinet Office and Inland Revenue. It also continues to help numerous organizations in the private and voluntary sectors to emulate its success.

THE EMN MENTORING PROGRAMME

The EMN mentoring programme was set up to develop individuals and help them discover their capabilities, understand the culture of the organization, remove barriers, break the glass ceiling, enhance their careers and achieve their full potential. The programme also helps to develop a diverse pool of talent from the ethnic minority employees from which BT can choose its future managers and leaders.

Initially the more experienced members of the network were asked to care for and train the less experienced, in a non-judgemental manner, by coaching, counselling and imparting knowledge. Over the years the mentoring programme has grown significantly, with mentors being recruited from across the organization with varying knowledge, experience and cultural backgrounds. The net result has been the production of numerous role models, higher aspirations, increased motivation, better cultural awareness and improved attainment.

THE ROLE OF THE MENTORS

The mentors have acted as advisers and guides by listening, motivating, supporting and acting as a link to the world and work. They have used their abilities to communicate effectively, acted as positive role models and been prepared to listen and relate to their mentees in order to help them realize their full potential.

They have also opened the eyes of mentees to opportunities outside their normal area of work and have helped these individuals develop new skills and break down perceived barriers, in order to take full advantage of these new-found opportunities.

Some of our current mentors have expressed the following views:

- 'The programme has really helped me understand cultural differences and has given me a real insight into my own personal filters and prejudices.'
- 'From my personal perspective, I believe the mentoring relationship contributes significantly in increasing the motivation, achievement and personal growth of the mentee whilst enhancing the skills of the mentor at the same time. It also provides major benefits to the organization by producing highly developed professional people who are its "life blood" for a successful future.'
- 'Mentoring offers you a great opportunity to develop others to their full potential whilst enhancing your own skills at the same time.'
- 'There is nothing more satisfying than to help people reach their full potential and make a difference in their personal and professional lives. I would like to take this opportunity to recommend and invite all of those people reading this report to become mentors and help make a real difference!'
- 'The mentoring programme has certainly opened up the world for me.'
- 'The programme has really helped me appreciate and value differences.'

THE ROLE OF MENTEES

The mentees who have joined the programme make up a diverse group encompassing all the different business units across BT. They are all at different stages of their careers but have a common goal to be more successful and achieve more in their personal and professional lives.

The following quotes have come from some of our current mentees:

- 'The programme has opened my eyes to new opportunities across the business.'
- 'I have a better understanding of different cultures and religions.'
- 'I now have a better understanding of senior management decision making and strategic approach.'
- 'I have received continued help, advice and guidance on how to develop new skills.'
- 'I can now objectively look at my strengths and weaknesses.'
- 'Without the mentoring programme I could not possibly have found such a great mentor in Rome, bearing in mind I am based in Leeds.'

BENEFITS OF THE PROGRAMME

The mentoring programme has provided considerable benefits for the mentees, mentors and BT.

The benefits to the mentees have included improved self-confidence, learning to cope with the formal and informal structure of the company, the receipt of career advice, extensive networking opportunities and of course managerial tutelage.

The mentors have also gained from the mentoring relationship. Benefits have included improved job satisfaction, a greater insight into their own level of knowledge, a new perspective on BT and the business case for diversity (provided by the mentee).

I have certainly benefited as a mentor, a mentee and a programme manager from the programme. The benefits have included, amongst others, better understanding of BT and its products and services, better cultural awareness, career advice and progression.

BT has gained by having a workforce with improved motivation, improved communications and a leadership development programme that not only develops participants but also ensures that key cultural values are passed on.

PROGRAMME MANAGEMENT

I, as the programme owner, plus a couple of helpers, manage the mentoring programme on a voluntary basis. We do this over and above our busy day jobs.

We all work as a team but do have agreed individual responsibilities such as database management, promotion, recruitment and matching. I have the overall management and accountability responsibility. The team generally uses audioconferencing to hold meetings but we do occasionally meet face to face to discuss and resolve any issues and/or make improvements to the programme.

Promotion and publicity

To attract new mentors and mentees and celebrate the periodic successes of the mentoring programme, the scheme is advertised and promoted in a number of ways, eg leaflets, flyers, EMN website, BT intranet, internal publications, at EMN open days that are held around the country and at the EMN annual conference.

Recruitment of mentors and mentees

Mentors and mentees are recruited in a number of different ways. These include face-to-face presentations, personal contacts, adverts in internal publications, via the intranet and through divisional campaigns organized by the various business units.

Those wishing to become mentors, mentees or both complete an application form online on the EMN website. The form asks for their contact details, grade, training and qualifications, achievements in the last two years, hobbies and interests, area of business interest and the type of person they wish to be matched up with.

Training and support

Support is provided for mentors and mentees on an ongoing basis by the mentoring team. A formal training workshop is also organized as and when required. The frequency of the workshop is currently under review.

Matching and support

The matching process is initiated once the mentor and/or mentee complete an application form online on the EMN website or send a paper copy through the post.

Mentors and mentees are matched on a regular basis to achieve best results, by sifting through the application forms, taking into account:

- *Grade.* The mentee is generally matched with someone two grades higher to ensure that the mentor has enough knowledge and experience to maximize the benefit for the mentee.
- *Location.* To avoid unnecessary travel and save time, mentors and mentees are matched close to each other wherever possible.
- *Shared interests.* These can help build rapport quickly and get the relationship off to a good start.
- *Career aspirations.* Aspirations of both the mentor and mentee are taken into account in order to find a good match for career progression of both individuals.
- *Development needs.* This is a key requirement and therefore a great deal of time and effort are spent to try to find a match that will best meet the needs of both the mentor and the mentee.

The matches are never made merely to get people off the waiting list. The policy is to wait until a very good match can be found to avoid premature failure of the mentoring relationship and any disappointment.

A letter of introduction is sent by e-mail to the mentor and mentee, asking them to make contact with each other. They are also encouraged to prepare for the first meeting to establish the ground rules of the relationship and to agree joint aims and objectives. The first meeting is mostly face to face but can also be conducted remotely via an audioconference.

The programme management team provides ongoing support for mentors and mentees, via the telephone, e-mail and, if required, face-to-face meetings.

Ending the mentoring relationship

Both mentor and mentee are encouraged to achieve closure – particularly if a mentoring relationship should break down. The reason for this is to avoid damaging the enthusiasm and commitment of both parties by such an occurrence.

Monitoring the mentoring process

The main aim of monitoring is to keep abreast of what is going on, to make changes in areas of difficulty that have been brought up by the participants, and to evaluate the scheme on a continual basis using anecdotal feedback, verbal and written reports and an annual survey/questionnaire. A comprehensive online guide is provided for both mentors and mentees as a reference for the monitoring of the relationship.

Statistics are regularly compiled and analysed to measure the performance of the programme. A close eye is also kept on the number of matched and unmatched participants, eg there are currently 160 matched mentor/mentee pairs, three unmatched mentors and six unmatched mentees on the mentoring programme. The unmatched people currently on the database will only be matched once suitable matches are found.

REWARDING MENTORS AND MENTEES

There is no formal reward but mentors and mentees are recognized for their work by having their details published on the Success Gallery, which is part of the EMN website. Their success and achievements are also celebrated in internal publications and at the EMN annual conference.

LESSONS LEARNED TO DATE

A number of lessons have been learned to date including:

- There is a need for robust end-to-end processes with clear roles and responsibilities defined.
- Continual cleansing of the database is an absolute must.
- Expectations particularly of mentees need to be managed very carefully to avoid disappointment.
- The matching process needs to be slick and efficient to maintain momentum.
- Every opportunity must be used to promote the programme and recruit new mentors and mentees.
- Progression of mentors and mentees through the organization should be tracked to help evaluate the effectiveness of the programme.

FUTURE PLANS

I have four key objectives for the year ahead as follows:

1. Formally review the programme in order to compare and analyse the feedback received from the participants. The results will be used to make any necessary changes to enhance the programme.
2. Continue to grow the scheme to broaden its appeal and extend its reach into more countries around the world. This will no doubt help more

people from many diverse cultures and backgrounds to develop and reach their full potential.

3. Develop links with other organizations that run similar mentoring programmes in order to carry out a benchmarking exercise and share best practice.

4. Gain a recognized accreditation for the programmes through organizations such as the European Mentoring and Coaching Council and Clutterbuck Associates.

CONCLUSIONS

The EMN mentoring programme has developed and grown steadily over the years and remains strong. The programme has helped countless people over the years to develop their careers and progress up the corporate ladder. It has also been instrumental in promoting cross-cultural communications, raising cultural awareness across BT and breaking down barriers.

I believe the scheme is highly respected within BT, and is recognized as a real success externally by other organizations. Many of these organizations are actively trying to create a similar scheme.

I have found clear evidence of mutual learning for the mentors and mentees and the development of a knowledge-sharing environment for individuals and the business.

THE IMPLATS PLATINUM LTD MENTORING EXPERIENCE

Peter Beck, Clutterbuck Associates South Africa and Leoni Van Wyk, Impala Platinum Ltd

COMPANY BACKGROUND

For many years Implats Platinum Ltd (Implats, formerly known as Genmin) has had formal development programmes that learner mining officials, junior engineers and learner officials in service departments were put through. These programmes are still being used today and, although all of them contain certain elements of mentorship, they tend to be very formal structured programmes with virtually no provision for customization. Nonetheless they are still very effective in that they deliver what they were designed to.

The need for a more focused approach became more apparent during the run of 2002–03. At that stage Implats was experiencing very high levels of labour turnover in critical positions. This came about to a great degree as the result of the boom in the mining industry, which raised demand for key skills.

There were a number of other factors that also contributed to this phenomenon as became clear in an employee loyalty survey focusing on the first-line supervisory staff and up – the areas where most of the labour turnover was experienced.

The survey covered issues such as remuneration and benefits, fairness at work, care and concern for employees, and training and development, as well as five core values that had been identified by Ken Berman, a management consultant, during a series of workshops that he conducted with Implats supervisory and managerial employees.

At more or less the same time, an international consulting firm, Monitor, was busy conducting a number of investigations in Implats to pinpoint areas to be addressed in order to make the organization more efficient than it already was.

Based on the data from both these investigations, top management decided to launch a major change programme, which it called 'The Third Wave'.

Gert Ackerman, the then operations executive at Rustenburg, South Africa, was the sponsor of the initiative. It comprised two legs, the one named 'Continuous improvement' and the other 'Top employer'. One of the sub-initiatives recommended under the latter was the implementation of a mentorship scheme.

THE MENTORSHIP SCHEME

The mentorship scheme is aimed at advancing the skills and careers of employees perceived by their managers as having potential – both previously disadvantaged black South Africans and white males. The organizational objectives – apart from meeting the requirements of the South African Constitution in general and the laws on removing unfair discrimination in particular – were to:

- attract, retain and develop HDSAs (historically disadvantaged South Africans);
- support the company's integrated diversity strategy;
- reinforce succession planning at both junior and senior management levels.

A literature study was conducted to identify best practices in mentoring and also to identify the most appropriate company to conduct the mentoring training, based on previous work and experience with the South African market. Implats aimed to develop a custom-made mentoring programme adjusted to the organization's culture and its employees. See Figure 2.10.1 for the process.

During phase 1 of the Implats mentoring process, we were invited to do a presentation to the human resource development team to get an overall feeling for the organization's need. This was followed by a workshop with current mentors and mentees to talk about their experiences and difficulties during the mentoring process. During this session it became clear that, while Implats was very strong on coaching, it needed to develop a formal mentoring system. People played the role of mentor and mentee without any formal training with regards to roles, responsibilities and competencies of successful mentors and mentees. During this workshop the overall objectives of the programme were identified. The next step was to do a presentation to the operating company management, who approved the programme.

Phase 2 started with the identification of the mentors and the mentees. For this purpose Implats decided to make use of the current senior and junior succession plan, to identify mentors. Those who did not want to be

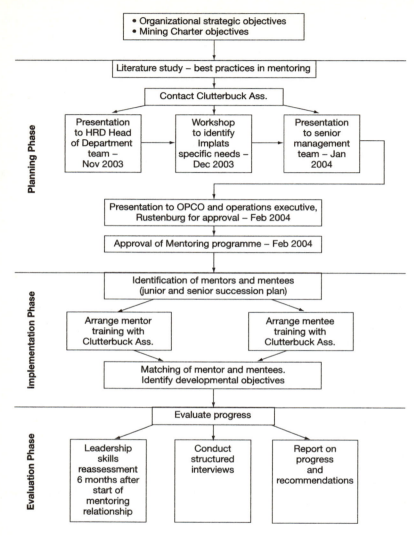

Figure 2.10.1   Mentoring process flow

trained as mentors had the opportunity to decline the training. The mentor training sessions started in March 2004 and were completed in June 2004. The identified mentees were trained between October and December 2004. The lag time here was due to the need for a review of the succession and talent pools. This proved to be a very worthwhile exercise. See Figure 2.10.2 for initial understanding of mentees' perceived needs for mentoring.

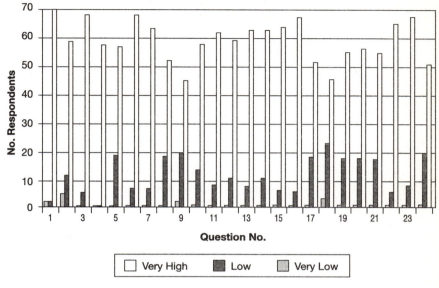

Question No.

☐ Very High   ■ Low   ▨ Very Low

Questions: Completed prior to the workshop.

1 Commitment to continuous personal and professional development.
2 Willingness to seize all opportunities for self-development.
3 Willingness to learn from someone else's experience.
4 Commitment to building mutually beneficial relationships.
5 Enthusiasm for gaining as much as possible from the relationship.
6 Willingness to be open and honest in asking for help and telling the whole story.
7 Willingness to listen to others.
8 Willingness to make time available for mentoring.
9 Comfort with gaining critical personal insights.
10 Willingness to accept constructive criticism.
11 Willingness to change attitudes and behaviour as a result of discovering that change is needed.
12 Desire to be open minded about information and opinions that challenge his or her own.
13 Willingness to rise to a challenge.
14 Commitment to a positive, determined, persevering mind-set (not negative, moaning, whingeing).
15 Willingness to take responsibility for managing his or her own career.
16 Desire to develop the 'good' into the 'excellent'.
17 Willingness to take increasing responsibility for managing the mentoring relationship.
18 Realistic about not expecting too much too soon.
19 Willingness to challenge others' views and opinions (rather than accept them without question).
20 Willingness to balance deference and respect for the mentor with a challenging/questioning/non-compliant attitude.
21 Willingness to accept rebuke, and take appropriate action.
22 Willingness to express gratitude.
23 Sense of humour.
24 Clarity of ambition.

As evidenced in the above graph there is a very high need, as perceived by the mentees, for development.

Figure 2.10.2   Mentee receptivity at Implats

Phase 2 also involved matching the mentors and the mentees. Mentees were encouraged to choose mentors from disciplines different from their own.

During phase 3, an evaluation will take place to determine the success and impact of the programme on the mentor and the mentees. The evaluation process will have several legs to it as identified in Figure 2.10.1. We will carry out structured interviews as well as asking participants to complete a six-month mentor/mentee questionnaire to measure the quality of the relationships.

This intervention is the only one of its kind in the mining industry and therefore required a unique and flexible approach.

The above forms the foundation for the implementation of the mentoring scheme. One can imagine the lively discussion that ensues within the South African context, given our history, when individuals are encouraged to discuss openly and enter into learning dialogue around issues that now are facing business on a daily basis. These issues are racism, discrimination, ethnicity and sexism. One cannot begin to introduce a meaningful mentoring scheme without first dealing with the inherent perceptions, stereotypes and prejudice that come as part of the baggage. Failure to do so will lead to a failed mentoring scheme! Appendix 1, at the end of the case, spells out the training workshop provided.

THE TRAINING PROGRAMME

The first morning is devoted to contextualizing and understanding the reality of business in South Africa, aligning thinking with the legislation and discrimination and gradually bringing the focus down to the personal level and helping individuals understand why the business is embarking on such a bold step. This section is vital and is experienced as a significant learning and turning point for many.

The main drivers for such an intervention were:

- attraction;
- retention and development;
- talent pool development;
- succession planning.

All of the above are currently focused on HDSAs (historically disadvantaged South Africans), and the section addresses the legislation in the Employment Equity Act, Labour Relations Act and The Skills Development Act to mention a few. Compliance with the criteria contained in the Mining Charter poses huge challenges for the mining industry in South Africa. Non-compliance is not on the radar screen!

KEY PRINCIPLES FOR THE TRAINING PROVISION

▪ Mentor training offered to those identified as potential mentors. (It is important to note that the participants were with one exception white and male.)

▪ Mentors were given the choice to select themselves out.

▪ Training would need to address:
   – diversity issues (our research revealed that a lot of emotional baggage existed around affirmative action);
   – the business reasons for such an intervention (we had found a distinct lack of clarity about this);
   – how progress would be measured and how the programme would be managed.

Prior to the training, all participants completed questionnaires examining how prepared they were to commit to the relationship and to behaviours that would help the relationship flourish. The responses are given in Table 2.10.1.

THE MATCHING PHASE

Matching took place at one-day workshops, where mentors and mentees received additional information and were reminded of the journey they were about to embark on. Unexpected delays had occurred between initial training and matching, so these workshops also helped to overcome effects of the time lag.

The workshops also provided an opportunity to conduct the first meetings of each pair, with facilitators present to guide and assist as needed.

In addition, we were able to gather information about how mentors and mentees had been able to apply what they had learned in the initial training to their day-to-day activities and responsibilities. Participants observed the following:

▪ Greater awareness of diversity issues had led to a more open and friendly working environment; people exhibited greater tolerance.

▪ Mentees had already taken more responsibility for their own development.

▪ They felt they had more courage to tackle personal barriers and to step outside their comfort zones.

▪ Communication had improved as a result of greater trust.

▪ Working across boundaries had become easier.

Table 2.10.1   Implats participant commitment

Response	Frequency %
Commitment to continuous personal and professional development.	98
Willingness to seize all opportunities for self-development.	83
Willingness to learn from someone else's experience.	97
Commitment to building mutually beneficial relationships.	81
Enthusiasm for gaining as much as possible from the relationship.	80
Willingness to be open and honest in asking for help and telling the whole story.	97
Willingness to listen to others.	89
Willingness to make time available for mentoring.	74
Comfort with gaining critical personal insights.	66
Willingness to accept constructive criticism.	81
Willingness to change attitudes and behaviour as a result of discovering that change is needed.	89
Desire to be open minded about information and opinions that challenge his or her own.	81
Willingness to rise to the challenge.	91
Commitment to a positive, determined, persevering mind-set.	91
Willingness to take responsibility for managing his or her own career.	93
Desire to develop the 'good' into the 'excellent'.	96
Willingness to take increasing responsibility for managing the mentoring relationship.	73
Realistic about not expecting too much too soon.	66
Willingness to challenge others' views and opinions (rather than accept them without question).	76
Willingness to balance deference and respect for the mentor with a challenging/questioning/non-compliant attitude.	78

- They were more self-aware.
- 'Helped me get rid of my stereotypes.'
- Mentees had greater business awareness.
- Listening skills had improved for both mentors and mentees.

One participant even observed a change in his relationship with his children!

IMPLATS MENTOR TRAINING WORKSHOPS: OVERALL OBJECTIVES OF THE WORKSHOP

- To provide prospective mentors with a contextual framework for the Implats mentoring scheme.
- To understand the breadth and complexity of the mentoring role.
- To examine the key stages of mentoring relationships.
- To understand the skills and competencies of a successful mentor and practise mentoring situations.
- To begin to plan the way forward for the mentors.
- To begin the design of the Implats mentoring scheme roll-out.

Mentoring workshop outcomes

- A contextualized understanding of mentoring in relation to the drivers identified by Implats.
- Mentoring programme framework developed to address the challenges at Implats.
- Clarified roles and expectations of mentors and mentees.
- Specific benefits identified for Implats with regard to mentoring.
- A plan of action for the trained mentors and Implats developed.

What has worked?

The following are verbatim quotes:

- 'The formalized structured system.'
- 'The formal support from the mentor and colleagues.'
- 'Informal support in understanding the "political system".'
- 'Feedback and communication to the trainees.'
- 'Development of confidence through the project work.'

- 'Met Head of Department of assessment after completion of training (technical competence).'
- 'Challenge of and exposure to top management.'
- 'Initiative from trainees.'

What has not worked?

- In-house politics.
- Quality of the mentoring process.
- Clarity of the purpose of the current scheme.
- Being 'given' a mentor.
- Matching the mentor with the trainee.
- The large number of trainees per mentor.
- Mentor has too many normal responsibilities and duties.
- Mentor not always available.
- 'Abuse' of trainees – used as skivvies, exploited and seen as 'cheap' labour.
- Loss of self-esteem.
- It was at times a case of 'trial and error'.
- The hierarchy was a problem – mentor and line manager.
- No authority at most times to do something for the trainee.

Measuring the impact

As the relationships become established, measures will be introduced to evaluate the contribution of mentoring to retention, attraction of high-potential and diverse candidates, and leadership development, and how well Implats is complying with the Mining Charter. There is a great deal to do before then, but simply launching mentoring in such a difficult and complex environment is a significant step forward.

APPENDIX 1: MENTOR/MENTEE TRAINING WORKSHOP

The learning objectives:

- to understand the business needs for installing the Implats mentoring scheme with a focus on diversity mentoring;
- to develop the measurement criteria for the Implats mentoring scheme;
- to understand the difference between training, coaching and developmental mentoring;

- to understand how to be a successful mentor and the mentor's role within the Implats mentoring scheme;
- to understand the developmental mentoring process with regard to talent pools, succession planning etc.

Outcomes:

- a contextualized understanding of mentoring in relation to the drivers identified by the Implats mentoring programme framework developed to address the challenges at Implats;
- clarified roles and expectations of mentors;
- specific benefits identified for Implats with regard to mentoring;
- to begin to clarify the way forward.

Table 2.10.2   Workshop: day one

Session	Objectives/exercises
Introduction and welcome	Introductions. Hand out workbooks and introductions note taking. Workshop objectives/outcomes. The road map for the workshop.
What will help us share and learn?	Ground rules for participation. Only need them when we face contentious issues. Experiential learning, not intellectual debate.
The business case (company spokesperson)	Setting the scene around the business case and the new challenges and obtaining 'buy-in' – right thing to do, sound business reasons. What does the law say? Implementation prescripts on this?
What is getting in the way of us achieving the business case?	Brief exercise to let the individuals say what they think – it will be issues largely out of their control.
What are the power relationships that exist in this room right now?	This is an experiential exercise that forces individuals to begin to look at their own behaviour and to realize that maybe this is what is preventing the achievement of the business case and not the earlier issues!
Reflection/learning	Time to record insights, learning, challenges. Allow sharing from one or two.
Tea	

The diversity awareness profile	To gain insight into our behaviours. To begin to draw up a personal action plan.
Personality styles questionnaire	An opportunity to gain insight into your ego states. Draw out how power and the ego states can be daunting for individuals. Draw out paternalism, dependence etc.
Change and transformation	This is about moving forward. Complete and reinforce the discrimination model.
Lunch	
What is mentoring?	Pose the question: what do we know about mentoring? Then work through the list of questions. Have you ever had a mentor, either formal or informal? What did you gain from that relationship? Note that not all learning is via formal training etc. Internal research said it is technical and not insight!
What is and isn't mentoring?	Small group discussions – not pairs.
Definition	Discuss definition and elaborate on phrases.
Comparison with other forms of learning	Mentoring vs coaching. Sponsoring vs developmental mentoring. Formal vs informal. Developmental role.
Benefits	This exercise to be done in small groups – not pairs. What are the benefits for Implats? What's in it for the mentor? What's in it for the mentee? What's in it for the line manager? What are the potential downsides, if any?
Success criteria	How would you measure success? To identify the fact that we may well have different definitions of success. Sharing this with your mentor to assist in better alignment and clarification of realistic expectation.
Closure	Plenary feedback. Handout on learning styles/emotional intelligence questionnaires. Mandela quote.

Table 2.10.3   Workshop: day two

Session	*Objectives*
Welcome back	Comments/questions/observations – we don't necessarily answer any of them unless we want to build or reinforce a learning point. Map for today.
Diversity mentoring	Yesterday – generic. Today focuses on process. Business driver for Implats – diversity and talent pool development.
The four key roles	Complete questionnaire in back of manual. Objective: – to provide a topic for discussion for the first meeting; – to show that we all learn differently; – to realize that whilst I have a particular preference I could become flexible and experiment or reflect more; – parallel this knowledge with the 'giving advice approach'.
The mentoring phases	Research has identified five key phases in the mentoring relationship – comments? Unpack each of the following with the group:
Building rapport	*Rapport:* How are we going to work together? Group to identify first. Trust, focus, congruence, empathy and empowerment. *Exercise:* Consider a case where you don't get on with an individual – how would you ensure that no barriers arise in the relationship with the mentee? *Exercise:* Write down your objective in wanting to become a mentor – use in first meeting as a discussion point. *Confidentiality* *Exercise:* Think of a situation that may occur in the relationship that would make the mentee feel uncomfortable about what is being asked of him or her – what are some of the boundaries? 'No fault divorce clause.'

Setting direction	*Exercise:* Question – what do you want to become? Discuss the issues around who sets the goals for the relationship and how. How to assess the level of commitment. How do individuals set career direction and how can the mentor help? Use the logic tree to show how goals need to be built step by step – use the SMART acronym. *Commitment* To emphasize that people are not always fully committed to development goals, New Year's resolutions etc. To provide some tools and processes.
Making progress	The mentee should be driving the relationship by now. Are we making the best use of this learning opportunity? Challenging effectively.
Winding up	What have we achieved?
Moving on	Where do we go from here? Discuss briefly how to recognize when the time has come to wind up and managing the transition effectively. NB Don't allow the relationship to fizzle out! Refer to checklist.
The mentor/mentee competencies!!	Pair off for discussion on how to identify the behaviours of each of the competencies – reflect back on this from the mentee's perspective. Read through the article. Where do you find yourself? Are there any gaps?
Learning styles	Questionnaire.
Tools and techniques	Reflective space. Talk through bullet points. Discuss the importance of listening, giving feedback, questioning. Understand your own issues around emotional intelligence – see appendix in manual. Are you there to be nice? Balance between challenge and support.

Practice session	Working in pairs, spend 15 minutes discussing a real issue – the mentee must feel that he or she has gained insight into the challenge. NO ADVICE MAY BE GIVEN. Use the material in the manual should you feel lost. After 15 minutes, give feedback and reverse the roles.
Getting started	Reiterate the first meeting objectives and discuss common reasons for failure: 10 minutes thinking about what you would like to share with your mentee about yourself and what you would like to hear from the mentee.
Design and roll-out plan for Implats	What are the group's recommendations for roll-out? The way forward – care on time lapse between mentor and mentee training. Read appendix.
Overview of workshop	What should we leave out of the workshop? What should we include?
Closure	Check achievement against the identified objectives. Post-evaluation. Closing circle.

A CASE OF CULTURE: A MENTORING CASE STUDY BASED ON DISCUSSIONS WITH THE UK TRAINING AND DEVELOPMENT MANAGER, ENGINEERING CO

Bob Garvey

This case study examines the key elements of the Engineering Co mentor scheme. Despite the great care taken in planning, the scheme didn't work. The case study describes the systematic approach taken to establish the scheme and discusses the possible reasons for failure. Engineering Co is an existing company but, at their request, all names have been changed.

BACKGROUND

In terms of market share, plant and international coverage, Engineering Co is a large multinational engineering company. It is also a market leader in its field although it is constantly aware of the serious threat of competition.

To tackle these threats, Engineering Co created a new corporate strategy. This meant introducing major change. The changes were underpinned by a number of slogans – 'The battle for supremacy in the market place will be won on the factory floor', 'Customer led', 'Learning organization', 'Continuous improvement', 'People are our most important asset' – and senior management recognized that change would only be achieved through the involvement and commitment of the whole workforce.

TRAINING AND DEVELOPMENT FOR CHANGE

To help support and progress change, Engineering Co developed a major training and development programme to run as an integral part of the Engineering Co production system. The programme was aimed at the whole workforce – senior managers to hourly paid workers. However, the main focus was on first-line supervisors and their team members.

Central to this programme was the notion of 'the common approach' for all people. This meant that the design, implementation and evaluation of all development programmes were carried out with constant reference to the worldwide company objectives. Through this approach of working to a common agenda, it was believed that all sections of the company would develop in the same direction and emerge with a shared philosophy.

BIRTH OF MENTORING

At the heart of the development programme was a mentoring scheme. In the UK, the training manager used an approach similar to Kram's (1985) model for achieving a successful mentor scheme. The Kram model involves:

1. defining the scope of the project;
2. diagnosis;
3. implementation;
4. evaluation.

THE SCOPE

The purpose of mentoring was, according to the UK training manager, to 'provide the yeast in the bread' for change. He saw mentoring as a key element in helping those on the development programmes to apply their learning in the workplace.

Mentors were also asked to discuss career opportunities and to help resolve learning difficulties in a supportive environment. They were briefed not to control events but to act as independent counsellors and guides for their 'clients'. (The term 'client' is discussed later.)

The mentor process was seen as two-way, in that the 'client' needed to influence the mentor's thinking just as much as the other way round.

The scheme was also for new recruits to provide them with the opportunity to gain a better understanding of the internal and formal structures of the organization quickly.

AND ANOTHER THING... !

The mentor scheme was also expected to address the following:

1. recent redundancies;
2. the need for improved individual effectiveness;
3. internal cultural change.

Redundancies

At the time of this initiative Engineering Co reduced its workforce. This was a result of the increased use of high technology and it created classic fears in the workforce of 'If we work hard and commission these new machines we lose our jobs, and if we don't lose our jobs we become deskilled.' The loss of trust and an increase in suspicion for management among those left after the redundancies was very strong. The workforce resented the insensitivity of management in making people redundant at the same time as introducing a major development programme. The mentor scheme was expected to help rebuild trust between management and the shop floor and help to address the deskilling issue.

The need for greater effectiveness

With fewer people and more technology, Engineering Co needed all individuals to be more effective and adaptable at work. The mentor scheme was also expected to help facilitate flexible working and enhance individual performance.

Internal culture change

The UK training manager identified the culture as heavily 'command and control' and believed that the new strategy would change this to a 'leadership culture', and mentoring was going to make this happen.

The scope of the mentor scheme was very wide and the reliance on it to help 'the bread rise' was considerable.

THE DIAGNOSIS

Some potential mentors had a poor comprehension of how development impacts on the career progression and personal growth of people and felt that learning and development were unimportant. Some potential mentors who had no positive experience of mentoring themselves were opposed to the concept of the scheme. Some were experiencing blockages in their own career progression and therefore were not very keen to help others.

It was felt that mentors might not consciously attempt to thwart the culture change but might be driven by a powerful subconscious force based on the notion of 'This is not the way I did it' and 'I did it the hard way and so should you'.

The UK training manager identified the following personal attributes for mentors:

- interest;
- support;
- position;
- influence;
- security;
- time;
- leadership.

Interest

Potential mentors needed to have a genuine interest in being mentors. Although this may appear an obvious statement, imposing the role on an unwilling individual could spell disaster for the relationship.

Support

The potential mentor needed to be an individual who supported the changes at Engineering Co or at least had an open mind towards change.

Position

The mentor was usually 'senior' to the 'client' but not the client's direct manager. In some cases, the mentor was somebody of equal status in the organization but with a greater, wider or different experience.

Influence

It was important that the mentor was somebody of influence within Engineering Co who was able to access the various networks and understand the political make-up of the organization.

Security

Potential mentors needed to be established in their career so that they would avoid the potential difficulty of seeing the 'client' as a threat to their position. The relationship needed to be one based on mutual respect, trust and a sense of 'camaraderie'.

Time

The mentor needed to be prepared to give time for face-to-face discussions of the issues raised and identified as part of the continuous improvement process.

Leadership

Successful mentors often possess good leadership qualities (Clutterbuck, 1992). They are able to motivate, listen, support and challenge. It was likely, then, that individuals who had previously displayed good leadership qualities would suit the mentor role.

As well as identifying personal attributes, the UK training manager identified key mentoring skills as follows:

- self-management abilities;
- ability to listen, interpret and comment;
- ability to manage time;
- skills necessary to facilitate good interpersonal relationships (often dependent on attitudes).

ADDITIONALLY...

Engineering Co felt it important for their mentors to understand the difference between the techniques of counselling and coaching. The UK training manager described coaching as being about instruction, teaching and feedback in order to achieve a specific end result and counselling as about exploring possibilities and ideas, and seeking solutions and mutual agreement in an open framework.

The UK training manager felt the scheme was dependent on a counselling skills approach.

IMPLEMENTATION

The implementation plans were a clear attempt to reflect the diagnosis. The UK training manager drew up a blueprint of the 'ideal' mentor using the diagnosed character attributes and skill list outlined above. Next, he asked the various plant managers to nominate potential mentors basing their nominations on the blueprint.

The 'client' then selected a mentor of his or her choice from the nominated list of mentors. Each selection was discussed with the line manager, mentor, plant manager and training manager and, where appropriate, agreed. There was no guarantee of agreement, although most selections were accepted. The relationship was then formally established.

The mentor nominees attended a one-and-a-half-day training programme to learn the principles of the scheme and to understand the mentoring role. This training was based on the assumption that nominee mentors already had the skills necessary to be mentors.

The scheme then started.

EVALUATION

The UK training manager identified the following issues:

- Mentors needed further training and development.
- The human resource development (HRD) specialists needed to support the process rather than force it.
- More collaboration was needed between the HRD people and the mentors.
- More educational inputs were needed to address resistance to change.
- Reward and recognition became an issue for the mentors.
- Mentors and 'clients' needed to review their relationships and the scheme.

In short, they needed a new implementation plan to address these issues. However, on the whole, mentors were not willing to give their time and, despite carefully identifying the problems and raising practical solutions, the commitment to mentoring had dissolved. The scheme withered and died.

THE POST-MORTEM

The UK training manager identified many of these problems in the diagnosis phase but some were insoluble. The following sections discuss these factors.

Hard-driving change

Engineering Co is in a highly competitive business, which needs to make certain that internal changes happen quickly. There is a conflict here, as mentor development cannot be hurried, particularly in a potentially hostile environment (Kram, 1985).

This driving competitiveness may have contributed to the macho management attitudes that were very evident within the business. It is likely that this management style and the culture it created were the real causes of the death of this scheme.

This can be demonstrated in many ways. The international strategy seemed to be formed 'lock, stock and barrel' behind closed doors and then imposed through a 'like it or lump it' approach. This top-down approach contrasts sharply with other businesses where the strategy is a more participative activity based on the application of information and business intelligence gathered from all employees (Garvey and Williamson, 2002). Although the 'leadership culture' was the desired outcome of the changes, it could not happen as the 'old' culture was too strong.

Understanding importance of culture in the mentor process

An 'autocratic' culture undermines the mentoring process or at least distorts it (Garvey and Alred, 2001). The natural inclination of autocratic management is to give instructions and advice, but mentoring involves supporting behaviours, challenging behaviours and a developmental approach. In an autocratic environment, this more person-centred approach is rarely the normal behaviour of senior management. In Engineering Co, such talk was seen as 'soft' and a 'waste of time'.

Shadowsides

Despite the sloganized 'positive' and 'people-focused' language from the strategic plan, there was plenty of evidence of 'shadowside' (Egan, 1993) language. Here, managers used aggressive expressions such as 'belly up, kick arse' when talking about working with employees, and one manager was heard to say that he was going to 'ream out someone's backside' and, when talking about going to the factory floor, 'visiting the animals'. These expressions, heard on a number of visits, simply reflected underlying management attitudes towards the workforce and management's position of control. It also demonstrated a lack of understanding of the implications of the 'new' strategy in terms of language and behaviour. This incongruence between the espoused language, the real language and management behaviour resulted in a cynical compliance by the workforce and is summed up very well by the following statement made by a supervisor: 'You can talk about development as much as you like, but if the product is not out the door on Friday you get your backside kicked.'

Clearly, if language is integral to the thought process (Bruner, 1990) and therefore to the resulting behaviour, the real language of Engineering Co rather than the public language had to change to reflect the behaviour if the strategy was to work.

The model of the 'new' culture was supported by the words but not the actions of the company. The language was that of development and change but the behaviour was of the past. Senior management behaviour needed to change in line with the language, but it didn't and the mentors, on the whole, simply carried on as before.

Another example of this problem is in the term 'client', which is used to describe the learner or mentee. This has confused and misleading meanings. This term implies a customer–provider relationship and seems to be born out of the 'customer-led' concept. However, whilst the term itself may have been an attempt to alter the existing relationships within Engineering Co, mentoring is not a customer–supplier relationship. The mentoring dyad may contain some elements of this form, for example dedication to 'customer' needs, commitment and trust, but most writers would support a form of the 'trusted counsellor and guide' definition of mentoring put forward by Gladstone (1988).

Further confusion about the term is that 'client' is used in counselling therapy. Perhaps some mentees and mentors may have found this meaning inappropriate, as it suggests some pathology in the relationship. The problem here is not one of semantics. It is that either the term 'mentoring' in this context was inappropriate or that the concept of mentoring was not fully understood by the users of the term. This is fundamental, for if the terminology is incorrectly used or misunderstood behavioural confusions will inevitably follow (Garvey, 2004).

Assumed skills levels

The assumption that potential mentors would have both the understanding and the skills of mentoring simply by being experienced was an error. Skills are acquired through the application of both knowledge and understanding. They are refined and enhanced with experience over time in an appropriate environment in which to practise them. As the appropriate environment or community did not exist in Engineering Co, senior managers could not develop the appropriate skills simply by being experienced (Lave and Wenger, 1991). The offer of one and a half days to develop the essential understanding and skills of mentoring was clearly inadequate.

Sometimes the two parties ran out of things to say because there was a lack of understanding of the three-stage process of mentoring (Alred, Garvey and Smith, 1998) – exploration, understanding and action. Mentors and mentees in Engineering Co tended to cut out the 'exploration' and 'understanding' and go straight for the 'action'. Had the two parties had sufficient development in the mentoring process, this might have been avoided. This is a common issue in mentoring in general.

Development minded?

Another factor that contributed to the demise of mentoring was the tendency of macho management to undervalue people development. This was evident through the mentors at Engineering Co agreeing that mentoring was a good thing in principle, but when it came to giving the time to their 'clients' they seemed unable or unwilling to make the time available.

Selecting mentors

Mentors were selected from an approved list and then paired with 'clients' on the basis of controlled choice. This is again an example of a heavily controlled and managed process for an activity that is essentially a voluntary activity. Some mentors were paired with 'clients' 300 miles away. This created serious communication difficulties.

Deskilling concerns

The issue of deskilling continued as a concern. As some mentors did not give the time to mentor discussions, these resentments were not resolved and the lack of trust in management continued. In the minds of the workforce, change equated with them either losing their jobs or becoming deskilled. People who found their skills replaced by technology remained resentful.

International dimension

The desire to achieve the common approach around the world and in different cultures is perhaps a misplaced ideal. People may find it difficult to alter their attitudes and behaviour for deep cultural or religious reasons and, indeed, the desire of the company leadership to push the strategy through seemed to be at the expense of local considerations.

It should be possible to achieve a global business by respecting and working with local cultures, customs and religions and making these differences a strength rather than expecting blanket conformity. The Tayloristic concept of 'one best way' is obviously a strongly embedded notion in Engineering Co.

All things to all people

The expectations on the mentor scheme were too great. It seemed as though the scheme was not only the driver for substantial change but also the mop for all the people problems in the business. All these things contributed to the decline of what essentially should have been a well-planned and well-organized scheme.

REFERENCES

Alred, G, Garvey, B and Smith, R (1998) *The Mentoring Pocket Book*, Management Pocket Books, Alresford, Hants

Bruner, J (1990) *Acts of Meaning*, Harvard University Press, Boston, MA

Clutterbuck, D (1992) *Everyone Needs a Mentor: How to foster talent within the organization*, 2nd edn, Institute of Personnel Management, London

Egan, G (1993) *Adding Value: A systematic guide to business-driven management and leadership*, Jossey-Bass, San Francisco, CA

Garvey, B (2004) Call a rose by any other name and it might be a bramble, *Development and Learning in Organizations*, **18** (2), pp 6–8

Garvey, B and Alred, G (2001) Mentoring and the tolerance of complexity, *Futures*, **33**, pp 519–30

Garvey, B and Williamson, B (2002) *Beyond Knowledge Management: Dialogue, creativity and the corporate curriculum*, Pearson Education, Harlow

Gladstone, MS (1988) Mentoring: a strategy for learning in a rapidly changing society, *Research Document CEGEP*, John Abbott College, Quebec

Kram, KE (1985) Improving the mentoring process, *Training and Development Journal*, April, pp 40–42

Lave, J and Wenger, E (1991) *Situated Learning: Legitimate peripheral participation*, Cambridge University Press, Cambridge

Case Study 12

E-MENTORING AND SMES: MENTORBYNET PILOT

Ruth Garrett-Harris

Acknowledgement: Kevin Hunt (KevinH@circle-squared.com), who was at the time of this evaluation the South East Regional Director of the Small Business Service (SBS), conceived, designed and drove the original SME e-mentoring pilot.

This case discusses some of the issues arising from the evaluation of an e-mentoring pilot programme for small and medium enterprises (SMEs) in the south-east of England. The pilot MentorByNet (MBN) programme was conducted with the aim of developing and growing the skills, knowledge and confidence of SME owner-managers to help them to succeed.

THE CASE FOR E-MENTORING

As with the fields of knowledge management and organizational learning, the impact of information technology has significant implications for mentoring. This is because, as Bierema and Merriam (2002) point out, in the case of mentoring 'successful mentoring involves frequent and regular interaction', but 'all sorts of barriers such as time, work responsibilities, geographical distance and lack of trust often reduce if not halt interaction' (p 214).

The issue of lack of time seems to resonate strongly for SME owner-managers. An e-mentoring scheme, therefore, is likely to appeal to such owner-managers, as it allows them access to important advice and assistance in a way that minimizes their time commitment and increases their flexibility as it makes interactions easier to manage. E-mentoring merges the approach of the traditional mentoring relationship with technology, and is increasingly used as the preferred choice of communication (*Realm Magazine*, 2002).

DEFINITION OF E-MENTORING

E-mentoring in this particular e-mentoring pilot was defined as 'a naturally occurring relationship or paired relationship within a programme that is set up between a more senior/experienced individual (the mentor) and a less experienced individual (the mentee), primarily using electronic communications, and is intended to develop and grow the skills, knowledge and confidence of the lesser skilled individual to help him or her succeed' (Single and Muller, 1999).

'The electronic communication that is favoured in these relationships includes e-mail; telephone; instant relay Chat (IRC); video conferencing' (SEEDA Fund, 2002).

INITIAL RESEARCH

Bianco and Bianco (2002) carried out an initial, extensive, primarily internet-based review of organizations throughout the world that were involved with e-mentoring or related practices.

This was to provide provisional guidance on the creation of a working model for an e-mentoring scheme for SME managers and entrepreneurs. This research included interviewing leading practitioners and academics in the mentoring and e-mentoring field.

Ultimately the MBN pilot structure was based primarily on the APESMA model in Australia (www.apesma.asn.au/mentorsonline) due to the fact that an evaluation report was to be published and was used as a benchmark for the evaluation of the MBN programme.

The structured e-mentoring pilot was set up within a formalized environment that was intended to provide:

- training for mentors;
- coaching for mentors;
- structure to increase engagement in the e-mentoring process.

An evaluation of the results of the programme was done to determine the impact on the participants and identify improvements for future programmes.

OVERVIEW OF PROGRAMME

The pilot MBN programme was conducted with the aim of developing and growing the skills, knowledge and confidence of SME owner-managers to help them to succeed.

The programme was conducted over three months, involving over 40 mentoring partnerships. A comprehensive evaluation was undertaken, which measured areas such as:

- perceived experience of the programme;
- programme outcome;
- satisfaction with contact frequency;
- satisfaction with online training.

These are areas that the Australian APESMA (2002) programme measured and were therefore used as a benchmark. In addition, this evaluation measured:

- expectations of benefits from the scheme;
- concern for the practical relevance of the programme;
- responses about focusing on the realization of specific goals and plans;
- expectations of the benefits of the e-mentoring programme.

There were also comparisons drawn between perceived benefits before and after the programme.

PROGRAMME STRUCTURE

Initially it was thought that participants would come from the agencies working with SMEs. However, that approach did not bring the level of response needed and therefore participants were recruited by cold-calling SMEs from membership lists of organizations such as the Chamber of Commerce and business directories.

SME owner-managers wanting to participate in the programme as either mentees or mentors completed a registration form. This formed the basis for matching mentors and mentees. The registration form explored:

- the nominated skills gaps of mentees;
- areas of expertise of mentors;
- geographical location (rural / urban);
- business sector experience;
- gender;
- personal interest and professional qualifications.

According to Megginson and Clutterbuck (1995), it is useful in the matching process to mix up, as far as possible, the secondary matching criteria in order to seek some diversity as well as commonality in the matching process. This was done when looking at elements of the matching criteria.

In the APESMA pilot, partners were manually matched according to the 'skill gaps' identified by mentees and 'areas of expertise' identified by mentors in their registration forms. Other factors considered included profession group, gender and education level.

A web-enabled online tutorial was provided and became the prerequisite of actively engaging in the mentoring relationship. The objectives of each module were as follows:

- Module 1 (generic) guides the participants through an overview of what mentoring is and is not as well as issues about expectations and benefits of participation.
- Module 2 (generic) discusses the mentoring relationship in terms of setting it up, keeping it going, winding it up and moving on.
- Module 3 (mentees) discusses identifying and analysing goals and tools of self-assessment.
- Module 3 (mentors) focuses on required mentoring skills and some of the dilemmas faced in a mentoring relationship.
- Module 4 (generic) outlines getting started, code of practice, support and FAQs, and further information about mentoring.

Ongoing communication from MBN was kept at a minimum throughout the programme although the centre did respond to specific requests from individuals within the mentoring partnership.

EVALUATION METHODOLOGY

The research was carried out in two phases – in the form of pre- and post-programme e-mailed questionnaires. The questionnaires were based on the one sent out by APESMA (Australia), for comparative purposes, as well as covering additional aspects that were of interest to the sponsors of MBN and the researchers.

On both occasions, parallel but differently worded questionnaires were sent out to mentees and to mentors.

The decision to send out both a pre- and post-questionnaire instead of just a post-programme one was founded on the desire to evaluate and compare pre-programme expectations with post-programme views.

A preliminary analysis of the pre-programme questionnaires was undertaken using the industry standard computer package for analysing data, called SPSS, and a preliminary report was produced. The data were analysed looking at both frequency of response and any significant correlations using the Spearman rho method.

PROFILE OF PARTICIPANTS IN SCHEME

All MBN participants were entrepreneurs and/or small business managers. The pilot comprised over 40 mentoring partnerships. Of the mentors, 78 per cent classed themselves as owners of SMEs, and 70 per cent of the mentees classed themselves as entrepreneurs and/or SME managers. Participants were drawn from business directories such as Chambers of Commerce membership.

Women represented 39 per cent of the population and males 61 per cent.

The mean age of female mentors was 47 while the mean age for male mentors was 50. This made the overall mean age for mentors 49. For female mentees, the mean age was 39 and the mean for male mentees was 44. This made an overall mean age for mentees of 41.

Of the mentoring participants, 51 per cent came from rural areas while only 49 per cent came from urban centres.

As the pilot had an equal split between rural and urban participants it is reasonable to argue that electronic access has included participants who might otherwise have been discouraged from participating in a mentoring relationship due to their rural location.

EFFECTIVENESS OF PILOT

The overall effectiveness of the MBN programme can be judged by the positive responses to the post-programme questionnaire. Some of those findings were as follows:

- There were 96 per cent of mentees and 80 per cent of mentors who described their e-mentoring experience as a positive one. This compares favourably to the APESMA study where only 82 per cent of mentees described the experience as a positive one, whilst the mentor response was similar at 80 per cent.
- There were 91 per cent of mentees and 84 per cent of mentors who indicated that they would participate in a similar programme at some time in the future.

■ Over 60 per cent of mentees and over 70 per cent of mentors cited convenience, flexibility and ease as the major benefits of e-mail-based mentoring, while 30 per cent of mentee and mentor responses indicated there is an element of impersonality about this type of communication.

■ Over 50 per cent of mentees and mentors indicated that they were planning to continue or thinking about continuing their relationship after the conclusion of the pilot.

Overall feedback from participants has been both broadly positive as well as explicit about the benefits, as illustrated by the following:

■ 'What the mentoring programme has done has "enforced" delivery of a business plan, enabled prioritization of different business opportunities, given me a clearer focus on what resources I need and given me more confidence in my own business abilities. The results of the mentoring programme are the birth of another business with another two waiting in the wings.'

■ 'I had been sceptical about whether I would be comfortable discussing business issues/concerns with a "stranger" by e-mail – thinking it would be too impersonal – but was surprised by how quickly it is possible to build a relationship of trust in this way. I believe, however, that some form of meeting would have instantly strengthened the relationship.'

■ 'It's a great programme in principle and one which I support and would continue to do so, provided that it gave me a sufficient number of quality mentees to support.'

SUMMARY OF KEY SUCCESS FACTORS

In reviewing the findings of this study together with the APESMA results we identified the following as key success factors in running e-mentoring programmes for SMEs:

1. the importance of appropriate matching;
2. the degree of desire that participants have to be involved in such a scheme in the first place;
3. establishing programme goals at the outset – mentee lead;
4. programme duration of at least six months;
5. pre-programme training that helps participants to manage their expectations;

6. setting a communication plan at the outset of the programme and regular contact between mentoring partners;
7. supplementing e-mail-based communication with other modes of communications;
8. assisting mentees to sustain motivation, eg frequent facilitator's messages of prompts and encouragement;
9. participant commitment to the programme and making the effort to give some priority to the relationship;
10. establishing a good mentoring relationship (eg rapport and trust).

PROGRAMME RECOMMENDATIONS

Features to be continued:

1. Positive benefits were widely reported and the scheme could usefully be rolled out in Surrey and adopted throughout the country.
2. The critical success factors outlined above should be a focus of attention in all future schemes.
3. 'Providing options' and 'listening effectively' are key skills developed by mentors and valued by mentees.
4. Using the business plan as a framework for discussion is considered valuable by some, and less so by others. It should be included as an option.
5. Frequent multi-mode, mentee-centred learning needs to be encouraged in future schemes to maximize benefit to mentees.
6. Addressing the skills nominated in the mentee's registration form was strongly linked to willingness to participate again in a similar programme. This is a useful reminder to mentors in future schemes to pay attention to the mentee's initial agenda.
7. Personal development of mentors was strongly linked to the development of mentoring skills, so this can be sold as a benefit to future mentors.

Features to be developed:

1. Many respondents would have preferred longer than three months. It is recommended that the scheme be set up for six months, with a review of progress made by the mentoring pair at three months.
2. A longer-term evaluation of the pilot groups to see if business competitiveness and growth were influenced by the scheme in the perception of participants.

3. Seek out reasons for a lack of referral from agencies working with SMEs (this is a pattern identified by Megginson and Stokes (2000)). Many advisers may be threatened by having volunteers do what they perceive as part of their job. The recruitment of committed mentees to schemes like these is a major challenge. Significant resources should be dedicated to this.

4. The opportunity to discuss issues and questions not available within a mentee's existing network could possibly be developed by using other modes of communication such as designated times for online chat with mentors and / or online chat with other mentees in the scheme.

5. More opportunities are needed for mentors to receive development. This could come from reviewing their practice with a skilled mentor or from networking among mentors. It would also be beneficial to review ongoing specific mentee feedback.

6. A process for involving the pairs in setting goals for their work should be more clearly established.

7. Establishment of a communication plan could be linked to mentees feeling that participation in MBN helped them develop professionally. It could give a sense of moving towards their programme goals and help establish trust between them and their mentor. Therefore, more encouragement could be given to the importance of creating a communication plan at the start of the programme.

REFERENCES

APESMA (2002) Mentors online: an e-mentoring program for professionals in small business, Report to Small Business Enterprise Culture Program, Post-program report, APESMA, Australia

Bianco, RS and Bianco, J (2002) *Small Business Scoping Study: E-mentoring for SMEs*, South East England Development Agency, Guildford

Bierema, LL and Merriam, SB (2002) E-mentoring: using computer mediated communication to enhance the mentoring process, *Innovative Higher Education*, **26** (3), pp 211–27

Megginson, D and Clutterbuck, D (1995) *Mentoring in Action*, 1st edn, Kogan Page, London

Megginson, D and Stokes, P (2000) Mentoring for export success, 7th European Mentoring Conference, Sheffield Hallam University, Sheffield

Realm Magazine (2002) Realm mentorship: electronic mentoring, http:/ /realm.net/ mentor /howment /ement.html (accessed 21 August 2003)

SEEDA Fund (2002) *Management Development Proposal*, Business Link, Surrey

Single, PG and Muller, CB (1999, April) *Electronic Mentoring: Issues to advance research and practice*, paper presentation at the Annual Meeting of the International Mentoring Association, Atlanta, GA

Case Study 13

MENTORING OWNERS OF MICRO BUSINESSES IN NOTTINGHAM

Jonathan Gravells

BACKGROUND TO ORGANIZATION AND SCHEME

Nottinghamshire Business Venture (NBV) is a not-for-profit company limited by guarantee. It promotes enterprise and offers support and training to individuals in Nottingham and surrounding areas who are planning to start their own business or who are already running a small business (up to 10 employees). It sees some 4,000 clients per year, and of these provides mentoring, via a bank of 100 or so trained volunteers, for 400 to 500 entrepreneurs every year. NBV works in partnership with organizations such as Business Link, the Chamber of Commerce and the local Learning and Skills Council.

In 2003 NBV was an award winner in the government's 'Inner City 100 Index', as itself one of the fastest-growing small businesses in the UK. Its stated mission is: 'To continue to be the acknowledged Centre of Excellence for entrepreneurship and business start-up support throughout the East Midlands.'

National government sees the small business sector as vital to its objective of closing the productivity gap with the United States, France and Germany, and has identified 'encouraging a more dynamic start-up market' as one of seven key actions in its quest to make the UK 'the best place in the world to start and grow a business' (DTI, 2002: 4, 7).

NBV'S MENTORING SCHEME – ROLES, DEFINITIONS AND OBJECTIVES

Our information for mentors describes the role as follows: 'Mentoring is a unique partnership set up for or by two individuals. It is shaped by the needs and aspirations of the client and the talents and resources of the mentor. A mentor is a wise and trusted guide.'

We cite the qualities of a good small business mentor as:

- a sincere desire to be personally involved with another person in business, to help that person achieve his or her goals, whilst avoiding emotional involvement;
- an ability to communicate with each other openly and non-judgementally;
- an ability to listen and establish a relationship based on equal responsibility and mutual respect;
- practical problem-solving skills and the ability to suggest options and alternatives;
- an in-depth knowledge of business support services available in the area.

We also lay down some clear guidelines as to what a mentor is and what a mentor is not (see Table 2.13.1).

Finally, we set out a number of benefits of mentoring for the start-up business owner:

- increased confidence;
- helps clients cope with change;
- improves their business skills;

Table 2.13.1   What a mentor is and is not

A mentor is:	A mentor is not:
An exceptionally good listener	A talker
Able to spot problems	The problem owner
Good at guiding, a facilitator	The decision maker
Able to provide an experienced point of view	A short-term fix
Able to offer choices and options	An emotional crutch
An identifier of resources	A provider of finance
Aware of his or her limitations	The fount of all knowledge
Informed, or knows a person who is	Jack-of-all-trades
Independent, with a fresh perspective	Part of the business
Credible and can empathize with the client	Judgemental or subjective

- reduces isolation;
- provides access to networks;
- encourages clients to try new ways of doing things;
- helps clients overcome barriers to growth;
- provides links to other forms of business support.

NBV'S MENTORS – SELECTION AND TRAINING

Volunteer mentors are selected according to their business experience, their exposure to running their own small business, and their motivation for wanting to mentor others. Training for mentors includes several elements:

- a half-day mentor induction;
- a two-day business counselling course, focused specifically on the mentoring role and practical skills needed;
- a one-day business awareness course, introducing the wider business support network and looking at factors involved in starting your own business;
- an observation of a 'live' mentoring session by an experienced mentor;
- a practical assessment, where the new mentor is observed conducting a session with a real client.

Volunteer mentors can only start to practise once they have been assessed as meeting the standard required, and they have signed up to the BVMA (Business Volunteer Mentoring Association) code of ethics.

EVALUATION OF THE SCHEME

Anecdotal evidence gathered over the years suggested that the mentoring we provided was both appreciated and effective, but until recently we had carried out no in-depth evaluation to substantiate these claims. So in late 2004, we did some research to try to answer the following questions:

- Can evidence be produced to support the belief that mentoring has an overall beneficial impact on micro businesses?
- What are the particular needs of start-up entrepreneurs when it comes to support, and how do these fit with our current views of mentoring?

■ What are the potential positive *and negative* impacts of mentoring in this context and how are they linked to mentor and mentee behaviour and scheme design?

A questionnaire was circulated to those entrepreneurs mentored by NBV over the preceding 18 months. Later, six mentees were interviewed in depth about their experience, and their mentors were interviewed separately.

RESULTS OF THE EVALUATION

Testing whether mentoring has an overall beneficial impact

We established that most of our mentored entrepreneurs reported stable or increased profit and turnover, and 90 per cent survived for at least one year, but there is a limit to how much we can legitimately attribute this to mentoring, as there are many other, independent variables affecting small start-up business success, which are very difficult to exclude.

In the absence of convincing 'experimental' evidence, however, other feedback helped us address this question. The questionnaires produced a number of plaudits for mentoring from respondents and, whilst only a minority of mentees chose to make a comment, this strength of unsolicited feedback indicated that a substantial number of entrepreneurs believed that the mentoring had had a positive impact. Reported benefits included:

■ providing a sounding board;
■ being a psychological or emotional safety net;
■ reassurance;
■ confidence;
■ learning to learn;
■ helping grow into a businessperson;
■ providing focus;
■ providing structure and a sense of progress;
■ networking and contacts;
■ skills and knowledge, eg marketing and accounts.

Mentees found it much more difficult, however, to isolate any beneficial effect that mentoring had had on their *business*. Half of the mentees interviewed reported either neutral or very little business impact and the majority were much more vague when trying to identify business benefits than when citing personal benefits.

The particular needs of start-up entrepreneurs for support

In the questionnaire, respondents were given a standard list of areas of help that a start-up entrepreneur might need, and were asked to identify what was most important to them when they set up their business, what mentoring helped with and where mentoring was more effective than any other source of help. In the case of over half of the help topics considered most important by entrepreneurs, mentoring was seen as not only helpful, but actually the *most* effective source of help.

Notably, the help topics that they considered most important (eg financial planning, marketing, regulation) fell exclusively into the career function side of Kram's well-known model (1985). The psychosocial benefits (reassurance and improved confidence and self-esteem) were among the topics for which mentoring was the most useful source of help, but were considered less *important* by our mentees.

So entrepreneurs generally described their needs more as career needs than psychosocial needs. But an interesting thing happened with those mentored several months into the life of their company. Career needs were much more balanced by explicit needs for reassurance and confidence, an empathetic sounding board. In many ways, this makes sense, as entrepreneurs at set-up stage are having to familiarize themselves with a lot of very specific factual and procedural information. Likewise, those who requested mentoring several years into their business generally did so in response to a precise need. They were about to employ someone, their market had disappeared, the enterprise needed to grow etc. In contrast, those who took part in mentoring several months after start-up had often sorted the early-days 'mechanics' of their business, but found themselves wondering if they were doing all the right things and whether their experience was 'normal' or not.

So, given these findings, are there any specific differences between entrepreneurial mentoring and the organizational mentoring models that dominate much of the literature?

It became clear that our mentors and mentees rarely stepped back from the process and discussed what they were doing and how well it was working. Mentors often failed to see the benefit of this, or were simply reluctant. Mentees, on the other hand, having not received mentoring training, were sometimes unsure as to the nature of the relationship. In itself this was a useful learning point for us, as it was also clear that some relationships would have benefited from such reflection. A basic, common structure to the mentoring process did reveal itself, and this was consistent with the kind of three-stage model described in the existing mentoring literature (Alred, Garvey and Smith, 1998).

However, the range of roles that our mentors seemed to play was much broader than this suggests. Some mentees clearly wanted little more than a non-judgemental sounding board, someone who might know where to get hold of useful information. A typical quote here might be: 'Jane wasn't there to make my decisions for me… They're not there to run your business for you. They're there to guide you and listen… but not to make your decisions… but it was the support really, as much as anything… just giving me that confidence to keep going, you know?'

Other mentees clearly felt they needed something much more 'hands-on'. One mentee requiring help with marketing and licensing a new invention had his mentor accompany him abroad on a visit to a potential partner, handling the initial sales pitch, in the belief that his own presentation skills would be inadequate to the task.

Undoubtedly, there are dangers in this approach, but the mentee in this particular case felt he had benefited hugely from what he had learned working with this mentor, and saw a clear distinction between the mentor's role and that of a business adviser or consultant: 'He has taken what feels like a more personal interest… You feel like you're on the same level… he tended to let us… to get it out of us rather than him do the talking.'

This mentee felt more able to face up to big, important customers having been helped through a couple of occasions by the mentor. So perhaps the result was more development than dependency. It seemed some mentees were frustrated that their mentor could not offer more specific, hands-on expertise, whilst others were horrified at the thought of someone 'interfering' in their business.

Positive and negative impacts of this mentoring

Only 22 per cent of mentees reported that they had at times found mentoring frustrating and/or unhelpful. But what made the difference between a wholly positive and an even partially negative experience?

The list of comments received in questionnaires reveals four main categories causing frustration amongst mentees:

- mismatched expectations;
- personal chemistry;
- behaviour of the mentor or poor commitment to the process by the mentor;
- no perceived requirement for a mentor.

A far higher proportion of mentees on NBV's new enterprise scholarship (NES) programme reported some frustration with their mentoring. Unlike other mentees, our NES programme graduates are obliged to have a mentor allocated to them as part of the terms of the grant they receive.

Previous research indicates that 'compulsory' mentoring is rarely successful and this result would seem to bear that out (Kram, 1985).

Surprisingly, those expressing some frustration with mentoring rated it just as highly for addressing the top six help topics as those who were entirely positive. This suggests that, whatever mentees may explicitly cite as causes, the principal drivers of 'less positive' mentoring experiences may lie in more than just poorly matched expectations about learning and other benefits.

The other most consistently cited influence, from the interview data collected, was personal chemistry. This is what one mentee said about his *new* mentor: 'The thing about Rosie is she understands the ME... within minutes she was my mate. We were laughing on the phone and joking the first time I ever spoke to her... She knows where I'm coming from.' A feature of all of the least successful partnerships was that the mentoring dyad did not 'connect' on a more personal level.

The research also uncovered some criticisms of the mentoring itself, although it should be said that what might be construed as 'poor practice' by the mentor, according to some experts, did not always result in dissatisfaction or frustration from the mentee. What seemed significant to us was what a narrow line divided good intentions from potentially damaging mentoring: how self-disclosure can become an 'ego trip' about one's own experience, inhibiting the mentee rather than establishing credibility. Wanting a business to succeed and improve can turn into a mentor applying his or her own standards and judging the mentee or, even worse, living vicariously through the mentee's business. Maintaining objectivity and emotional detachment can become aloofness and formality, undermining rapport.

Significantly, a unifying characteristic of the mentors whose mentees had expressed some frustration was their apparent lack of awareness of the impact that their behaviour was having on the entrepreneur. This, together with a reluctance to step back from the business agenda and explore the relationship, generally prevented any mutual adjustment.

LESSONS LEARNED

Whilst this evaluation generally reinforced our belief in the usefulness of mentoring as a crucial part of our support to new start-up entrepreneurs, we have also learned some useful lessons.

It has highlighted for us the crucial importance of matching mentors and mentees, and we are taking several actions to improve this part of the process, not least of which is working hard to recruit mentors who represent a broader mix of ethnicity, gender and age. The evaluation has confirmed for us how important personal chemistry is to the success of a mentoring relationship.

Likewise, we have looked again at the allocation of mentors to our NES scholars, replacing a 'one size fits all' compulsory mentoring approach with a range of options tailored to individual needs. This includes providing additional training rather than mentoring, where the primary need is for improved skills.

Finally, a number of improvements have suggested themselves with regard to training mentors and mentees. Clearly relationships would benefit from greater reflexivity and self-awareness, on the part of mentors especially. So we are looking at ways of briefing mentees as well as mentors on the mentoring process and roles. We are encouraging a more open attitude to discussing process and relationships amongst mentoring pairs by focusing on this during continuing professional development sessions with mentors. And finally, we are using these same sessions to introduce debate around questions of ethics and how we manage the boundaries of the mentor's role.

REFERENCES

Alred, G, Garvey, B and Smith, R (1998) *The Mentoring Pocket Book*, Management Pocket Books, Alresford, Hampshire

DTI (2002) 'Small Business and Government – A way Forward', DTI Small Business Report

Kram, KE (1985) Improving the mentor process, *Training and Development Journal*, April, pp 40–42

Case Study 14

MENTORING THE TOP TEAM IN A DYNAMIC, ENTREPRENEURIAL COMPANY

John Lambert

INTRODUCTION

This is a study of a mentoring scheme for the top team in a dynamic and highly entrepreneurial company. My purpose is to compare this scheme with published studies of schemes in other organizations, and to draw comparisons, which might arise either because this is a company of a kind not typical of the published literature or because of the particular characteristics of this mentoring scheme.

THE COMPANY

The company is a privately owned service provider. It is high in the list of the fastest-growing British companies. Founded about 10 years ago, it now has a turnover of over £30 million and over 1,000 employees.

The company's founder is now its non-executive chairman. Its group chief executive, who has been in post for seven years, is still in his early 30s, and only one of the top executives is over 45. This is reflected in the company's culture.

The company has a number of operating arms, and my study was of the largest of these, which accounts for over 90 per cent of the company's turnover. The mentoring scheme covered the chief executive of this operating arm, and his immediate reports, now seven people in total.

The company had recently experienced a significant setback, losing a number of major contracts. However, it remained confident about both its future growth and profitability.

The company has a number of particularly interesting characteristics. A number of observers described it to me as chaotic. The chief executive, who has been with the company for three years, having previously been marketing director of a major PLC, said that the company had been chaotic, but this was now improving rapidly.

The company's rate of growth has been impressive by any standards, and it remains very ambitious for further growth. It has had charismatic and mercurial leadership, and has lived with a culture of constant change, though the chief executive believes that he now has a top team and structure that may remain stable for some time.

Though the company is now a substantial one by any standards, it still behaves in many respects as a small one. The chief executive, with large company experience, has been attempting to introduce structure, systems and discipline, but this has not been easy.

Because of the company's products, it is however, in the words of one of those I interviewed, 'people centred'.

BACKGROUND TO THE MENTORING SCHEME

The story begins about three years ago. At that time the chairman and group chief executive recognized the need for top team development, and called in a consultancy firm whose head was a personal friend and informal mentor to the chairman. Following discussion about the need to improve the leadership of the company, two consultants met the chief executive, who found them 'inspirational' and agreed to work with them. The outcome was a two-day workshop for the then top team (only three of whom now remain with the company). Further monthly workshops, which focused on the development of the team as a group, followed over a period of eight months.

One of my interviewees described the outcome of the first workshops as being an improvement in how members of the team felt about and interacted with each other, but with little improvement in performance in the workplace. The emphasis later moved to exploring models for more cohesive group working. A common action plan was drawn up for the group, and this made a 'huge difference'.

In the course of these workshops, the company and the consultants identified a need for help with personal as well as team development. The consultants and a member of the top team were jointly commissioned to produce a formal proposal for a mentoring scheme. This happened at the same time as the company lost a significant part of its business.

An additional factor was the presence of an existing coach within the company who was already working with some of the top team. Although a consultant, the coach spent a great deal of time in the company and, in some respects, was seen as a 'company man'. Some greatly valued his help, but others were concerned about confidentiality. There was also concern that he was being used by the group chief executive to deliver messages to those he was coaching.

A significant aspect of the proposal was the use of external, paid mentors. According to the participants, there were a number of reasons for this:

- a lack of capacity and expertise within the company;
- the complexity of organizing internal mentoring;
- a desire to bring in outside experience and expertise;
- using external mentors would have less impact on internal relationships and would be easier to sell to the top team.

DESCRIPTION OF THE SCHEME

One of the two external consultants became scheme organizer. The first task was to draw up a list of external mentors. An immediate issue was that the company felt that it needed people with coaching rather than mentoring skills. However, the organizer recognized, through his knowledge of the company, that there was at least as much need for mentoring as coaching, defining coaching as being about skills, and mentoring as being about the inner person. He therefore drew up a list of people with mentoring and coaching skills. (Subsequent experience showed that a mixture of coaching and mentoring in fact took place.) The scheme organizer commented that he could have found cheaper people – and cost became an issue later – but that he felt that the company needed the sort of challenge that could only be provided by senior and experienced people.

Each of the mentors was asked to provide a brief CV. Based on his knowledge of the top team, he then offered each of them a choice of two possible mentors. Mentoring was not compulsory, and some members of the team chose instead to continue their relationship with the existing coach. Each of those who chose a mentoring relationship picked one of the two mentors offered. Each pair had an introductory session at which to decide whether to continue the relationship. So although mentees had at least an element of choice in their choice of mentor, mentors had no choice, although they were free to pull out after the first session. Garvey and Galloway (2002) reported that mentors in the HBOS scheme were largely indifferent to who they mentored, in an internal scheme that did not involve paying mentors.

The mentors were offered little briefing on either the company or the individuals who had selected them as potential mentors. The scheme organizer would now, with the benefit of hindsight, offer 'more briefing, but not too much', based on his experience of setting up a mentoring scheme with another company, where comprehensive briefing was given but, as a result, the mentors were seen as 'company people'.

The scheme was bounded by few rules. Mentor/mentee pairs could meet as frequently as they wished. In effect, they were free to construct their own rules to govern their relationships. A uniform payment (per hour) was paid to every mentor. My own knowledge of several of the mentors suggests that generativity as well as money was likely to have been one of the main motivators for the mentors (Levinson, 1979).

Unfortunately, the company suspended the scheme after only a few months as part of cost-cutting measures following the loss of contracts. Some existing members of the top team (seven people, all but one male) are continuing existing mentoring relationships, but new members of the team do not have mentors. Facilitated team workshops continue, and these are having what was described to me as 'a profound impact on the business', with a much greater sense of collective responsibility.

As well as meaning that the mentoring relationships were short-term ones, this has also meant that plans to use the top team as coaches/mentors for the next tiers of management have not yet been implemented. One of those I interviewed felt that the top team is now much better equipped to take this on; another felt that 'we are still miles away from this'.

The company hopes to reactivate the mentoring scheme in a few months. The hope is that this will then include more junior people; this is perhaps the reverse of the view of Wilson and Elman (1990) that mentoring is not and should not be a phenomenon restricted to lower-level personnel but, rather, that it has a place at the very highest levels of the organization.

IMPACT OF THE SCHEME

My interviews revealed no negative results from mentoring. The scheme organizer believes that mentoring helped some mentees to survive and blossom in the company, whereas without mentoring they would not have done so. One mentee was helped to cope with cost cutting. Another was well coached in quality management techniques. Another had felt less lonely in a difficult set of circumstances. Overall, the full benefits of mentoring would only become apparent over time.

Those I interviewed felt that there had been significant benefits from being able to talk openly ('safely') with someone from outside the company. One relationship had focused particularly on coaching on process management techniques. Mentoring had led to an improvement in the mentee's relationship with his line manager. However, his discussions with his mentor could have gone deeper, and his mentor had not offered much challenge. Mentoring had not yet had much impact on the business.

Another was much more positive. Mentoring had had 'a tremendous impact on me personally'. Family relationships and the work–life balance had improved. In the workplace, he now had a much better understanding of the impact of different behaviours. He had learned to become more controlled and focused, and to slow down. This resonates with the discussion on 'slowing down' in the mentoring scheme in HBOS (Garvey and Galloway, 2002), and with the prominence of time management and personal or domestic issues in an NHS mentoring scheme (Garvey, 1995).

In the recent restructuring, the same mentee had been under great pressure and his mentor had helped him to keep sight of the long-term benefits in the midst of the short-term difficulties. The benefits of mentoring were visible in the whole team, which was thinking and working differently. 'I instinctively know that mentoring has contributed to this.'

EVALUATION OF THE SCHEME

I believe that this scheme had a number of interesting features not normally found in the mentoring literature:

1. The company is not typical of those found in other studies, which are usually very large, established corporates or, if smaller, mentoring is confined to one or two individuals.
2. A strong focus on external mentoring is unusual in company schemes.
3. Mentoring was taking place at the same time as group development for the top team; while this makes it difficult to disentangle the impact of mentoring from the group activity, it is perhaps a model that should be followed and studied elsewhere.
4. The shortness of the mentoring relationships was unusual.

At the very least, I believe that this study has demonstrated that mentoring can bring significant benefits to dynamic, entrepreneurial and fast-changing organizations that represent the growth points of the economy. The combination of mentoring and group workshops for the top team seems to be leading to the development of a corporate curriculum within the company (Kessels, 1996). Megginson and Clutterbuck (1995) suggest that mentoring seems to work best when it is going with the grain of other initiatives in the organization. Alred and Garvey (2000) suggest that the contribution of mentoring to organizations, rather than individuals, going through transitions has been little discussed and researched. This study may be a modest contribution to this research. (One might question whether there is now any significant proportion of organizations that are not constantly changing (Garvey, 1999).)

As noted above, the shortness of the mentoring relationships in this study was unusual. Megginson and Clutterbuck (1995) say that, if goals are specific and participants are highly motivated, then much can be achieved in a few short meetings. However, Hansford, Tennent and Ehrich (2002) comment that, in many cases where mentoring programmes had negative outcomes, success appeared to have been jeopardized by lack of time or lack of training. I believe that this study has shown that benefits can flow from even very short-term mentoring relationships, though this is not to say that proportionately even greater benefits would not have come had the relationships been longer lasting. Perhaps the 'dark side' of mentoring (Long, 1997) has insufficient time to emerge in short-term relationships.

Based on this case, those organizing top-level mentoring schemes in organizations should consider:

- the benefits of using external mentors;
- the potential impact of even a short-term mentoring scheme;
- being aware of too much pre-briefing of the mentors;
- the potential benefit of group feedback from the mentors;
- the benefits of mentoring the individual and developing the team simultaneously.

REFERENCES

Alred, G and Garvey, B (2000) Learning to produce knowledge: the contribution of mentoring, *Mentoring and Tutoring*, **8** (3), pp 261–72

Garvey, B (1995) Healthy signs for mentoring, *Education and Training*, **37** (5), pp 12–19

Garvey, B (1999) Mentoring and the changing paradigm, *Mentoring and Tutoring*, **7** (1), pp 41–54

Garvey, B and Galloway, K (2002) Mentoring at the Halifax plc (HBOS): a small beginning in a large organisation, *Career Development International*, **7** (5), pp 271–78

Hansford, B, Tennent, L and Ehrich, LC (2002) Business mentoring: help or hindrance?, *Mentoring and Tutoring*, **10** (2), pp 101–15

Kessels, J (1996) *The Corporate Curriculum*, Inaugural lecture, Leiden University, Netherlands

Levinson, DL (1979) *The Seasons of a Man's Life*, Alfred A Knopf, New York

Long, J (1997) The dark side of mentoring, *Australian Educational Research*, **24** (2), pp 115–23

Megginson, D and Clutterbuck, D (1995) *Mentoring in Action*, 1st edn, Kogan Page, London

Wilson, JA and Elman, NS (1990) Organisational benefits of mentoring, *Academy of Management Executive*, **4** (4), pp 88–94

WOMEN AND LEADERSHIP: A DEVELOPMENT PROGRAMME IN DENMARK

Kirsten M Poulsen, KMP & Partners, Denmark

This section describes a development programme to support women's careers that used the role of the mentor as the central catalyst for learning. The section also shares the lessons learned from designing and implementing the programme, which may be useful for other programme organizers in other contexts.

BACKGROUND

The idea for the programme started with the Association of Business Women's (ABW) local chapter in Herning, a centre of commerce and innovation out in the moors of Jutland. The local chairwoman is an experienced mentor, and through mentoring a person working with fundraising she realized the opportunity to apply for funds to create a programme supporting women's careers. The chairwoman herself has been in management positions since 1984 and is very interested in promoting the development of young people, especially women. As a long-time member of ABW she was very aware of the lack of women in top management and on company boards – especially in Jutland. For this reason, she wanted to create a programme that would promote young businesswomen as well as motivate them to move on in the hierarchies of their companies. And since the purpose of ABW is to motivate women to take larger responsibilities in the business world and in the world in general, it made perfect sense to establish a programme like 'Women and leadership'.

The Association of Business Women then allied themselves with MTC – a self-financed centre for supporting local companies in developing quality assurance, environmental issues and leadership, as well as other relevant skills and competencies. Together they designed the programme called

'Women and leadership' and secured funding from FUTURA, an initiative created by Ringkøbing County to support development and growth of local small and medium-sized companies. Key to the programme was mentoring.

The purpose of the programme was:

▨ to create a learning arena for the mentees to clarify their own ambitions about taking on more leadership responsibility – preferably to move into top management;
▨ to develop the leadership qualifications of the mentees through personal development and insight into theories and tools;
▨ to give the mentors more insight into being, and the skills needed to become, board members of companies in the area;
▨ to encourage networking among all the participants for their further career development.

For ABW the objectives included spreading the message that women both can and will become top managers and promoting ABW as an important player in this arena. The association wanted to create a 'ripple effect' in the local area through word of mouth and through media attention.

PROGRAMME DESIGN

The programme included the following activities, all implemented in 2004:

▨ marketing the programme – finding the right participants as mentors and mentees;
▨ matching the participants;
▨ kick-off for all mentors and mentees;
▨ mentoring education for all mentors and mentees;
▨ four leadership development days for all mentees in the spring with approximately 14 days between each development day;
▨ a seminar on becoming/being a member of a board of directors;
▨ three networking days for all mentors and mentees in the autumn with approximately four weeks between each networking day – one was dedicated to new input on and discussion about mentoring.

Participants were found through a combination of advertising or direct marketing and directly contacting potential participants – mentors and mentees – in the area. There was great interest among potential mentees for participating in the programme, but the resources were limited to only 14 pairs.

Several mentors came through ABW. However, men applied too, and they were invited into the programme as mentors. Most mentors had never formally tried the role of mentor before.

Eventually, the group of mentors included:

- seven managing directors of small, medium-sized and larger companies;
- two HR managers;
- one purchasing manager;
- one chartered accountant;
- one department manager from the local union;
- one business consultant from the local trade council;
- the principal of a local school (Scandinavia's largest institute of education within design fashion and lifestyle);
- the chairwoman of ABW.

The mentors were between 35 and 65 years old. The mentees selected were women between 28 and 45; all were in middle management positions, though not all with responsibilities for managing people.

OUR APPLICATION OF THE MENTORING CONCEPT

In this programme the mentor is a catalyst for learning and a learning partner, who helps the mentee find as much as possible within him- or herself. However, the mentor is also a supporter, a story teller and an adviser, when relevant. The mentor motivates, asks the 'stupid' and 'difficult' questions, and follows up and remembers from one meeting to the next what the mentee has decided to do. The mentor's role is to be the conscience of the mentee. Sometimes it is just too easy for the mentee to postpone things; the fact that the mentee has committed him- or herself in front of the mentor is part of the accelerated learning process. Being a mentor involves the art of listening and the art of always being a bit ahead in the conversations, thinking about where the conversation is leading and whether to support this direction or to try to turn the conversation to another track.

The participants, as part of the evaluation, said the following about what mentoring is and what defines a good mentor: 'Mentoring is to think out loud – and to think big with no limitations.' A good mentor is 'open, honest, listens, asks questions, follows up, motivates, is available, shows his or her own insecurities and doubts openly, is patient, a guide, a coach etc.'

To get to know the participants and have a good basis for matching mentors and mentees, MTC did interviews face to face with all mentees.

Mentors were mainly interviewed by telephone since many were already well known by MTC.

On the kick-off day, mentors were given in-depth information about the leadership development event the mentees were going to attend. This ensures that the mentors understand development processes, so they can help the mentees use their new learning in their daily lives. At the same time, the mentees were given an introduction to mentoring – the concept, the ground rules, the potential benefits and outcomes – and they were given the opportunity to discuss in groups their own expectations of the programme and to start defining their goals for the process.

All mentors and mentees attend a one-day mentoring education event. They spent the day together, getting to know each other better, looking at barriers to establishing effective mentoring relationships, learning about the definitions and phases of the mentoring work, receiving training in communication and active listening, and exploring how assumptions and values can trick us into judging others wrongly. Finally, after being introduced to their respective mentors or mentees, they worked specifically on defining their own contract and goals.

The next day devoted to mentoring took place approximately five months later. During this day, the mentors and mentees exchanged experiences and learning with each other. It was interesting to see how the couples had developed differently according to their personalities, motivations and development needs. Many subjects came up that day, eg several mentees were in the process of changing work and the mentors felt this to be an ethical dilemma for themselves: the mentees' companies were sending their employees to a development programme and the result would be the employees leaving the company! Other mentors really wanted to get in contact with the mentee's company to push them into action and into supporting the mentee better. And a general issue was the 'closeness' of mentors and mentees. There were major differences among the pairs. Some were very close, talked to each other very often using all kinds of channels (telephone, mail, meetings); others would meet perhaps every six to eight weeks and sit down formally for a couple of hours and talk. It did not seem to have anything to do with the mentor being a woman or a man. It seemed to be more an issue of feeling secure in the role of being a mentor and understanding the role of the mentor, and of the mentee feeling an actual need for and understanding of the potential value of using the mentor to his or her fullest.

In January 2005 ABW invited all participants and representatives from the companies of the mentees to an evening of talking about mentoring. At this meeting two of the mentor/mentee couples presented their evaluation of participating in the programme.

Eighty per cent of the participants were there for this event. The atmosphere was vibrant and full of energy, and the connections between people were almost visible. But there were very few company representatives present, which fits quite well with not having involved the companies during the programme.

There is, however, no doubt that this programme has started a development process and made a difference in the lives of the participants. Everybody seemed quite confident in recommending mentoring programmes to friends and colleagues.

LESSONS LEARNED

Lessons learned for the mentor

Before you sign up as a mentor, you need to think about:

- How to make yourself worthy of the trust and openness – you as a mentor need to be very open about yourself, your strengths and weaknesses, professionally and personally, to encourage the mentee to be so too and to create the atmosphere for learning.
- Mentoring should have a goal, and the mentor's role is also to follow up to keep the process going, as otherwise it will end up as a 'cosy tea-party'.
- Taking on the huge responsibility of somebody telling you things that he or she is not telling anybody else in the professional or private network.

Mentoring is also a great opportunity for the mentors to apply new learning: 'when I coach my mentee around better time management and setting and following priorities, I feel that I must apply it to my own work too to be a good role model'.

Mentors also become more open about themselves through the mentoring programme. The mentoring programme lets the mentor see the world through the eyes of the mentee, which gives new insights into the mentor's own personal behaviour and leadership style.

One mentor has realized that he is now hiring more women managers. He subsequently realized that he has gained a better understanding of the strengths and weaknesses of women in the workplace.

Lessons learned for the mentees

- A male mentor can be great for setting things into perspective for a woman working in a very male-dominated company.
- It is tough to do leadership development and mentoring at the same time; however, the combination also gives great opportunities for learning.

- If the mentee does not feel he or she has a challenge that requires a mentor, you should not try to construct challenges or problems.

Lessons learned – for mentor and mentee

- Preparation is important – keep a log and remember what you have talked about at the last meeting to follow up between meetings or at the next meeting.
- It takes time to create trust and openness.
- You will probably always be nervous during the first phase of getting to know each other. The expectations are high and you do not want to disappoint your mentor or mentee.
- Mentor and mentee do not always agree. However, they find this is the challenging and fun part of the programme – disagreeing and then agreeing to disagree.

Lessons learned about the programme

- Leadership development linked with a mentoring programme is a strong combination – and an opportunity for lots of synergy and anchoring of learning through the mentoring process. The timing of the activities in this programme might have been changed for better effect. The leadership development days were too close in time for proper 'digestion'.
- It is very important to screen the mentees going into the programme to ensure that they actually have a situation or ambitions where they will benefit from both the leadership development and the mentoring.
- Involving the companies of the mentees more would have facilitated the process and ensured that the companies also achieved visible and relevant benefits from the process.
- It is also important to screen the companies beforehand to ensure that they really support the programme and the participant; otherwise it might be too much of an uphill battle.
- Starting a programme like this will accelerate changes in the lives of the mentees: several mentees have changed jobs during the programme – or have initiated major changes in their professional and/or personal life.
- Networking among the mentees is much stronger than any of them expected. Strong relationships have formed, including both professional and personal subjects. This is an area to be aware of in the design of such programmes.

■ It is an advantage when the mentor does not know the people that the mentee talks about. The fewer the connections with each other's worlds, the easier it is to open up and talk about your world as a mentee – and mentor.

WHAT WE MIGHT DO DIFFERENTLY NEXT TIME

Both ABW and MTC are positively interested in running more programmes in the future. So what will we do differently? On the basis of the lessons learned, four key areas will need future work:

■ There could have been more results for the mentors in their own professional development if the programme had had more focus on education for board directorship – this activity did not receive enough attention.

■ Mentors need more education and preparation to understand their own role and overcome doubts.

■ Mentors need to be more informed and involved in the leadership development programme to understand what the mentees are learning – to have the same framework and coach the mentees better on the learning.

■ It would have been a benefit to have more specific goals for the programme and for the individuals. An idea for another time would be for the programme management to coach the mentees in setting individual goals that could be evaluated at the end. Also other and more specific measurement and follow-up methods might have been used midway through and at the end of the programme.

Case Study 16

WEIR WARMAN LTD MENTORING PROGRAMME IN SYDNEY, AUSTRALIA

Imogen Wareing

Wherever there are beginners and experts, old and young, there is some type of learning going on, and some sort of teaching. We are all learners and we are all teachers.

(Gilbert Highet, *The Art of Teaching*)

COMPANY BACKGROUND

Weir Warman is an organization based in Australia that manufactures, sells and services pumps for the minerals industry. This includes coal mining, alumina refineries, gold mining and paper production. Weir Warman also provides pumps for power stations, distributed around the world.

The organization commenced in Kalgoorlie and has just under 500 employees. It has sites around Australia, including the Sydney head office and factory, Newcastle, Brisbane, Mount Isa, Rockhampton, Perth, Kalgoorlie and Adelaide. Its major site is the Artarmon (Sydney) operation, which has 350 employees.

Weir Warman is part of Weir Minerals, a division of the international Weir Group. Weir Minerals' reputation is based on engineering excellence applied to innovative, customer-focused solutions for processing minerals and aggressive materials. This reputation is founded through the merging of the previous global operations of Warman International and Envirotech.

REASONS FOR INITIATING MENTORING

The Weir Warman equal employment opportunity committee originally considered mentoring to assist with the development of women. An employee survey that highlighted a 'silo culture' and leadership issues led to revisiting the idea of a mentoring programme along with management training in 2001–02.

Weir Warman sourced an Australian mentoring firm, The Growth Connection, and invited its principal, the author of this case study, to present an information session. The concept of an integrated mentoring programme was explained and the ultimate aim for mentoring was expanded to apply to all employees.

It was agreed that a pilot study would be undertaken in 2003, and then the opportunity and benefits of access to a skilled mentor would be rolled out across the organization.

The second group is currently completing its programme.

Cameron Bott, the human resources manager and instigator of the programme, 'championed' the cause on the executive committee, and senior management were advised about the programme and then kept informed about its progress. There are currently two of the executive committee managers involved in the programme as mentors.

PROGRAMME OBJECTIVES

The objectives of the Weir Warman mentoring programme are to:

- assist self-management of careers;
- enhance organizational skills and knowledge;
- develop leadership skills;
- assist with staff retention;
- share the best of the company's values and culture;
- improve communication and understanding across the company.

Figure 2.16.1 illustrates the main features of the mentoring programme.

WHAT DO WE MEAN BY MENTORING?

Mentoring is primarily defined within Weir Warman's programme through a description of the history of the term. This, The Growth Connection asserts, places the practice not amongst new management techniques but instead as an age-old, natural way for people to learn and develop. The following description is explored in the mentor and mentoree preparatory workshops:

> Mentoring is a relationship between two people where one is knowledgeable and more experienced and assists the other to grow and to learn. It is not a new management technique. Since humans have lived in social groups we have learnt our norms, values, skills and behaviours by example, story and coaching. It is arguably the most effective way to learn the desired way to do things and pass on a culture.

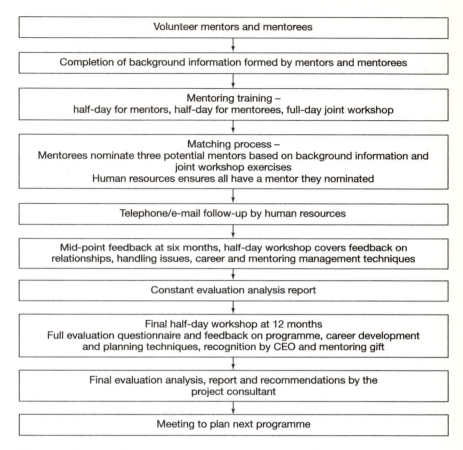

Figure 2.16.1   Weir Warman mentoring programme plan

The purposes mentorees selected for working on in the mentoring relationship reflect their understanding of the Weir Warman mentoring definitions and programme objectives:

- interpersonal skills development (80 per cent);
- professional skills development (60 per cent);
- clarifying career direction and opportunities (60 per cent);
- contacts, networking and understanding company functionality (40 per cent).

PREPARATION FOR THE RELATIONSHIP AND PROGRAMME

The pilot programme had 12 participants and was restricted to head office (in Sydney), and the second has 18 participants and includes employees from across Australia. These participants ranged from supervisor level through to the executive committee, and two of the partnerships are distance mentoring relationships.

The pilot programme was initially promoted through the organization using noticeboards, the company magazine and the Lotus Notes platform. A brochure was designed for this purpose. These were appropriate media to target the selected group – supervisors and above – and encourage volunteers. For the first programme, 14 volunteers were chosen. Over the period of the programme one mentor was made redundant and one mentoree resigned, leaving 12.

One mentoree became a mentor in the second group.

Training was undertaken both times for the mentors and mentorees prior to the matching process. The first group was trained in September 2003, and the second in August 2004.

The mentoree training focused on mentoring definitions and roles, developing mentoring objectives and communication skills. The mentor training also examined core mentor skills and how to manage the relationship. The combined workshop contained more detailed information about the programme with highly interactive 'getting to know you' and mentoring techniques exercises including goal setting, mentoring agreements and managing the mentoring discussions. The Myers Briggs Type Indicator was used to highlight differences in operating and communication styles and 'broke the ice' for the sharing of career stories.

During the joint workshop the mentorees nominated their choice of three preferred mentors. These mentors could not be in their direct supervisory line.

In both programmes, Cameron Bott, the human resources manager, undertook the final matching process from the three choices, in consultation with Imogen Wareing. This ensured no one mentor was overloaded. All mentorees received one of their preferred mentors. The participants were notified and partnerships began.

WHAT HAPPENED OVER TIME

In both programmes, two relationships struggled initially to meet regularly. From the mid-point onwards all partnerships met as frequently as needed, and most settled into a pattern of a formal meeting monthly, backed up by 'corridor meetings', telephone and e-mail. The interstate 'distance' relationships are of necessity more structured (including incorporating time differences) and are often fortnightly telephone discussions. Use of e-mail is discouraged, other than for exchanging factual data, ie contacts, references or organizing meeting times.

All but the distance mentoring relationships moved from meeting in participants' offices to more informal 'neutral' meeting venues such as local cafés or the company cafeteria.

The relationships all grew and strengthened over time. No relationships have failed. In one case, a combination of ethnic cultural differences and challenging work situations has been particularly hard work for the mentor, who has applied himself with commendable focus and time commitment to provide the best support to his mentoree.

The role of the human resources manager and his team has been critical in monitoring, communicating, removing road blocks and generally providing smooth running of the programme administration.

MEASUREMENT

'It is an opportunity to achieve more in everything you do and learn from the best' (mentoree).

The results of the pilot group were formally measured with a mid-point analysis. This group also had a final meeting and celebration, and informal evaluation occurred at this stage.

The second group has had a mid-point evaluation and a final, formal evaluation. The evaluations for both groups have consisted of confidential surveys completed and returned to Imogen Wareing for analysis, reporting and recommendations.

Some of the results and benefits reported by both groups include the following:

- One hundred per cent of mentors and 80 per cent of mentorees felt comfortable discussing sensitive work and career issues.
- All participants rated the mentoring programme as 'useful to very useful'.
- One hundred per cent of mentorees thought the programme supported their career development.
- All but one mentoree stated that the programme extended their contacts through:
  - time spent in other sections;
  - discussions with different department managers about their involvement in the business;
  - sharing with the other mentoring participants in the workshops.

■ Examples of what mentorees are doing differently as a result of mentoring included:
- growing themselves professionally;
- approaching tasks and challenges differently (better);
- working better with people;
- working better with other departments;
- standing up for themselves.

■ One hundred per cent of mentorees stated that their mentors made enough time available. One commented: 'I like making the most of every session we have.'

■ Areas listed that worked well for the mentorees were:
- better national and international knowledge of group business and processes;
- the set-up and maintenance of the mentoring relationship;
- the rapport between people in the mentoring group;
- support from human resources with follow-up and feedback;
- career goals and communication learned;
- working together with the mentor to develop strategies in handling difficult issues relating to work.

■ Mentors' gains included:
- an opportunity to review their own career path and reflect on organizational life, whilst gaining the satisfaction of developing others;
- better understanding of activities and problems;
- as a manager, a better understanding of a person's work and their aspirations;
- a focus for and an opportunity to reflect on their career development, and consider the career aspirations and work environment of others.

THE PILOT PROGRAMME

In the pilot programme, the participants demonstrated commitment and support for the mentoring programme. They were focused on making the programme successful.

Both mentors and mentorees stated that having partners come from separate areas allowed for 'cross-pollination' of ideas and greater understanding of different areas and wider perspectives in decision making.

Lack of time was the only issue raised as a difficulty. The pilot group agreed that with commitment on both sides this could be managed and they worked to continue their relationships despite this issue.

THE GROUP 2 PROGRAMME

'Mentoring is the best thing that has happened for me at Weir Warman' (female mentoree).

The participants are again committed to making mentoring work. The participants really appreciate the chance to meet and discuss their progress as a group. Two partnerships that were struggling to maintain momentum have been re-energized by the mid-point meeting and were determined to give mentoring a higher priority.

The mentoring group also helps with ideas on how to clarify objectives, intentions and ways to find time to meet.

Time to meet is again the major difficulty that has been uncovered. The partnerships largely meet in their own time (lunch, before work etc) and this demonstrates the commitment of those who have volunteered for the mentoring process.

LESSONS LEARNED

- There was low awareness about the programme throughout the rest of the organization. This can be addressed in future through a monthly newsletter, e-mails and other channels. This will allow for a greater pool of volunteers for future programmes – once they understand the benefits; and it will allow current managers of mentoring participants to understand and support their people's commitment to the programme.

- A briefing for participant managers and supervisors about the programme may be another way to inform those indirectly involved about the programme's benefits.

- Mentoring needs to be linked formally to the organization's management development programme.

- An allocated budget may assist in interstate partnerships being able to meet at least once face to face.

- The training for the second group needed to be fine-tuned to emphasize points raised in the pilot: importance of goal setting, more structure for early meetings, how matching takes place, balance between mentoring and coaching.

- The mid-point workshop has proved to be extremely helpful to the mentoring process in both programmes through:

  - re-energizing and refocusing some of the relationships, eg in group 2, two floundering relationships were completely regenerated and are continuing to be successful;

  - learning tips and insights from other partnerships;

- reinforcing the empowerment and self-driven development messages through including career development techniques with outcomes to be progressed in the partnerships, as well as enhancing mentoring techniques;
- providing qualitative feedback on successes and any road blocks so that human resources could address them rapidly.

CONCLUSIONS AND NEXT STEPS

The Weir Warman mentoring programme will now extend to more supervisory-level employees and will call on the experience of the two existing programme participants for support.

Group 2 has extended its 'formal component' by a further three months by general agreement.

In successful organizational programmes, the dedication and care taken by the mentors who generously share their time and knowledge are an impressive feature. The Weir Warman mentors are no exception, and it is notable that they expect much of themselves in the mentor role and are concerned whether they are giving enough. Their mentorees are in no doubt that they have continued to benefit in a wide range of ways and value and acknowledge their mentors' gifts.

Significant personal development is readily observable in both the mentors and the mentorees, and communication and respect across the 'silos' is enriched with each programme.

This is an example of a well-planned programme, with sufficient resources provided for training and resources, good will, good humour and commitment from the participants, and the development of closer work relationships and measurable increasing knowledge, skills, self-confidence and realistic career goals.

MENTORING FOR LEADERSHIP IN HBOS

Tom Riddell, Executive and Organizational Development Team, HBOS

Executive mentoring at HBOS is seen as a key component in growing and developing leadership capability at the most senior levels in the organization. The overall aim is to broaden the mentees' business knowledge, grow their networks and prepare them for progression to even more senior roles. To achieve this, the mentees, who are identified as high-potential people, are matched with current executives from outside their own division of the business.

BACKGROUND TO MENTORING IN HBOS

In earlier work in the same organization with a different level of participants, Garvey and Galloway (2002: 271) noted that: 'Mentoring is an enriching activity which offers the participants the potential to reflect and act through developing understanding through dialogue in a supportive and sometimes challenging relationship.'

Although this previous scheme involved different people at a different level in the organization, there are a number of common features. These include:

- leadership development as the focus for mentoring;
- development for mentors and mentees;
- voluntarism;
- high-level support for mentoring;
- offline mentors.

Given the success of the previous scheme and the early advances made in this current arrangement, it is possible to speculate that these seem to be important features in the successful implementation of mentoring schemes within large organizations.

HBOS background

HBOS was formed from the merger of the Halifax and the Bank of Scotland in September 2001. HBOS is a leading provider of financial services in the UK. The company currently employs approximately 68,000 people. Many senior managers and executives across the business have involved themselves in the executive mentoring for leadership programme.

PURPOSE OF EXECUTIVE MENTORING

The executive mentoring programme was developed and is managed by the executive and organizational development (EOD) team.

The executive mentoring programme is seen as a key part of the drive to grow and develop internal leadership capability at the most senior levels in the business. This is part of a clearly developed career progression, succession and leadership development strategy within the group.

A main feature of the programme is that the participants are matched with a more senior colleague outside of the line management function (in line with Clutterbuck's (1992) recommendations for matching mentors), division and specialist area. This provides a cross-divisional element to help improve communication, understanding and knowledge sharing across the HBOS group.

From the mentor's perspective, it gives him or her the opportunity to work with a talented colleague from another part of the business and have the opportunity to contribute to the development of the leaders of the future. This develops a strong mutual learning and networking opportunity for the participants.

The programme focuses specifically on the top three layers of leaders in HBOS (levels 6, 7 and 8). Typically, the mentor participants will be directors and board members of various HBOS businesses at grade 8, and the mentees will be, in terms of the grade structure, at grade 6 or 7. There are some small variations to this.

IDENTIFYING MENTORS

All level 7 and 8 executives in HBOS work closely with a consultant from EOD in the creation of a personal development plan, and during these discussions the possibility of acting as a mentor to a level 6 high-potential colleague is discussed. Many of these executives responded positively to the idea and an initial group of 10 were identified who all agreed to participate.

The motivations of the executives to participate are interesting and relate well to other research in the field (Alred, Garvey and Smith, 1998) with executives giving the following reasons:

- 'I see it as my job.'
- 'What else can I do if I don't help to bring someone else along?'
- 'I want to develop my own knowledge of the business.'
- 'I believe it is important for the future progress of the business.'
- 'I want to give something back to the organization that has been good to me.'

Some of these motivations resonate well with Erikson's (1995) concept of 'generativity': 'Generativity, then is primarily the concern in establishing and guiding the next generation' (p 240). This notion would seem fundamental to mentoring and a core element in the psychological motivations of potential mentors. Perhaps we simply can't help but to want to mentor at some stage in our lives.

IDENTIFYING MENTEES

Level 6 managers who have been identified as high-potential by the divisions attend a two-day career development centre (CDC), which consists of a number of activities including psychometrics, group discussions, presentations and case studies.

During the CDC, participants discuss mentoring and are given the opportunity to indicate the type of mentor they would wish to work with. Following the CDC, the participants are offered an executive mentor. This is not compulsory and so far only two have declined – both on the basis that they were already in mentoring relationships.

MENTOR AWARENESS

To help prepare and orientate the mentors for the programme, EOD developed a one-day workshop. The workshop was designed to run in the 'mentoring way' using the three-stage process (Alred, Garvey and Smith, 1998) – exploration, understanding and action. Participants develop a personal view of what mentoring means to them through exploring the mentoring process. This is of vital importance because mentoring can take many forms, involve a variety of techniques and have a range of styles (Gladstone, 1988). If a potential mentor is not clear about the form of mentoring in which he or she wants to engage, early confusion can create later difficulties. This understanding also enables the mentors to establish ground rules and to explore the dimensions (Garvey, 1994) of the relationship with their mentee.

For the practical element of the workshop, mentors work in groups of three, with one taking the role of mentor, another that of mentee and the third observes. All participants are asked to come to the workshop with at least one issue that they would like to discuss in a mentoring conversation – we call this 'real play'.

Mentors generally find the skills work very helpful on two levels: the first in raising his or her awareness of the mentoring process – explore, understand, action; and second in helping some of them to work through real issues of concern that they were facing in the workplace. This, we believe, is one of the hidden benefits of 'real play'. The topic, being live, takes on special significance to the participants. Here, the programme participants develop an understanding of mentoring processes and skills as well as experiencing the outcome of mentoring real play as authentic and relevant. This enables the mentors to be fully aware of the power of mentoring through personal experience.

As support material, all mentors are given a copy of *The Mentoring Pocket Book* (Alred, Garvey and Smith, 1998) and a collection of articles about mentoring. An important part of the ongoing support for mentors and mentees is open access to the EOD team and the workshop facilitator to discuss mentoring process and skills issues. All participants are able to access this support on the basis of individual need.

At the close of the awareness workshop, mentors are invited to think about their own development as mentors. Some mentors wish to take a mentor for themselves to assist them in their development as mentors.

ORIENTATION FOR MENTEES

Mentees are assisted in their choice of mentor and are helped to prepare for mentoring in two ways.

First, each mentee has the opportunity to discuss mentoring with an EOD consultant. Here, issues of concern are raised and clarified. Most see the offer of an executive mentor as a real and positive opportunity.

Second, mentees are given a copy of the video 'Mentoring conversations' (produced by The Greenwood Partnership, www.greenwood-partnership.com) to watch. This video illustrates the three-stage process and key mentoring skills. Following this viewing, mentees participate in a telephone conference call with the workshop facilitator and the EOD consultant to discuss the video and any other issues of concern.

While it is probably better getting the mentees together for a meeting, often they are at great distances apart and consequently there are time and cost implications. The telephone conference is a good compromise.

GETTING STARTED

The EOD match the pairs and confirm that both parties are willing to go ahead with the relationship. It is then the responsibility of the mentee to schedule the first meeting. At this stage, an informal contract is drawn up, which agrees the ground rules of the relationship and the length of the relationship (normally 12 months), agreeing confidentiality and an initial draft agenda of meetings. Sometimes the agenda is influenced by the outcomes of the mentee's career development centre.

Typically, meetings last one to two hours per month and are usually face to face, although telephone sessions do happen, particularly once the relationship is established. Given the travel commitments of many of the executives, meetings are often scheduled to coincide with other business activities.

As part of the process, the pair agree to review the relationship at the end of the third meeting and, if either party feels it is not adding value, they may part. In general, regular review of the relationship is encouraged.

CONTENT OF DISCUSSIONS

Discussions are normally around work-related issues identified by the mentee, as well as organizational issues, career development activities and behavioural issues. A common behavioural issue raised by mentees is their ability to influence their peers. In an equal-status environment, this is an important element of leadership. Other topics commonly discussed are:

- behavioural aspects of time management;
- personal issues;
- conflict with others;
- team performance issues;
- business decision making.

At the end of the meeting, the pair may agree a course of action that the mentee will take. This will be reviewed and updated in a later mentoring meeting. Sometimes the mentor may suggest someone in his or her network whom the mentee could approach for information or advice.

PROGRESS

The first relationships are now quite well established and the feedback has so far been positive. To date, more than 30 relationships are active.

Owing to the success of the programme, the EOD team mirrored the process to allow high-potential level 7 executives who were seen as having board potential to be matched with a member of the HBOS executive (this is the top 25 leaders in HBOS). Nine senior executives from the HBOS executive have attended workshops and are now in mentoring relationships with level 7 colleagues from other divisions. There are plans in place to involve more of this group in mentoring over the coming months. Additionally, the success of this scheme has encouraged other people, for example the HR community within HBOS, to investigate mentoring as part of an effective development strategy.

EVALUATION

All the mentors and mentees are encouraged to review their progress throughout the life of the relationship, and if they need support this is provided by EOD. The EOD team also informally evaluates the programme as part of the development relationship with the executive population.

It was felt that policing the scheme would be counter-productive to a positive relationship and would lead to an overemphasis on counting the number of meetings, agendas and action plans. The EOD team feels that it is important to allow the participants to use their own judgement over what is most appropriate and adds most value for them. In this way, mentoring activity does not become part of a management control mechanism but a genuinely autonomous and developmental activity that is managed with a 'light touch'. It works if the participants want it to work, and the EOD team provides support to give mentoring the best chance of survival.

A further element under consideration is the development of mentor support groups and, possibly, mentor supervision (Barrett, 2002). It is felt that these activities may provide the mentors with vehicles for their continued development as mentors.

A case example of the benefits

This brief case example illustrates the benefits of the cross-functional nature of executive mentoring within HBOS. The EOD team suggested that two executives from different parts of the business might benefit from being in a mentoring relationship. The mentor was from the retail banking division and the mentee from the business banking division. They met and agreed the agenda for the relationship and this included some work-shadowing activity. Leadership issues were discussed and progress was made in this area. However, a real and tangible business benefit emerged from the mentoring interaction. Both realized that some individuals who approached, for example, the retail banking division for mortgages to purchase high-value domestic properties sometimes also had business mortgage needs and vice versa. Consequently, the two executives created a cross-divisional referral process and thus developed important new business opportunities for both divisions.

LESSONS LEARNED

There seem to be a number of features in the HBOS executive arrangements that give the scheme a good chance of working well and help it to meet its business objective of developing leadership capability.

These include:

- a strong element of voluntarism;
- ongoing support for mentors and mentees if they require it;
- light-touch management of the scheme;
- strong participative influence on the shape of the scheme;
- attention to mentor development and orientation;
- attention to mentee development and orientation;
- further resources available, ie books, articles and videos;
- responsive EOD consultants to participants' needs;
- informal evaluation;
- regular review within the individual mentoring arrangement.

REFERENCES

Alred, G, Garvey, B and Smith, R (1998) *The Mentoring Pocket Book*, Management Pocket Books, Alresford, Hampshire

Barrett, R (2002) Mentor supervision and development: exploration of lived experience, *Career Development International*, **7** (5), pp 279–83

Clutterbuck, D (1992) *Everyone Needs a Mentor: How to foster talent within the organization*, 2nd edn, Institute of Personnel Management, London

Erikson, E (1995) *Childhood and Society*, Vintage, WW Norton, Reading, first published by Imago Publishing Company in 1951

Garvey, B (1994) A dose of mentoring, *Education and Training*, **36** (4), pp 18–26

Garvey, B and Galloway, K (2002) Mentoring at the Halifax plc (HBOS): a small beginning in a large organisation, *Career Development International*, **7** (5), pp 271–78

Gladstone, MS (1988) Mentoring: a strategy for learning in a rapidly changing society, *Research Document CEGEP*, John Abbott College, Quebec

Case Study 18

EXECUTIVE MENTORING IN UBS

Chris Roebuck

COMPANY BACKGROUND

UBS is the world's largest wealth manager, a top-tier investment banking and securities firm and a key global asset manager. In Switzerland, UBS is the market leader in retail and commercial banking.

UBS, headquartered in Zurich and Basel, is present in all major financial centres worldwide. It has offices in 50 countries, with 39 per cent of its employees working in the Americas, 38 per cent in Switzerland, 16 per cent in Europe and 7 per cent in the Asia Pacific time zone. UBS's financial businesses employ over 68,000 people worldwide.

UBS serves a discerning client base and, as an organization, it combines financial strength with a culture that embraces change.

The bank has a clear vision: to be recognized as the best global financial services company.

The business is made up of four business groups: Investment Bank, Global Asset Management, Wealth Management US, and Wealth Management and Business Banking. These are supported by a corporate centre based mainly in Zurich. All, except Wealth Management US, operate globally.

From 1992 until 2002 UBS had grown through a number of mergers and acquisitions. The bank then entered a period of consolidation and expansion through organic growth. A critical part of enabling such growth was to deliver all the services from all business groups to all clients as appropriate: from the client perspective to be in effect 'one firm' operating an 'integrated business model'. It was decided that to achieve this objective the leadership of the bank, a group of about 600, needed to be fully behind this strategy, to be aware of what other parts of the bank could do for their clients and to become one united leadership team. It was agreed that mentoring was a key element of this and that, to deliver awareness, it should operate across business group boundaries, ie mentors would have mentees from business groups other than their own.

THE MENTORING SCHEME

As the mathematics did not allow all 600 to be covered, a mentoring programme was designed to engage the top 200 of the leadership group. It was proposed that the group executive board (GEB) (group CEO, business group CEOs, group CFO, general counsel and two others) would mentor the next level down, the 50 members of the group managing board (GMB) (the heads of significant business units), who would in turn mentor 160 of the next level down, called 'key talents' (senior managers often in key positions in the bank). The mentoring would thus be between adjoining rank levels. The decision was taken that, given their leadership role, those at GEB and GMB level should all be mentors without exception.

The structure of the mentoring programmes is shown in Figure 2.18.1.

The objectives of the mentoring programmes were to:

- help create one aligned leadership group to build the 'one firm' concept;
- drive forward our integrated business model by improving business performance through cross-business and cross-cultural communications and teamwork;
- enable the UBS vision and values to live across the business by creating a common culture;
- improve individual performance of both mentee and mentor;
- provide ongoing career development and increase retention of talented leaders;
- enhance the potential of cross-business group talent movement.

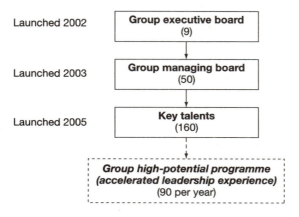

Figure 2.18.1   The structure of the UBS mentoring programmes

The mentors and mentees would come from a culturally diverse group of individuals resulting from:

- *Nationality:* the nationality of senior managers was about 43 per cent Swiss, 31 per cent US, 19 per cent British and 8 per cent other.
- *Business group culture and practice:* where there was variation in factors, eg operational timescales and decision-making styles. The bank contains a number of different business models: retail and private banking, currency, equity and other trading, mergers and acquisitions, asset management, commission-based financial services sales, and specialist, strategic and group management activities. Within each area there are also often cultural variations between trading, client-facing and support functions. Whilst this cultural diversity is a strength in developing innovation, during mentoring it can make building rapport more difficult.

Prior to planning the implementation of the programmes, a set of principles was drawn up to make the implementation effective:

- Focus mentoring on delivering personal and business benefits, not just as HR best practice.
- Cultural diversity to be a valued element in the partnerships.
- Minimize time taken to train mentors and mentees to be effective by using a clear, simple and practical framework for mentoring. Additional support materials to be provided to add further support.
- Minimize bureaucracy but ensure effective implementation, management and monitoring of the programme.
- Ensure all participants and stakeholders are informed and involved.
- No specific time limit to relationships so that ongoing development would continue.
- All mentees to be given information on being an effective mentor as well as a mentee, as many would be mentoring in their business group role as senior managers.

In terms of implementation this meant that, for the GEB/GMB-level mentoring, all GMB members would initially be mentored by a GEB member. This meant that most GEB members had five to six mentees.

For the GMB/key talent-level programme the selection of mentees was based on an assessment by the CEO and head of HR of each business group who identified those within their senior-level management who they thought would benefit most from a mentor from another business group.

Once nominations for mentees were submitted, matching was based on three criteria in order of priority:

- mentor and mentee to be in different business groups (compulsory);
- mentor and mentee to be in the same location or region (if at all possible);
- personal needs of the mentee (where possible).

Given the variation in global distribution of business groups, and hence the distribution of mentors and mentees, it was difficult in some cases to find enough mentors to cover all the required mentees in some locations. GMB mentors were restricted to three or four mentees.

Mentor and mentee training took place in Zurich, London and New York. On the GMB/key talent programme, over 90 per cent of all mentees were briefed and 100 per cent of the mentors. Within three months of launch, an e-mail-based check was made to ensure that all partnerships had met.

Subsequent feedback on both GEB/GMB mentoring and GMB/key talent mentoring has been obtained via a number of means:

- face-to-face feedback – verbal feedback from ad hoc meetings with participants collected on an ongoing basis;
- simple e-mail during the early phase – a short e-mail requesting the number of times met and any benefits identified;
- online survey after 18 months – providing detailed feedback.

Results so far show that:

- Most partnerships have met an average of three to four times.
- On both levels 50 per cent of participants have identified a specific benefit from the programme.
- GMB/key talent: 96 per cent wish to continue to be mentored going forward.

Direct benefits: A wide variety of benefit has been identified: solving operational issues, career planning, initiating cross-business group contacts for effective communication or development of new business, and dealing with significant personal issues. Whilst compared to 'normal' mentoring programmes the number of meetings seemed low, the highly focused approach of the participants has led to more benefits than normally expected for this number of meetings.

Secondary benefits: The profile of the strategic mentoring programmes has led to four specific effects:

1. Some of the participants have initiated mentoring activity in their own business areas.
2. The profile of mentoring has been raised within the bank, so that in other areas it is now being considered as a development option where it might not have been.
3. This has had a positive impact on building a learning and development culture in some areas where mentoring has been initiated.
4. The transfer of mentoring skills into coaching skills by line managers for use with their own teams has further enhanced the value.

During implementation a number of predicted challenges were confirmed:

- *Matching*. The geographical spread of mentors versus mentees led to high numbers of mentees per mentor.
- *Working with senior management who have very busy diaries*. The difficulty of getting time for training and meetings means this time must be optimized. Further, the high number of mentees made finding time for mentors to meet all of them more difficult.
- *Best practice versus business reality*. The participants have priorities other than mentoring. This needs to be accepted and worked with.
- *Nominations not volunteers*. Some mentees and mentors were initially not keen to be involved. In most cases after initial meetings they identified the potential value of mentoring and became positive about their involvement.
- *Keeping up the momentum of the programme*. After time the programme could become a lower priority and might eventually cease to function. It was necessary to raise the profile on a regular basis via newsletters, meetings and other activities.
- *Cultural differences*. It was made clear to all involved that these would be present but were an opportunity not a threat.
- *Closeness of mentors and mentees*. In organizational-level terms, mentors and mentees were closer than in normal mentoring programmes, so more two-way learning was expected and a more 'peer learning'-based approach was taken by many.
- *Effective communication*. E-mail communication to gain commitment from participants, particularly mentors, is insufficient. Communication needs to be face to face to gain real commitment.

Within a dynamic organizational environment changes such as promotions, departures and inter-business group moves occur on a regular basis and these have to be monitored and the programme adapted to deal with them. With a constituency of 200 this can be difficult.

In 2004, changes in GEB membership and new appointments to the GMB resulted in two fewer GEB but 10 more GMB members to mentor. This caused the numbers of GMB mentees per GEB mentor to become unrealistic. A full review was conducted and GMB members were asked to rate their personal need for a mentor. Some of the more experienced GMB agreed that the newly appointed GMB needed a mentor more than they did, so they offered to conclude their current formal relationships. As a result the number of GMB being mentored was reduced by 19.

In 2004 it was decided to introduce a programme to develop high-potential junior managers. As part of the accelerated leadership experience (ALE), participants would be supported by a mentor, their line manager and HR teams after an intensive three-and-a-half-day programme. Again the mentoring would be across business groups. During the survey of the GMB/key talent participants the mentees of the GMB were asked if they would like to volunteer to mentor the ALE participants. Eighty-five per cent of key talents volunteered. The ALE mentoring was launched in May 2005 in the same way as the GMB/key talent with briefing of both mentors and mentees.

NEXT STEPS

Through ongoing verbal feedback and periodic formal reviews, steps will be taken to develop further and embed mentoring and coaching within UBS. These are likely to relate to:

- *Linkage to the strategic organizational agenda.* Ensure key organizational issues are discussed within partnerships and awareness of them increased.
- *Development of the coaching and mentoring culture.* Expand the number of people being mentored and coached and build understanding of the commonality of skills between the two and their application to enhancing all working relationships.
- *Further activities for both participants and stakeholders.* Enable mentors and mentees to meet and discuss their progress and create a mutual support network.
- *Enable human resources teams to deepen knowledge and raise skill levels.* Mentoring works best when driven from within the business. To enable this to happen, HR teams working with the business must be able to help the line implement mentoring and coaching.
- *Link with other talent development activity.* Mentoring does bring benefits as a stand-alone initiative, but benefits are significantly greater when integrated with other development activity.

■ *Use as a further driver for mentoring elsewhere.* Enthusiasm spreads fast, and mentoring becomes popular, but it needs to be stressed that mentoring is not the answer to everything and bad-quality mentoring is worse than no mentoring!

LESSONS LEARNED

There are a number of lessons that have been learned, which may be of benefit to others about to run mentoring programmes:

■ *Importance of training.* Mentors and mentees must be given enough training to make the relationship effective from the start. This means that both partners must be fully aware of what they have to do. Issuing support materials is not a substitute for face-to-face training.

■ *Need for senior sponsorship.* A high-level senior sponsor acts as a powerful motivator to both mentors and mentees to have initial meetings and keep the relationships going.

■ *Volunteers.* Where possible mentors and mentees should be volunteers. This will increase the chances of positive relationships. However, although senior managers, who were obliged to mentor as part of their role, were initially not fully happy, once they started to mentor they discovered the benefits and some even offered to undertake more mentoring in other environments.

■ *First meetings.* Once the mentoring programme is launched it is important to get people together as soon as possible. The first meeting must be effective to drive the relationship forward.

■ *Managing expectations.* Mentoring is not a quick fix, nor will it change the organizational landscape overnight. Many of the benefits of mentoring appear slowly and are not always obvious to begin with. This means that data collection to demonstrate benefits to stakeholders has to be carefully planned.

■ *Importance of keeping up the profile of the programme.* Within any organization, mentoring is unlikely to be the key operational priority. It has to compete with other time demands and participants must be reminded from time to time about it.

■ *Cultural diversity and differences.* If these differences exist it is essential to explain them to people and treat them as opportunities, and to give people tools to help them to do this.

■ *Keeping in touch.* Programme managers must know what's going on – mentors and mentees need to know that someone is interested in their success, and this also allows the programme managers to monitor progress.

■ *Need for a credible programme manager.* There must be a programme manager who has a good knowledge of mentoring and a working relationship with the key stakeholders and participants. He or she must be able to influence effectively both mentors and mentees and therefore needs to be of at least a similar rank level if possible.

The strategic mentoring programmes at UBS have been successful in delivering benefits to those involved and to the organization. They have demonstrated that top management can become personally involved in developing talent, that they can be effective mentors and that mentoring across business area boundaries can bring commercial benefits. Within UBS, mentoring is starting to flourish, but it is still work in progress, and further enhancements and resultant benefits will occur in the future. Mentoring is more a marathon than a sprint!

Part 3
Individual Cases

3

Case Studies

INTRODUCTION

The cases in this edition are as varied as the ones in our first. For the first time we have a thoughtful account of an e-mentoring relationship, analysed by the mentee; and we also have three cases from the first edition updated by the participants and in one case (Mike Allen and Ray Hinchcliffe) with an added contribution from the person who started as the mentee. This case may stand as one of the longest active relationships of its kind – as it has now been going for more than 22 years. If any of our readers have tales of longer relationships then we would like to hear from them.

We found that many of the issues arising from individual and organizational cases have been the same, so the analysis of these individual cases has been incorporated into the organization cases for this edition and will be found in Part 4.

Case Study 1

VERY LONG-TERM PEER MENTORING: MIKE ALLEN WITH RAY HINCHCLIFFE, CBE

Mike Allen and Ray Hinchcliffe, CBE, interviewed by David Megginson

In our first edition Mike Allen described what was already a 12-year-long rela-tionship with Ray Hinchcliffe. We include his account in this edition, updated for what has happened over the last 10 years. We have also added a separate account by Ray of what is one of the longest and most successful peer mentoring relation-ships that we know about.

Mike Allen said this 10 years ago in our first edition:

I came into the Employment Department as a Clerical Assistant, acciden-tally, from being unemployed, after an abortive attempt to become a teacher. So I have moved up from the bottom rung, and I know what it is like to be managed both well and badly. My peers now (Grade 5 in the Civil Service structure) tend to be very bright people, who have joined at a high level, so I emphasize people management, as this is the key thing inside me that differentiates me from them.

Throughout my career I found it important to be able to go and talk to people: to ask 'How do I do this? How do you do it?' I have had variable success. One boss, three layers above me, was always prepared to explain why he was doing things. This was very valuable. If I had bosses who weren't willing to give the time, I had to reach out for others. In my career, I could usually find someone. Knowing the value of this to me, I have tried to do the same with others.

The longest mentoring relationship I have had is with Ray Hinchcliffe, with whom I have worked closely on and off since 1983. We are currently on the same grade, and so it is peer mentoring, and both of us benefit from it. We first met when I came to Sheffield on completion of a full-time MSc at Shrivenham. I was given a big project to deliver a new financial management system for the Manpower Services Commission. My team of four included Ray. I was completely lost; I knew about management and about the field part of the organization; but I knew nothing about accounting and little about large mainframe computer systems. Ray appeared to have this expertise and we formed a partnership.

At this stage he was a Higher Executive Officer (HEO) and I was the next grade up – Senior Executive Officer (SEO) – but acting up as a Grade 7. He had the ability to see both the big picture and the detail, but he wasn't able to work the politics of the system. So I dealt with the rest of the world, and I could trust him to give me sensible things to say. The relationship, the project and our careers all flourished.

We kept getting into situations where we needed to lean on each other. In time we made this a more explicit mentoring relationship: we sat down and advised each other. We became nervous about being separated, though at times we were in separate commands, and I spent six months working in HR. However, the relationship continued. Every time Ray has been promoted, we have had a period where he has had some explicit mentoring. For example, when he became a Grade 6 (the first Senior Management grade, with a secretary and all the trimmings) he had a crisis about how you operate at that level – how you get away from the detail, and remain confident that things will still happen; how you handle the politics. We identified competences like persuasion and negotiation that he had not developed. Up until then he had relied on the force of the argument. I helped him reflect on what being a Grade 6 meant. I made sure that I didn't just give him the things that I do, because we are so different, but we concentrated on the things that are essential for the job.

Now we are both Grade 5s, and I am Chairman and he is the Managing Director of the Information Systems Branch (ISB). When he became a Grade 5, he had to do more presentations at conferences, and he has found it difficult to enjoy and use these occasions. I have helped him use networking as a major asset in this position.

The mentoring relationship has helped me when we have had some really difficult decisions to make, for example over market testing. Would I lead the bid? What if we lost? We examined different scenarios and how we felt. It became clear that I didn't have a role in the detailed planning. Ray was able to be very explicit about what my role was. He said, without hesitation, that I had to be the figurehead, the leader who people know and will follow; I had to do the visionary things, go and be seen, listen to the staff, and handle partnerships and competition.

One thing about this relationship is that it is fun. With Ray it is really good, and we have both benefited in our careers and in doing our jobs better. It is difficult to know whether it is a friendship or a working relationship. We have great arguments when we are under pressure, which worry people outside. But the strength of ISB during market testing was the Allen/Hinchcliffe relationship – understanding each other's thinking made us almost unbeatable.

Because we both got such a lot out of this, we realized that we needed other people, so we now look at and work with our skills and preferences and those of our two colleagues in the management team. In turn, we spend quite a lot of time discussing the performance of others and what to do about it, so we have ended up helping others.

Then we became involved in the Hybrid Manager course (an MSc in Information Technology and Management at Sheffield Hallam University), and I started reading about mentoring and making it a formal arrangement for people doing the course part time. We were very aware of the differences between people and the strengths of others that they could use. Mentoring would not have developed had we not talked about people a lot.

The Hybrid programme made me think about mentoring and we discussed it a lot. Up until then I had not realized the power of hierarchy, how there seemed to be no option if a senior boss suggested it. We have now raised the issue of blame-free divorce. The chapter on male/female relationships in *Everyone Needs a Mentor* (Clutterbuck, 1992) was deeply worrying. What was worrying was that I hadn't thought about it. Before that, the decision on choice of mentor was very loose, and this raised the importance of not taking a power position.

We have learned the importance of taking a contractual position. Before, with Ray, it hadn't seemed necessary. Sometimes with the Hybrid managers we seemed to get on all right. You could allow a long period to get to know each other and gradually adjust. With others, if you lack that rapport, you need a definition of what you will do, and a process for agreeing this.

It has helped having training sessions with other mentors at the university. I started without an understanding of how to help people on the course. Now part of what I do is provide the context. They often come with their thoughts about an assignment, and I offer the wider picture. I draw this on the electronic whiteboard and some of them take a print-off and find this helpful. Others seem to want more specific help – references, reports, a look at the structure of what they are doing. They all get a good insight of what it is like to have the wider perspective from the top of the pyramid. Ray is also doing the course, so I act formally as his mentor for this.

I have also mentored a woman not on the course. I have taken a fatherly interest in her career. Occasionally, I set out my problem to her and ask her what she thinks. It helps me and it helps her. I highlight how my job is not easy – perhaps that's why I do it! I do it with management issues for her, and with more technical issues for the Hybrids.

With one of the Hybrids, who was a project manager of the old school – 'this is mine, this is yours' – Ray and I have both mentored him. He has changed enormously. He has built a support relationship in his team. It has worked and it has had an effect on other teams too. They have the makings of a really high-performance team.

Another benefit of mentoring to the organization came from the fact that we were early to de-layer. Status shouldn't come from position, but the people I mentor have helped me to realize how many landmarks we have taken away. So, we have had to give them a better compass. Mentoring is an important part of that. I have learned a lot about my organization from the people I mentor.

Mike Allen added the following in the light of the last 10 years' experience:

My vision, after the market test, was to take the organization into the private sector, to keep the sharpness. A number in the management team and among our private sector partners were interested in working with us to compete for other work. In the week I was going to go to Senior Management with the proposal, I was called and asked to manage another very large project. I was talked into this – it was an 18-month project. Ray took on my role, and two months later there was a Cabinet reshuffle and two departments of state merged. Ray applied for and won the job of heading the combined IT function.

We remained supporting each other as friends. Ray outsourced some applications. I implemented my project (Jobseeker's Allowance) in April 1997. I realized I wanted to go into the private sector, and became one of the founders of Oakleigh Consulting. There were two of us at the time. There are now 70 employees and 100 associates. We focus primarily on change management in the public sector. We do mentoring and coaching within this, mainly as a component of other assignments. What excites me is the application of programme management to the end-to-end policy process. Deliverability is an important criterion for policy formation. We have developed tools – the 22 questions and outcome relationship mapping – to support this. It stops policy people thinking a White Paper is a useful outcome!

We often find that mentoring and coaching of senior managers (senior responsible owners) is useful. I run mentoring sessions in DfES and colleagues do the same in DEFRA and other departments.

With Ray, we still talk a lot, but it's more informal now. Our position is reversed – we are now one of his approved consultants.

I have also found that, if it isn't working, one must be prepared to let it stop.

As one's circle of mentees becomes wider it emphasizes the importance of thinking oneself into their mind-set.

Ray Hinchcliffe, CBE, Head of Programme and Project Management, DfES:

The shift in role – me being pushed into Mike's role – made me realize how the way you have to look at things is shaped by the job you have to do, rather than your personality. With Mike, I valued being able to talk through how he had done things, but not to copy him. Instead we thought about how I might do it.

It was a peer relationship, because he had help from me on a number of occasions about his big project.

Jobs we did were one-off in our organization, and our influence depended on high credibility. Mike had it, and I developed it. So, I am still consulted on IT issues in the Department, though I ceased to be Head of IT two years ago.

I needed help from Mike to become able to do things that were not natural to me – being the frontman and networker (my natural talent was being the problem solver). In a sense, this was like coaching, but we didn't have the time to do it in a coaching way. So he increased my confidence and gave me the encouragement to do it. He also provided insight into what people were looking for. Being able to be open with him about what I didn't know was important. The issue of establishing your own credibility is the way things work in government.

During this time the Department for Employment merged with the Education Department. In the first 18 months in my new job, I faced some big challenges (downsizing by 30 per cent, reducing costs by a third, re-establishing our reputation when in-house IT was very unpopular in government). Mike had faced them all before.

Mike had realized he had almost a parental responsibility for the organization's long-term future – developing the next generation of managers. We increased the number doing the Hybrid Manager programme and other courses. There was a big gap in age between people of my age and those 15 years younger, and there was nobody below the age of 24. So we established a regular intake of graduates. For the middle managers, we got them involved in management development with an IT directors' forum – and they got coaching and mentoring through that. My successor has continued with that.

All this must have worked because I was awarded a CBE four years ago. Mike got the money; I got the gong.

From the foundations that Mike laid, the organization – and its people – have been extraordinarily successful. When we merged with Education, we got together and liaised with opposite numbers and put together combined IT facilities extremely quickly. It's been a very resilient structure with a very capable set of people.

I've worked with Mike over 20 years, and I wouldn't have been able to do what I've done without that relationship.

Templeton College did a study of successful CIOs and they asked how I got where I am and I said, 'Luck.' I was in the right place at the right time. They said, 'It's funny, no-one else has suggested this.' They must have a higher view of their abilities than I do of mine.

It was important to Mike and me that we got on well together, but we were also aware of our differences.

DISCUSSION

- *Natural to formal.* One of the reasons that the formal mentoring scheme in ISB works so well is that the two senior managers both have a strong, positive experience of natural mentoring on which to build. They have used the training opportunities offered by the university to help them hone their skills and fit the way they approach mentoring to the particular task of the formal scheme.

- *Mutual.* Long-term mentoring soon seems to become mutual, and in this case the relationship between Mike and Ray has been highly bene-ficial to both of their careers and to the work of the branch.

- *Transitions.* Mike noticed how Ray particularly needed mentoring when he was making certain key transitions, such as becoming a senior manager. He was able to focus his effort on these transitions, while avoiding the trap of imposing on Ray his perspective of what that tran-sition had meant to him.

- *Mentoring in a de-layered organization.* The metaphor of navigation is a powerful one; de-layering takes away a lot of the landmarks, so indi-viduals need their own compasses. Mentoring helps them to get this sense of being able, self-sufficiently, to chart their own course.

- *Multiple mentoring.* Mike is as busy as most senior managers, yet he still has time to mentor several staff. Perhaps this is because he does not see mentoring as additional to his other management tasks, but integral to them.

- *Friendship and fun.* There is no mistaking that Mike finds a lot of friendship and fun in his working life, and mentoring is part of the context that makes this possible. Ray and Mike, not surprisingly after the time that they have worked together, see friendship as an important part of mentoring.

REFERENCE

Clutterbuck, D (1992) *Everyone Needs a Mentor: How to foster talent within the organi-zation*, 2nd edn, Institute of Personnel Management, London

MENTORING USING TWO MENTORS AT A4E WORK

Richard Field with contributions by Peter Field

BACKGROUND

The years from 2001 to 2004 were a period of strong growth and rapid change for A4e Work, part of A4e, a major training, development and consulting company. During this time the number of people within the company almost doubled to just under a thousand.

In May 2001 my brother Peter and I were asked, by the CEO of A4e Work, to mentor the team to assist in making it even more effective and professional as the speed of change within the organization accelerated. This was seen as a successful strategy, when measured by both the company's results and the recorded perceptions of the team, until July 2003 when the team confronted us and said that developing them during two-day workshops, which averaged out at about once every two months, was fine for dealing with business issues but not enough for their own personal growth.

WHY THIS MENTORING WAS DECIDED UPON

Peter and I have different views on the world; Peter's experience has been gained with the British armed forces whilst mine comes from being an industrialist; also his lifelong learning process and spiritual journey has been parallel and different to mine.

So we recommended to the team that we could jointly mentor each member for an hour at each of our workshops. This proposal was accepted by the team; so our early mornings, lunchtimes and evenings were set aside for this specific purpose.

WHAT DID THE MENTORING CONSIST OF?

All team members followed the same process, which was initially to produce a holistic picture of them, and at each subsequent session to focus on the perceived most urgent and important aspect of their lives that needed attention. To this base information, we added questions to understand their journey from our last meeting and agreed homework for them to address before the next session.

Specifically, this was the procedure followed at the first session:

1. How do you feel?
2. Produce a personal fishbone (see below) with the mentee.
3. Decide upon what is most urgent and important, and focus upon how to address that issue.
4. Agree actions (homework) to deal with 2 above.
5. How do you feel?

And this was the procedure followed at subsequent sessions:

1. How do you feel?
2. In each area of your life, as defined on your fishbone, how do you score yourself, out of 10?
3. Are there any enhancements that you wish to make to your fishbone?
4. Address the homework: has it been completed? What were the outcomes? What are the likely consequences?
5. What has gone well since we last met? What has not gone so well?
6. What are the issues you would like to discuss? (These could be anything, remembering that our fishbone is holistic and all aspects of the mentees' lives were open for discussion, if they wished.)
7. Homework given alternately by each mentor.
8. How do you feel?

Personal fishbone: I discovered this process many years ago after visiting Komatsu in the north-east of England where they were using a traditional Ishikawa diagram within their factory; it has been adapted to be used as a mentoring and coaching process, and can be used as a guide to personal decision taking. Mine is drawn on an A4 sheet of paper, which is kept in my wallet, and when a difficult decision needs to be made then reference to the fishbone can guide me upon whether it takes me towards or away from my personal goals – it is simply a cause-and-effect diagram. This is how it works.

Draw two boxes at either end of your A4 landscape sheet, join them up with a line; draw two more boxes at the top of the page and two at the bottom, and join them to the centre line – the result should be something resembling a fishbone. Now to the questions:

- *Question one.* When you become who you want to be, who are you? Answers might include: 'Fulfilled' Ben, 'World Class' Helen etc. Put this in the right-hand box, for this is the effect, the goal that you are seeking to achieve.

- *Question two.* What do you perceive as the key areas of your life? Mine are: health, family, work, student and social/spiritual. Put the headings in each of the remaining unfilled five boxes.

- *Question three.* In the area of (take one of the five boxes, say health), what would have to happen for you to become (whatever you put for the answer to question one, say 'Fulfilled' Ben)? Write the answer on the spine/line of the fishbone.

- *Question four.* What else? Write it as in question three.

- *Question five.* Keep asking question four until the mentee says 'That's all'; and then go through all of the answers as follows: You are now who you want to be (for example, 'Fulfilled' Ben), and in the area of (whatever you have been focusing on, for example health) you are now (list all of the items listed by the mentee, for example running three times a week and drinking no more than seven measures of alcohol a week). What else would have to happen? If there is more then add it to the list and if there is no more then move to each of the other areas.

- *Question six.* When all areas are covered, go through them all as in question five to give the mentee the opportunity to add anything he or she might have missed.

- *Question seven.* Having gained the mentee's agreement that nothing needs to be added, then ask 'What of all that you have shared is the most urgent and important item needing attention by you?' You will probably have an indication of which item it is, for the mentee will probably have shown emotion or some physiological change when mentioning this point. Underline the item and work with the mentee to decide upon what actions are needed to progress that issue. It is this action plan that will be addressed at the next meeting. Incidentally, the mentee is informed that there will be no story accepted for not doing what has been agreed, unless circumstances change, in which case the mentors need to be informed immediately so that they can assist if appropriate or at least change the agreed goalposts; this may sound hard but, in our experience, being uncompromising on these action plans gives mentees a sense of certainty and resolve.

HOW THE MENTORING WAS CARRIED OUT

Times were agreed with each team member, during the breaks, from seven in the morning to eight at night. All three present, the two mentors and one mentee, found a quiet spot where they would not be disturbed, and the session began and ended by asking how he or she felt.

The mentors prepared by writing down their initial questions, and mentees did likewise. This preparation usually ensured that the mentees had thought through their most urgent and important issue needing to be addressed, so the hour together became increasingly more focused as the process was repeated at each session.

What surprised the mentors was the variety of subjects that they covered: from holidays to detailed work problems, from hobbies to family; as the process progressed so did the depth and trust gained by all present.

CONSEQUENCES

To work throughout the two days without a break was exhausting for the mentors, and also exhilarating; for as the workshop progressed then so did the closeness of the team – we found ourselves part of the team rather than assisting from the outside.

When the team was eventually disbanded under a group reorganization, all members gained promotion, and we parted as close and 'lifelong' friends. And from the mentors' perspective the sessions could have gone on indefinitely, for it was from the mentees that the will-force to accomplish more came.

Learnings from the experience

Top management team members need someone to care for them personally. It is frightening leading an organization with stakeholders who rely on your decisions; for now there are few right and wrong answers – certainly at a strategic level – so much relies on one's own values and intuition. To have two mentors is a luxury, for as one of us perceived a certain need by the mentee – perhaps an action that the mentee needed to carry out in his or her homework – the other would notice something completely different. For example, one of us noted the need for the mentee to find time for photography, whilst the other noted that an aunt was in need of a phone call; other examples include making space for hobbies, family and holidays.

Perhaps most importantly, the added dimension of the mentors having the space to stand back and just observe and listen with no pressure to respond or interact enhanced the quality of the input and feedback, something that neither of us has been able to quantify and both of us valued greatly.

So does dual mentoring work?

That depends, we suggest, first upon the two mentors. We know each other so well and trust each other's judgement having worked closely together for at least 10 years. The process needs to flow, to be seamless for the mentees as well as for the mentors. Second, before this process can be embarked upon, there needs to be a high level of trust between the mentors and mentees, for such a potentially intense session could be intimidating to someone who didn't feel at peace with their fellow travellers.

We recommend the process highly if there is a close bond between those individuals involved. After two or three sessions it is like being in a family conversation where the love that passes between you seems to accelerate and enhance the process.

MENTORING DIMENSIONS

Bob Garvey

This case explores the detailed workings of a mentoring partnership within a semi-formalized mentoring scheme. The scheme is linked to a two-year part-time MBA programme (Garvey, 1994).

THE MODEL

Mentoring is a complex relationship between two people. Trying to pin it down to one definition is difficult, but this case example shows it is possible to identify certain 'dimensions' within mentoring (see Figure 3.3.1). These are described as follows:

- *Open.* This dimension relates to the content of the relationship – what they talk about. If the relationship is open, the two parties feel able to discuss any topic in a free atmosphere. There are no 'off-limits' subjects.
- *Closed.* This is the opposite end of the continuum of the open dimension. In a closed relationship there are specific items for discussion and an understanding that certain issues are not for debate. For example, there may be a strong focus on work-related issues with personal issues not on the agenda.
- *Public.* Other people know that the relationship exists. In organizational schemes it can sometimes be helpful to have a strong public

OPEN	CLOSED
PUBLIC	PRIVATE
FORMAL	INFORMAL
ACTIVE	PASSIVE
STABLE	UNSTABLE

Figure 3.3.1　Mentoring dimensions

dimension to minimize colleague speculation about the nature and purpose of the relationship.

- *Private.* Few people will know that the relationship exists.
- *Formal.* This is about the operation and administration of the relationship. In a formal mentoring relationship the parties may agree appointments, regularity, venues and timescales. They may take notes or record the meeting in some other way. The members of the partnership in this formalized relationship are also likely to establish ground rules.
- *Informal.* The relationship is managed on a casual basis. There are unlikely to be ground rules. The parties are likely to work in close proximity to each other. This tends to encourage a 'pop in any time' foundation for the relationship. The informal relationship can operate in both a wider social context and within an official scheme.
- *Active.* This is where both parties are genuinely active and the relationship is 'live'. This may involve either party taking some sort of action as a result of the mentoring discussions. It may involve agreements to think about issues or research something between meetings. It may be possible that one party is more active than the other. Active can also mean that contact is regular.
- *Passive.* This is where there is little action taken by either party as a result of mentoring discussions. Contacts between the parties may have lapsed. It may be possible to have a mentoring partnership in which one party is passive and the other active. If the relationship is constantly passive, it may be time to review the relationship.
- *Stable.* Both parties feel secure in the relationship. Both behave consistently and meetings are honoured. This is linked to a sense of commitment, which helps to build trust.
- *Unstable.* The relationship is unpredictable and insecure. Trust may be lacking and the commitment may be questionable. Meetings may be regularly missed or changed at short notice.

CASE EXAMPLE

The names of the people have been changed to protect their privacy and confidentiality.

The mentor
Name:	Jane Smith
Gender:	Female
Age:	32
Position:	Training and Development Manager

Learning Style:	Developing activist tendencies from a theorist base
Background:	Total Health Service experience – seven years, and three years' experience in training in a commercial organization

The mentee

Name:	John Jones
Gender:	Male
Age:	32
Position:	Surgical Services Management
Learning Style:	Theorist
Background	Total Health Service experience – 10 years plus

This relationship has a number of interesting features about it.

1. The mentor is female and the mentee is male. This makes it an example of cross-gender mentoring. It is also still the least common form in terms of gender.
2. They are the same age.
3. They have a similar status in the Health Service.

   (Points 2 and 3 make this an example of peer mentoring.)
4. Initially they worked in the same trust but now they are in different trusts and are separated by about 30 miles.
5. The relationship had its problems but they were resolved.

The mentor's view

After 10 months of the relationship, Jane admitted finding the mentor relationship with her mentee 'difficult'. She believed that John chose her for the following reasons:

- They had quite a good working relationship.
- John wanted somebody inside the organization.
- John did not have a good relationship with the general manager. (The GM didn't want him to do the MBA.) Consequently, the general manager as mentor was not an option for John.
- Jane was a 'last resort', and he felt that she would not be as critical of him as others might be.

Jane agreed to mentor John to:

- develop her understanding of mentoring so that she could implement a similar programme for other managers within the trust;
- help John develop his understanding of work-related issues through the MBA;
- provide John with career support so that he might be in a better position to gain employment outside the Health Service if he needed to (Jane sees job security for the mentee as a major issue);
- help John to understand the difficulties he has with relationships at work so that he might develop into a 'better' manager.

The mentee's view

John agreed with most of Jane's observations. However, he added that Jane was accessible and available and he believed that Jane had a different knowledge and skills base to his own. He felt that Jane had a 'head start' in her understanding of the mentoring process.

The mentor and the mentee did not see the relationship in the same way, particularly in the open/closed and active/passive dimensions (see Figure 3.3.2).

The closed/open dimension

In their early meetings they agreed ground rules. John was keen to have a strong MBA focus but he did agree that other work-related issues could be discussed. John interpreted this as being an open relationship.

Jane was particularly keen that the relationship was indeed open. She did not see her role as 'an extension of an MBA tutor' but as having an all-round development focus. She wanted to help John explore his other developmental issues and not just his MBA learning. John's interpretation of 'open' was more limited than Jane's.

OPEN	Y		X	CLOSED
PUBLIC			YX	PRIVATE
FORMAL	XY			INFORMAL
ACTIVE	Y		X	PASSIVE
STABLE	XY			UNSTABLE

X = mentor's perspective; Y = mentee's perspective

Figure 3.3.2   The relationship

At 10 months into the relationship, John's interpretation, in Jane's view, had the upper hand, and discussions around other developmental issues had not happened. She described the relationship as 'the opposite of openness' and John controlled the agenda of their discussions.

At this point Jane was feeling frustrated with John. Jane said 'He loves to show me his assignment plans and timetables', but she believed that he needed to widen his thinking beyond the MBA course.

John's perspective was interestingly different. He believed that Jane's counsel on the MBA was exactly what he needed. Indeed, he believed that the relationship was progressing along the lines of the agreed ground rules. He felt that it was as open as it could be.

The relationship had a problem. Jane recognized that aspects of John's behaviour at work were unhelpful to his career prospects and felt that she was able to help him modify his approach through the mentor discussions but the relationship needed to become more open. She found this shift very difficult and was ready to stop mentoring John.

The trust was under financial pressure and John was asked either to move to another trust on temporary secondment but with his job closed behind him or to be made redundant. The closed dimension, from Jane's perspective, was compounded by this enforced move to another trust. As Jane put it, 'The potential for common ground and common understanding was reduced by the move', as they no longer shared the same workplace.

The private/public dimension

Jane may have put her own position at some risk by agreeing to be John's mentor. This was because, despite the opportunity within the mentor scheme to include the role as part of her performance review, Jane did not discuss the role with her line manager (the general manager) or with the HRD director. She believed that they would feel she was 'wasting her time' with John. John was not seen in a positive light by senior management in the trust.

This pressure to keep the relationship private caused Jane difficulties. She was not gaining any recognition or support for her efforts with John. Indeed, she might, if discovered, have received a reprimand for starting and then continuing the relationship after John left the trust. Therefore, their meetings tended to be arranged out of office hours and in a neutral venue. However, she was committed to the concept of mentoring and it was this commitment to both the process and John that kept her going. John was unaware of this private dimension and the pressure it put on Jane.

The formal dimension

They agreed meeting times, dates and venues. This dimension did not create any significant issues in the case.

The active/passive dimension

John was clearly gaining as an active partner. He was, through Jane's obvious skill as a mentor, widening his understanding of MBA-related topics. John said that Jane 'helps me to step away from things and look at them in order to clarify a few things in my own mind'. He also confirmed Jane's perception that he heavily controlled the agenda, saying 'The relationship is pretty much logistical and about planning things around my MBA work.'

Jane felt unable to influence or contribute to what she saw as the priority issues for John – his response to change, his behaviour towards others and his poor interpersonal skills. This put Jane in the passive dimension, which contributed to Jane seeing the relationship as a 'deadlocked relationship'. These different perspectives on the active/passive dimension contributed to Jane's frustration with John.

This may be a cross-gender issue. Sheehy (1974) sees male behaviour as broadly 'initiating' and female as 'responsive'. To stereotype: John dominated the relationship with his lack of self-awareness and practical insensitivity and Jane accepted the passive role to facilitate John. This debate is generalist in nature, and neither behaviour is exclusive to men or to women. However, Jane listened and responded to John and she did not challenge him.

The stable dimension

John moved jobs twice over this period. He was seconded to another district and then seconded again to another trust in yet another district. John's original job no longer existed and the secondments had a time limit on them, so John was facing redundancy if he didn't find another permanent position. John admitted that Jane was a strong stable influence in his life through this period. He said he felt 'very bitter and upset' by the changes, that 'Jane's ability to be objective about that and not take sides but to push me to think positively about it was significant' and that she 'reassured me of my own self-worth'. This type of outcome in mentoring is well documented (Gladstone, 1988; Clutterbuck, 1992).

Stability was obviously crucial to John, and clearly Jane enabled him to feel some security in uncertain times. As John put it, 'I think that it has been useful at times, in particular doing the MBA programme as being a sort of stability, and in a way Jane's done the journey with me... It's been a bit of a constant which has been necessary.'

It may be that this desire for stability in an uncertain situation pushed John into keeping the agenda closed and focused, as this provided him with safety. Perhaps the prospect of Jane tackling his behavioural problems threatened his security further and therefore he controlled the agenda to preserve his sense of security.

Jane recognized this point later in the relationship but for now she wanted to become more active in areas other than those John would allow.

Learning styles

Both parties had completed a learning styles questionnaire. Jane believed that John's learning style contributed to his 'entrenched' views and to the creation of the closed dimension. She also believed that John's strong theorist style contributed to his behavioural problems with others. Jane said that John 'is a strongly principled person who sticks to his principles, no matter how small the issue'. She believed that this led others to believe that he was rigid and immovable – the criticisms levelled at him by the general manager.

Jane's learning style leans towards theorist but, by her own admission, had changed through environmental necessities. She believed that she had developed another style of learning and behaving that was more appropriate for a 'fast-changing and reactive' Health Service. Jane felt that it was important in this work environment to become more activist/pragmatist in style, particularly in her role in training and development.

Jane was clear that John was a 'nice person, very hard working and a good employee for any organization' but he had become a victim of cultural change. The new culture is one driven by targets and measurable end-results. Jane believed that John's thinking was locked into the ideology of the 'old' Health Service where service was the most important thing. She clearly empathized with John's position and perhaps it was this empathy with John that explained both her feelings of despair with him and her willingness to pursue the relationship. Jane was demonstrating some key characteristics of a good mentor:

- empathy and objectivity;
- strength of character;
- reliability and determination;
- commitment;
- self-awareness and an awareness of her learning needs.

Jane decided to revisit the ground rules using the dimensions framework. She also used the learning styles profiles as a vehicle to discuss their dead-locked relationship. Jane believed that these two tools would provide the 'objective' information and 'evidence' that John needed as a theorist to understand the deadlock.

The outcome

Jane said that using these tools 'opened up the discussion' and helped John to appreciate and understand their different perceptions of the relationship.

Both agreed that the meeting was 'very productive'. They had further meetings at informal venues and Jane said that, whilst the meetings retained an academic element, they were able to discuss other issues concerning John's future. She also reported that, over a period of six months, John seemed more 'confident, outgoing, assertive and business minded'. These observable changes in John probably contributed to him gaining a promotion and a new job.

Also, at the time of the 'turning point' meeting, Jane discussed her mentor role with her own boss and gained his agreement to it continuing. This changed the relationship from the private dimension to a public one. Jane felt relieved that the pressure of secrecy was lifted. This new openness with her boss did Jane some good as he started to recognize some of Jane's strong qualities and she gained a promotion.

Jane also observed that, as the discussions became more open, she moved from a passive listener to a more active participant.

Conclusion

The changes in John may also be attributed to a number of factors:

■ the threat of redundancy and consequent feeling of insecurity;
■ his desire to adapt to the Health Service changes to survive;
■ a series of limited secondments building experience and confidence;
■ the influence of the MBA course.

However, the constant through this period was his mentor. She provided him with support, guidance, coaching (specifically in interview techniques for his new job), counselling and honest feedback. Jane was also a neutral figure to 'bounce' ideas off. Jane was the one truly independent element in John's life during this two-year period. John said that he discussed work-related issues with his wife but sometimes there was 'too much emotion involved with the possible insecurity that the conversation generated' for these discussions to be helpful.

This case example demonstrates that a mentor relationship can transform itself provided there is the will on both sides. Jane needed to change her approach just as much as John did. Gladstone (1988) suggests that 'successful mentors accept change willingly' and that 'mentorees are encouraged to devote their talents and energies to attainable goals and as a result they develop self-confidence'.

This seems to have been the case here. Jane's positive view on change conveyed itself to John with dramatic effect. The case also demonstrates the depth of impact mentoring can have on the individual participants.

The relationship evolved and changed over time, to become as shown in Figure 3.3.3. The dimensions outlined in Figure 3.3.3 may need to be in place for an effective mentoring relationship to develop. However, it is also clear that a combination of the elements of trust and commitment to the process was crucial to this ultimately successful partnership. The relationship continued for two and a half years.

MENTOR SUPPORT

The case clearly identifies the need for mentor support within any scheme. There was some limited training (half a day) for mentors offered at the start of the programme. In my view, if this was all the support offered to mentors, it was inadequate.

Often it is assumed that mentors already have the skills of mentoring by virtue of their experience and status within the organization. Undoubtedly, more development would have assisted Jane. This is where the issue of mentor supervision (see Barrett, 2002) becomes very important. In this case, supervision would have helped Jane to develop her practice and the frustrations might have been avoided or at least dealt with sooner.

Additionally, perhaps mentoring could form part of an organization's standard management development programme. In this way, mentoring potential would be identified and developed early in managers' careers. This approach would also help mentoring to flourish at the same time as instilling the concept of 'mentoring for development' in the minds of future managers.

OPEN	XY		CLOSED
PUBLIC	XY		PRIVATE
FORMAL	XY		INFORMAL
ACTIVE	XY		PASSIVE
STABLE	XY		UNSTABLE

X = mentor's perspective; Y = mentee's perspective

Figure 3.3.3   The evolved relationship

PERSONAL QUALITIES AND SKILLS

There can be little doubt that the personal qualities of trust, empathy, openness to challenge, and commitment (Alred, Garvey and Smith, 1998) played an important role in the development of both Jane and John. Both seemed to realize that learning involves a certain amount of risk.

Counselling skills, coaching skills, listening skills, and an ability to analyse the relationship, the issues and situations and take appropriate action to keep the discussions on track also seem important in mentoring.

Further, both parties need to feel they are gaining from the relationship; it should not be a 'one-way street'.

Ground rules do seem to be helpful but it is also important that these are regularly reviewed.

It seems that here is further evidence to support Neilson and Eisenbach's (2003) finding that high-quality feedback within the mentoring relationship, well-developed interpersonal skills and shared values contribute more to mentoring success than any other factors.

MENTORING TOOLS

This case example provides tools to help mentoring pairs:

- to establish and agree the dimensions of their relationship;
- to create ground rules;
- to review their relationship.

It also expands the use of an already existing tool, the learning styles profile (Honey and Mumford, 1986).

FINALLY

It is clear that time plays a crucial role in the dynamics of the relationship. Over time, the relationship changes and develops into a new form. The dimensions of open, public, formal, active and stable appear to offer the best combination for success, but it is probable that other combinations will also raise challenges to discuss within the relationship.

REFERENCES

Alred, G, Garvey, B and Smith, R (1998) *The Mentoring Pocket Book*, Management Pocket Books, Alresford, Hampshire

Barrett, R (2002) Mentor supervision and development: exploration of lived experience, *Career Development International*, **7** (5), pp 279–83

Clutterbuck, D (1992) *Everyone Needs a Mentor: How to foster talent within the organization*, 2nd edn, Institute of Personnel Management, London

Garvey, B (1994) Ancient Greece, MBAs, the Health Service and Georg, *Education and Training Journal*, **36** (2)

Gladstone, MS (1988) Mentoring: a strategy for learning in a rapidly changing society, *Research Document CEGEP*, John Abbott College, Quebec

Honey, P and Mumford, A (1986) *The Manual of Learning Styles*, 2nd edn, Peter Honey, Maidenhead

Neilson, T and Eisenbach, R (2003) Not all relationships are created equal: critical factors of high-quality mentoring relationships, *International Journal of Mentoring and Coaching*, **1** (1) (electronic journal of the European Mentoring and Coaching Council, www.emccouncil.org)

Sheehy, G (1974) *Passages: Predictable crises of adult life*, Dutton, New York

Case Study 4

MENTORING START-UP ENTREPRENEURS: INTERVIEW WITH BRIAN MARTIN

Jonathan Gravells

I got into the mentoring because I was put into the mentoring. I went through a scheme called the NES. At the end of it there was a sort of graduation ceremony and we were assigned a mentor, so that's why I got into mentoring. The mentoring has not given me any specific highs or specific lows. That's not what it's there for as far as I'm concerned. I mean, yes, I've got contacts from my mentor, and I've followed these contacts up, but that's not what I look at mentoring as doing. It's a bit of a psychological, emotional safety net, as much as anything else. It's very easy just to get quite lonely... In the first six months certainly I stopped calling my mentor, I stopped meeting him, because I felt I was a bit of a... not a failure... I just felt that I didn't have anything to give him.

I was afraid he would look at me and think I was pointless, afraid that I'd be wasting his time – oh, and feeling a bit awkward that this great business idea of mine wasn't happening.

Now you've got to know Stewart better, do you think you were right about that?
No, I was totally wrong. We met in… one of these pubs down by the canal… and he said, well look, let's meet every two weeks regardless of what happens. And so for a while I was hammered into this having to meet him. But that was really useful, and even if nothing was happening he could talk to me in general terms about whatever we might want to talk about.

So, if you had to summarize what you've got out of that mentoring relationship?
Well, a friend first of all, a knowledgeable friend, somebody I can talk to about my business without feeling like I'm boring them, somebody who can give me contacts, somebody who's willing to help me if I ask him to, and who's got a bit of gravitas. He's effectively a bit of a safety net for me, a psychological and emotional safety net. At some point you always come

across something that you're not sure about, you know… It's almost like it gives you a staging post… and if you have these staging posts you feel that you're moving somewhere… So I don't look at the mentoring system as giving me anything specific, in terms of highs or lows, but it does do a job.

How do you prepare for your meetings?
They vary. If I've got something specific to talk about, I'll tell him about it and we'll go. If I don't we'll just sit down and have a cup of coffee and we'll chat. More often than not he'll bring in something that he's found that he thinks is useful for me, and we'll discuss it. And more often than not we'll discuss what I've done since we last saw each other. Occasionally he'll ask me where I am in business, where I am in relation to where I thought I'd be. But more often we'll just sit and it'll be very informal… that might be frustrating, but the mentoring process isn't necessarily that x, y or z gets done. It's that… there's somebody there.

Before I went to America we had some case studies to go through. And there were just some things about them that I didn't understand, and he and I sat and talked about them… And that gave me a lot of confidence… it's more of a background noise than a palpable bang, if you see what I mean.

When asked what help you needed, you talked about marketing and pricing, product development and networking/contacts. That looks like practical, skills-based kind of help, but what I'm hearing from you today is something much softer than that…
Absolutely, yeah, yeah. There's nothing in that that says Stewart and I have sat down with marketing books and gone through them formally. What I mean is we've discussed where my business is going, the people I'm marketing myself to and how I'm marketing myself… We've discussed the problems I've had in doing it… In terms of pricing, it's always useful for Stewart to give me a kick up the arse… I mean I underprice myself all the time… And he gets quite… well, he does get angry… If I exasperate him at all, it's probably about that. He's a kind of anchor into reality for me.

Let me ask the question in a different way then. What have you actually learned from your relationship with your mentor?
It's like speaking to a child and saying, OK, you're three years old now. What have you learned from your mum? And the child could sit there and go, I've learned how to make myself an orange squash, I've learned how to open doors, I've learned how to… I don't know, what three-year-old kids do… But the chances are the child wouldn't say anything of the sort. The child would look at you and go, whoa, I'm becoming more grown up, slowly, but eventually through this process of mothering I will become a grown-up… Say to me what have I learned from my mentor, and I feel I'm growing in that respect… as a businessman.

I'm becoming better as a businessman all the time. I know that. Accompanying that is a mentoring relationship. But accompanying that is also getting my feet dirty, speaking to more businesses, going to America, talking to other people who are starting up in business, my experience, a whole wealth of experience. Mentoring is part of that. I believe it's an important part, but to talk about it in terms of causal result... I dunno. I believe it's sufficient. I don't believe it's necessary.

Would you have reflected on all this experience as much if you hadn't had a mentor?
No, I don't think so. One thing I said about the mentoring process was these staging posts... it gets me to think about the business... It's difficult to meet your mentor without doing that... Because of the relationship you've got, regardless of how formal it is or how well understood it is, there is an understanding [that forces you to talk about what you've been doing].

Did mentoring ever seem to have a negative effect?
Certainly it's been frustrating when I've had nothing to say to the guy. It's almost been like it's put a big marker pen over the word 'useless'... We all go through it, we all feel that... Yeah, sometimes speaking to Stewart is frustrating because I'm not quite sure what I've got to give him. I'm not quite sure where I am... Sometimes also I've wanted some help, and not been quite sure what it is... and nothing's really come of my questions... and that's been quite frustrating...

You seem to be saying that the times that you found the relationship most difficult was when you were struggling with the business because you had least to say, but arguably that was the time you needed your mentor the most...
Clearly, yeah, absolutely, yeah.

Do you and Stewart ever find yourselves talking about the process, about the relationship?
No, we don't. We did once or twice at the beginning, I think... We only touched upon it... partly because it was a bit embarrassing in the first place. I didn't know whether I was expected to know. Because there was never any hammering down of what the roles were, I feel almost responsible for the relationship that we have.

Is there anything your mentor does you find frustrating or unhelpful?
I suppose we all like to be 'Daddied' or 'Mummied' occasionally. It would be nice if he came and said, right, this is what we're going to do today. But I don't expect that's his job... So I suppose, yeah, I would like someone to tell me what to do sometimes. I suppose we all would... Because when you have your own business, you spend your life telling yourself what to do, and it would be really nice if someone just said, do this.

So you wouldn't resent that?
No, I'd love it. I'd worry he'd resent it if I asked him to! I suppose also I worry that I would feel too childish asking him that…

So how important do you think personality mix or chemistry is?
Frankly? Immediately we didn't click. No there's never been a click. When I first met him maybe I wasn't sure what I was supposed to do. I don't know, but I felt quite uneasy with him. The first couple of sessions I felt quite uneasy. I also felt uneasy when I didn't have anything to report to him. Over a period of time… I couldn't tell you a point at which I became easy with him… but I feel really easy speaking to him… I feel that I could probably tell him almost anything. But there was never a moment when anything clicked.

If you were being mentored now by someone you didn't get on with would it be doing the same things for you?
I wouldn't see the point. Because a lot of it is the safety net, the psychological and emotional support. If you don't have a relationship with somebody then you can't have that support.

What would happen and how would you feel if mentoring finished tomorrow? Would it have any effect?
(Long pause) Yeah, I don't know what it would be though. One of the first things I would do, I think, is to look around for somebody who could fill the gap. But it would be interesting because, as I pointed out, I'm not too sure what that gap would be.

Would you be trying to fill a personal gap, or do you think there would be some sort of critical impact on your business?
I think there would be some impact on my business. Actually, that's a really interesting question… I think it might have a material impact on the business. I don't know… but I wouldn't like it… I would immediately want to fill the hole… and I think there would be a slight element of… not shock… because he's become such a part of the furniture. A brilliant question. What it does is shows me I don't know what Stewart and I do… I don't know how he helps me, but I wouldn't want to lose him… because there's something there that I get from him.

Case Study 5

KATE KENNETT IS E-MENTORED BY DAVID CLUTTERBUCK

Kate Kennett

I attended the part-time Master's in Organizational Change and Consultancy at Sheffield Hallam University, specializing in mentoring and coaching. I approached David Clutterbuck after his lecture during the first taught module and asked him if he would consider being my mentor, to which he agreed. The majority of communication has been conducted by e-mail largely due to geographical distance and the flexibility that this arrangement provides.

After two years, I am left with an invaluable trail of ideas, advice and questions that are transferable to enable effective thinking in many different situations. I have found that e-mentoring – that is, using the normal internet e-mail system – has offered time and space to reflect on the questions and suggestions received in response to e-mails sent.

There have been multiple challenges presented through the mentoring e-mail exchanges at different levels in all dimensions of my life – professional, academic and personal. In particular, largely because of the time factor, they have exposed me to consider the usefulness (or otherwise) of my own approach to reflection – *what* and *how* I reflect and respond.

I have struggled at times with the dilemmas thrown up by the e-mails sent to me. Certainly at the outset, I was beset by doubts about what and how to write about a mentoring issue. In face-to-face meetings, there is the potential for finding a gradual way in to the issue and defining it in an evolving way. There seems to be less scope for this in virtual mentoring and a sense of needing to get to the point more directly. The result of this for me was, at times, paralysis and I simply stopped writing for periods of weeks at a time, the reason for which I found difficult to convey in writing. In a regular mentoring meeting, I think that it would undoubtedly have been easier to explore such 'stuckness'.

One of the most valuable elements of the e-mentoring relationship has been the feedback about how my dilemmas/issues/problems/crises are perceived by someone external. All being delivered in *writing*, this process leaves a recorded trail of thoughts to which I can regularly return for further reflection. In this respect, I have found that e-mentoring has a definite advantage over face-to-face contact, for which an excellent memory may be required to recall an accurate account of a conversation.

One of my personal key themes has been around the development of confidence in me as an independent coach, mentor and consultant. The e-mentoring relationship has been invaluable from the point of view of exposure to a wide range of different materials from which to learn, as well as providing opportunities to meet with other practising consultants.

Most valuable, though, has been the steady trickle of ideas, advice, support and challenging questions that I received in return for every e-mail sent. The promptness of the replies also meant that I could begin to act on suggestions whilst situations were still 'hot'. I now have a collection of influential interventions, some of which, at least, have become ingrained into my own self-talk. It is in this gradual internalization of learning at a deep-thinking level that virtual mentoring makes an exceptionally effective contribution.

Surveying the volume of e-mails exchanged, I can observe the wealth and variety of the different sorts of questions that I received. Whilst some were definitely in the MDQ (massively difficult question) category (Megginson and Clutterbuck, 2005), many others were distributed between critical, incisive, experimental, reflective, clarifying, challenging, creative and practical. All provided a rich menu of accessible options and 'thought food', which meant I was (to continue the metaphor) digesting them for extended time periods. Where I could come up with no answer to a question, I was often inspired and stimulated to seek more information that took me forward in the situation anyway.

The questions were interspersed with snaps of advice, often profoundly astute, relevant and helpful in practice. Advice occasionally had a 'rescuing' function and this was always noted as a point for reflection after the crisis had passed. For example, I once sent a long and panic-stricken e-mail in respect of help with managing a complex situation at work. The reply, received back within hours, identified that I needed 'some quick responses and some advice rather than contemplation', which was provided in seven points. I found that the most enduringly inspiring of these was the last, which suggested: 'Remember the Golden Principle of SODIT (Simply Opt for Doing Interesting Things) – chuck all your energies into what you instinctively feel is right, don't worry about making a fool of yourself – ACT. And when you do act, do it with confidence (voice, posture, mental state) and a certain sense of devil-may-care.'

Although I think that the value and benefits provided by the virtual mentoring outweigh the disadvantages, it is important to acknowledge the *differences* between face-to-face and virtual mentoring and not to imagine that one is an equal replacement for the other.

Although I consider myself to be reasonably articulate and able to express myself fairly well in writing, participation in an e-mentoring relationship has been quite challenging for me. I have puzzled considerably about this and come up with a number of potential contributory factors. Probably the most significant of these is the value I place on face-to-face contact for non-verbal communication in conversations. Virtual mentoring inevitably does not offer the wide range of communication and information that is available in face-to-face mentoring, depending as it does pretty much solely on the written word.

I think that this lack of opportunity to observe the mentor in action, 'read' his non-verbal messages (and he mine), and sense and hear complex intonation in the communication has affected the potential richness of the mentoring relationship.

In terms of written communication being the primary medium for the mentoring relationship, I suspect that a mentor without considerable competence may not achieve the necessary degree of expressed interest and warmth to generate reciprocal trust and understanding to create effective mentoring rapport. As Fagenson-Eland and Yan Lu (2004) explain: 'It is not easy to establish trusting relationships in face-to-face mentoring relationships and it is much more difficult to establish trust in a virtual relationship.' For example, the assumptions about the mentor that inevitably germinate (for example, estimates about the other's time available for the mentoring relationship and importance assigned) are hard to explore and resolve.

On balance, the experience of e-mentoring is something I would probably recommend as a valuable adjunct to face-to-face mentoring, rather than a replacement for it. I would qualify this by saying both that this is a personal judgement and that, where choice is limited, e-mentoring could definitely 'stand alone' as a form of mentoring. For me, I enjoy the experience of being with people for real, as it were, gaining a lot from interacting with their subtle communications as much as their direct ones.

However, I would argue that the question of whether the virtual relationship bears more fruitful learning and development opportunities is different. There is a definite power and influence that an e-mail communication exerts that has lasting impact, not replicated by words in a usual sort of conversation. My experience of many face-to-face helping-type relationships indicates that these can be transitory. Much of what is shared can be quickly forgotten, and even important ideas, questions and guidance lose their energy and zest with the passing of just a few hours. The accurate record of the e-conversation (brief though it may be compared with an hour-long mentoring meeting) is a concentrated and tangible reminder to be proactive in creating opportunities and to be creative at dealing with challenges.

REFERENCES

Fagenson-Eland, E and Yan Lu, R (2004) Virtual mentoring, Chapter 13 in *The Situational Mentor: An international review of competencies and capabilities in mentoring*, ed D Clutterbuck and G Lane, Gower, Aldershot

Megginson, D and Clutterbuck, D (2005) *Techniques for Coaching and Mentoring*, Elsevier Butterworth-Heinemann, Oxford

Case Study 6

IS COMMUNITY MENTORING PINK AND FLUFFY?

Kim Langridge, Greenwood Partnership

The title for this section comes from one of the early European Mentoring and Coaching Council conferences when, after an interesting presentation about volunteer mentors working in their community, a professional mentor who only worked with CEOs made the observation that community mentoring was all well and good but was, at the end of the day, pink and fluffy and did not add as much value to society as working with chief executives.

Astounded, I felt angry and then, as I thought about it, I could only laugh. My own background in mentoring spans corporate, public sector and community projects but what came to mind was one of my earliest experiences as a mentor.

During the 1989–91 recession when work was a bit thin on the ground, I was asked if I could help out with a small local project (as what we would now call a volunteer). It wasn't called mentoring, and there was certainly no training. I'd just meet up with people who were going through a difficult time and we would chat through what the issues were and look at some possible alternatives.

The people I worked with came from a cross-selection of society and the issues ranged across redundancy, relationships, coping with long-term illnesses and substance abuse. It was an incident from one of these that sprang to mind. Pink and fluffy? I'll let you decide.

CLICK!

I watched in amazement as the blade leapt out of the handle. It looked very shiny and very, very sharp.

'This is what they'll get,' he said, as he made stabbing gestures with the knife.

It didn't comfort me that, although I was apparently not the target, as the knife was pointing at me it kept getting closer and closer with each stabbing motion. Totally alert and totally bereft of what I should do or say, I eventually opened my mouth and tried to say something wise and calming.

'Errr, right, yes, err, who are we talking about, Terry?'

Terry looked at me as though I was an idiot.

'The bastards that got me at the service station. No one's ever going to get me like that again.'

CLICK. The penny dropped. Two years before, he had been badly beaten by members of a rival football club in front of his girlfriend; I suggested that he put the knife away and talk me through what happened.

This mentoring conversation took place in the early 90s and has always stayed with me. Interestingly not because of the knife, but because I came to know and like Terry and wish that I had been able to assist him more in his struggle with his personal demons.

Terry, at the time of our meeting, was in his late 30s, unemployed, and had been in and out of trouble with the police and courts for substance abuse (alcohol and drugs) and involved in fights for all of his adult life. In between social workers, probation and courts, he had committed himself three times for treatment at the local psychiatric hospital and had emerged each time heavily sedated and confused from intensive electrical shock therapy.

We met weekly for three months and life did become calmer for Terry. He found work in a major warehouse, bought a car and had started a new relationship. He still got out of his skull when life became too hard for him but he, and then his new girlfriend, would phone me and I'd try to pop round to have a chat with him.

We practised breathing, counting to 20 (we tried 10 but he counted to 10 very quickly and then hit the door, so I decided it would be better to up it!) and just chatting about life, mainly in the present. The past we could only dip into, as he seemed to have ring-fenced his childhood in his mind and only came out with what sounded like rehearsed soundbites about how good his family were. As for the future, one week at a time was more realistic and achievable.

As I came to know him, I realized that he had grown up in a highly dysfunctional family where beatings for the slightest mistake were common. He was also dyslexic at a time when the word wasn't recognized in schools; instead, he was labelled as being either stupid or lazy.

Increasingly I found myself wondering how I would have fared with a childhood like that. Would I too be scarred and damaged for life?

I recall asking him towards the end of one of our meetings, what did he get from our meetings, why did he find them so useful?

The answers surprised me at the time simply because I was conditioned by my earlier working life to value thinking solutions above all else; now, of course, most mentoring literature quotes these points as though they have been common knowledge throughout all ages.

The benefits for Terry were:

- I didn't judge him.
- I never criticized him.
- He didn't feel belittled by me.
- He felt safe.
- I gave him time to think through problems.
- I believed in him.

I lost touch with Terry over time but our mentoring relationship always remained a pivotal learning experience for me. I heard some three years ago that Terry was in prison for assault; the learning for me continued into the present. As much as I wish that I could go back in time with the skills and knowledge that I have since developed, ultimately each of us has responsibility for our own lives.

As a mentor, I aim to do my utmost whatever the situation, and constantly look to reflect on my own practice: 'What could I have done better?' This approach bears fruit because many years later I was working with a so-called 'disaffected' 17-year-old in Luton called Chris.

Chris is a very intelligent young man with a very realistic and mature grasp of his situation. Despite this, I was struck by the similarities with Terry. Chris had been placed in care from 9 years old where he stayed until he was 16 with little contact from his family (despite social services doing their utmost to effect this and re-establish Chris in the family home). He too had ring-fenced his family in his mind and saw them in a radiant golden hue.

I arrived for what was to be our third meeting to be met by Chris who told me he didn't want to talk today. I could see that he was very agitated and that he couldn't stand still but moved around the reception area like a cornered tiger.

'That's no problem. We can always meet next week,' I said, and then continued, 'but I do need a couple of minutes of your time to run through something. That's OK, isn't it?'

He stopped and seemed to consider this from all angles before saying OK.

Stepping into the meeting room I asked Chris directly what on earth had wound him up so much.

'I'm going to put a screwdriver in his eye!'

CLICK!

Still no great words of wisdom but this time, 'Who, Chris?'

'My sister's boyfriend. I'm going to teach him a lesson.'

I looked at him, holding the silence and tension, before asking 'Why?'

'He gave her a beating,' he replied.

'Will it make her happy if you stab him in the eye?' I asked, still holding eye contact with Chris.

He too looked at me as though I was an idiot (I'm used to this by now) before saying very quickly, 'What are you talking about?'

'Well,' I said slowly, 'if you stick a screwdriver in his eye will it make your sister happy and will she thank you for doing it?'

He looked away, thinking about this. After a brief pause (which felt like ages!) he said, 'No.'

'So, Chris,' I asked him, 'who are you doing it for, if not your sister? Certainly not her boyfriend.'

By now he was getting very uncomfortable and starting to move around again. I stayed still and kept my voice slow and calm. 'Who are you doing it for, Chris?'

'Don't know what you're talking about,' he replied.

'Yes, you do, Chris. You're not thick. Who is going to feel good if you do it?' After a bit more squirming, 'Me,' he eventually replied.

'So you're going to put a screwdriver in someone's eye, go to prison, hack your sister off and all just to make you feel good for a while, is that right?'

'He shouldn't be allowed to get away with it!' he said defiantly.

'No, he shouldn't, but have you talked to your sister about what she wants to do about it?'

The conversation carried on. Chris didn't attack his sister's boyfriend and has since become a lot closer with her; one of his parting comments to me was, 'We now talk as equals. I'm not just her nuisance little brother any more, we're friends.'

His responsibility, his change and his benefit. He now has the beginnings of a real family relationship with his sister and feels valued by her as a person.

I might have only helped to bring a temporary period of calm into Terry's life but now, thanks to him, Chris and all the other mentees that I have learned from, I have greater skills and certainly more experience to call upon to help other people achieve profound changes in their lives.

These are two extreme examples of mentoring in the community; most are not in the least linked to violence or such overt drama but are still about people being trapped by lack of self-esteem, skills or a personal vision.

One of my colleagues, Julie, started working with a 15-year-old single parent with no home and no apparent future. Twelve months on, the mentee and her daughter have a flat, she is going to college, her abusive ex-partner now has an exclusion order on him (that the mentee decided upon and organized), she has a clear vision of what she and her daughter are going to be doing in the years to come and, most importantly, she and her daughter are happy.

The mentee herself told Julie at the final meeting, 'It's amazing what I've achieved and I now know I can do even more. I've had to do it all myself but all the time it felt as though you were there, holding my hand and telling me that I could do it. I'll never forget you.'

CLICK – pink and fluffy, I think not.

CLICK – breaking dysfunctional patterns and being a gateway to people realizing their potential, I think so!

MENTOR TO EX-EMPLOYEES: FRANK LORD

Frank Lord, interviewed by David Megginson

Frank Lord is one of the most inspiring entrepreneurs that we know. At the time of our first edition, we told the story of his success in the motor industry, breaking records for sales market share and profitability by supporting and developing people. He moved into private education provision, his success continued, and so did his commitment to those who worked for him.

Frank has enjoyed two successful careers, one in the motor industry and the other in education. He puts his rise in both of them down to one common denominator, helping people around him become magnificent, and he believes the best starting point for this is in becoming a better listener.

Frank has a powerful commitment to development, which was apparent in many ways in the Appleyard Learning and Education Centre (ALEC), which was formed when Frank was managing director of Appleyards of Chesterfield, a Peugeot dealership that he established a new site for in 1989. ALEC obtained a National Training Award (NTA), with the NTA Patron's special commendation for encouraging self-development. Frank has not made this a one-off experience. He has built on it and gone on to become a UK judge and regional chair for NTA so he can learn from others what makes them magnificent and apply it.

Frank has been a witness to a parliamentary enquiry into employee development schemes, and as managing director of Education Lecturing Services he was presented in 1999 with the Investor in People award at the House of Commons by Baroness Helena Kennedy. Frank's IiP accreditation had several unique features. As a pilot for IiP UK's STAR project, there was no paper portfolio presented. Instead assessors looked at a system of online learning logs used by employees at the company's head office, together with an internet-based lifelong learning network that supported the continuing professional development (CPD) of all 62,000 lecturers in the IiP process. Frank went on to lead the management team through an institutional buyout, and ELS was sold for £34 million and rebranded as Protocol.

Frank now operates a portfolio career as an independent director in a variety of organizations across the private and public sector and is retained by clients such as General Motors for interim general management assignments and troubleshooting. He also enjoys doing business turnarounds of medium-sized companies.

With such a variety of assignments, being a committed developer is something that you may think that Frank has moved away from and become more task driven. Not so, he says: all the failing businesses he gets involved in are in that position because they have not been locked on to developing their people.

One of the potential problems about being a committed developer is that some of the people whom you help will grow out of the roles that are available in the organization. This has happened on a number of occasions to Frank.

Rather than seeing this as an inevitable cost of a commitment to development, Frank has continued to support, through a mentoring relationship, a number of people who left him to move on to bigger jobs.

Frank's model for mentoring is a simple one. He recalls the process with the acronym 'ARAFAB'. This stands for:

- **A**ccomplishment in all that you do, which comes from
- **R**esults that you achieve, which are built on your own
- **A**ction, which is fuelled by
- **F**eelings, which generate movement, deriving from
- **A**ttitudes, which each of us hold, based on our
- **B**eliefs, which need to be thought through.

Frank continues to use the basis of his ARAFAB model and has since included in his mentoring agreements with corporate clients the establishment of where the boundaries are.

A positive example of this process is Andy Machin, who used to work for Frank as a vehicle technician and then a supervisor. Andy left the organization because there was no further opening, but Frank continued to coach him and help him develop his skills, even helping him to enrol at college to gain further qualifications. Andy now has a service manager's job in a large vehicle dealership and still comes back to talk to Frank about having difficulties in building a team in his department. Frank took him through the process of thinking deeply about his feelings, attitudes and beliefs, and this had the very practical consequence of helping Andy to recognize that he had to address issues of teamwork company-wide.

Andy has kept in touch, and whenever he goes for a job he telephones Frank. He doesn't get solutions from Frank, but questions that encourage him to seek out his own way rigorously.

Sometimes ex-employees contact Frank and say that they are demotivated by the regime they are working in under their new boss. Compared with how it was with Frank, they say that work does not feel right; there is no fun to it. In exploring feelings, attitudes and beliefs, Frank encourages his ex-employees to think broadly about the whole of their lives – business and home. Often this brings out non-work worries that are draining energy away from work performance. Then he returns to the issues at work and encourages his learners to be responsible for creating their feelings from within. Rather than people being unduly influenced by the external environment, Frank challenges them to create their own influencing factors, to generate their own feelings. Only then does he turn the conversation to the specific issues about how to win this or that account or how to achieve next month's target.

His message is: 'Don't add your own negatives to someone else's. Don't miss your budget month after month because of the way you are being treated, but create your own feelings and then go for what you know you can achieve.' Frank's reward is when people ring him back and say that they are grateful for his concern, and that they have gone for it and are achieving again.

DISCUSSION

- *Mentoring ex-employees.* Frank does this because, for him, development and love of people are deeply held values, which he encourages others to find for themselves.

- *Mentor pay-offs.* Frank mentors ex-employees because it is a worthwhile activity in itself, and one from which he derives great satisfaction. For other people, it may be that networking and having long-term feedback on the impact of their development efforts could also be benefits.

- *Holistic approach.* Frank deals with feelings as well as action, home as well as work, and support as well as tough challenge.

Frank puts a great emphasis on listening, as mentioned at the beginning of this case. He realized it was a skill he needed to work on, so for the past three years Frank has honed these skills by becoming trained as a Samaritan, seeing helping others as a way of helping himself. His favourite saying is from St Francis of Assisi: 'It is in giving that you receive.'

Case Study 8

LIS MERRICK IS MENTORED THROUGH TRANSITION

Lis Merrick

This case study is about my experience of being a mentee over the last two years, during a period of immense change in my life, and how the mentoring relationship has supported my successful transition into a consultancy career.

I met David Megginson, my mentor, at a voluntary sector mentoring meeting and was very impressed with the calm manner in which he facilitated the event. Afterwards I approached him and asked if he would be my mentor. I felt that his gentle, yet assertive, style and reflective manner were reassuring and his knowledge of mentoring and coaching was very relevant to my career objectives. He agreed to be my mentor, and we have met every two or three months since then.

Our mentoring relationship began during a period of enormous transition for me. In recent times, I had been at home in Yorkshire, looking after three young children and with no intention of returning to work. My previous career in the City working in human resources within investment banking was a very dim memory after five years as a full-time mother. I was offered an opportunity to lecture in interpersonal skills to women returners at Bradford College for two hours a week. Despite severe trepidation and with a lot of support from my husband, I accepted the position, and over the next three years became increasingly involved with the Let's TWIST and JIVE projects based at Bradford College. A few months later, I accepted the challenge of setting up a mentoring programme for the Let's TWIST project and, by the time I met David, I was operating as the national mentoring coordinator for JIVE Partners, running a national mentoring programme for women in the engineering and construction industries.

I decided to enrol on an MSc in mentoring and coaching in order to develop my learning and gain a credible qualification in mentoring and coaching. By the time I asked David to be my mentor, I had begun some consultancy work outside of JIVE and was feeling ready to spread my wings further in my independent consultancy work. My major barrier to proceeding to a consultancy career was the safety I felt working within the project versus moving outside to what I mistakenly perceived as 'real' work. I was hopeful that the transition to becoming a consultant would give me more flexibility in balancing the demands of my career and the responsibilities of family life, but I was wondering how I would manage the transition.

I felt I needed a mentor for support around the dual strands of my work as a growing mentoring practitioner and my career aspirations of developing into a consultant in the field of mentoring and coaching. David seemed to fit that bill.

Looking back over the last two years, I realize that I have achieved enormous growth in my self-esteem and self-confidence and a more realistic perception of my own self-image. I have also made a successful transition into a consultancy career, although not without some significant pain and grief on the way!

In our first few encounters I was not entirely sure what to bring to the meetings and raised a number of task-focused issues, which David was incredibly swift at helping me clear up. This left space for him to support me in the real issues in my life, which I had been loath to focus on previously.

A good session with David leaves me feeling as if I have been mentally pummelled, but with that glowing sensation of having worked hard and achieved. He makes my head and my heart work hard and is very astute in challenging my responses. Zachery (2000: 25) describes challenge as a 'creative tension that seeks resolution, a stretch opportunity, or a threat'. This challenge is so rich and valuable. I feel the creative tension so acutely with David's questioning. It cuts to the core and can completely stop me in my tracks, but it is also so inspiring and developmental. David's questions are very simple and often move me into a place of discomfort enabling me to face up to the reality of a situation. Sometimes this involves looking at an issue from another angle or another person's perspective, or it may be that the question provokes deep self-reflection, which stimulates me to confront my own cosy sense of reality.

Initially David quite terrified me. A major difficulty to me was my perception of this enormous gap I viewed between us, in terms of education, learning and intelligence. Sadly, I let this intimidate me to begin with. Once I began to relax and feel more confident, I believe our rapport grew and so did my learning. With David, I also worked initially on slowing down the pace of our meetings so I felt more in tune with him and the pace he was operating at. I am sure this helped our rapport-building process.

In Clutterbuck and Megginson (1999: 163), Richard Field is quite definite in his views about building trust in a mentoring relationship: 'A mentor is a friend, a coach, a judge and an encourager. You have got to have enormous trust and a long-term relationship – which can be created in moments. To do this you have to be totally vulnerable – when I have given trust, I don't think I have ever been let down.'

Richard is correct here. You cannot trust someone else without being totally vulnerable and it can be quite terrifying if it is an individual you are in awe of or do not know well.

With David, initially I was too conscious of the 'distance' between us and this made me quite nervous in what I disclosed to him. My true vulnerability was not exposed totally at first and this probably impeded the pace at which I was learning. After our first session when we had talked about my lack of confidence, David came back to me with a wonderful model of Jack Canfield's to help me with my sense of developing my ERSI (extraordinarily realistic self-image) (Inglis, 1994). The model contains a diamond, surrounded by horseshit and a layer of nail varnish. I can remember being horrified by it initially until the penny dropped and I realized he was not really insinuating I was full of horseshit, but actually being complimentary about the layer of nail varnish, which he had thought was a super-competent confidence, not a façade hiding other things underneath and indeed the diamond at the core!

I know in working with David on my self-image I have seen a different 'me' after our sessions. This is probably the single most important outcome of our mentoring to date, that David has supported me in reflecting on some of my experiences and the terrific changes I have undergone in the past few years to develop a more realistic awareness of myself, a realization of what I have achieved very quickly and the exciting awareness that I now possess of how much I can go on to achieve in the future, both in my career and in other areas of my life. I have also moved very successfully into full-time consultancy, setting up my own company, as well as working for two other well-known organizations in the field of mentoring and coaching.

A final, very tangible example of David's mentoring support is illustrated by our discussions whilst I prepared for the mental battle of running the London Marathon. Drawing on some of his long-distance running experiences helped me enormously in confronting some of my fears about being unable to complete the course, and knowing David was 'willing me on' was instrumental in stopping me from walking when I hit the 'wall' at 19 miles.

David's enormous commitment to self-development and the growing of self-awareness are to me his most valuable qualities as a mentor and these have had an enormous impact on me during our mentoring conversations as he has acted as both a role model and a coach, but most importantly these attributes in David have impacted hugely on my own self-confidence and supported me in realizing just what I am capable of achieving in my life and opened up completely new horizons for me to work towards. His skills in asking deeply insightful questions that cut to the core and his ability to create a safe reflective space for me to enter in our meetings, which is not always entirely comfortable but very productive, are the key skills that have contributed to my learning and developing within the relationship. But most of all, David's incredible enthusiasm for people and joy of life are his most infectious qualities, which have contributed in inspiring me to believe that I can achieve what I want to do in my own life and career.

REFERENCES

Clutterbuck, D and Megginson, D (1999) *Mentoring Executives and Directors*, Butterworth-Heinemann, Oxford
Inglis, S (1994) *Making the Most of Action Learning*, Gower, Aldershot
Zachery, L (2000) *The Mentor's Guide*, Jossey-Bass, San Francisco, CA

Case Study 9

KEITH METCALF MENTORS ELEANOR WILLIAMS

Keith Metcalf and Eleanor Williams

INTRODUCTION

I first met Eleanor Williams in 1995 in a meeting room in the House of Commons where she was giving a speech on the benefits of the supported placement scheme for people with disabilities, known as Interwork, which was pioneered by Remploy Limited.

The occasion was the 50th anniversary of Remploy Limited, which was a government-funded non-departmental body, and at the time I was the company personnel manager of Remploy. Eleanor made a superbly witty, poignant and entirely relevant speech that put all of the more senior official speakers in the shade. I decided to watch her career development with interest.

Sometime in 1996 Eleanor moved from her placement as a trainee solicitor to work for the company training manager who was a colleague of mine. Following the implementation of the Disability Discrimination Act 1995 from 2 December 1996 onward, one of the tasks that Eleanor carried out was to analyse employment tribunal cases that involved disability discrimination issues, and these reports were added to my regular employment law bulletins to personnel managers and to factory managers. In this way Eleanor's name became more established in the company.

I visited Eleanor at her home in Wales to reinforce the relationship that was developing and we got on very well. Clearly this was a key step in that both parties need to be comfortable together and to commit to the mentor/mentee relationship, as emphasized by Clutterbuck (1985, 2004) in his seminal work. The relationship was also 'offline', as identified by Megginson and Clutterbuck (1995), in that there was no direct reporting line, although Eleanor's direct supervisor was on the same status level as myself within the company.

MENTOR'S ACCOUNT

The relationship continued to progress but really took off when I left the company in June 2000 to work as a self-employed HR and employment law consultant and lecturer. I was conscious, in leaving the company, that there was a void in terms of handling employment tribunals and recommended that Eleanor be given the responsibility. The company accepted this proposal and I was asked to continue the mentoring relationship and help Eleanor become confident and competent in handling tribunals, which although she was a qualified solicitor was an area in which she had no experience.

Eleanor took over all tribunal work with a relish but initially I accompanied her to help build confidence and to assist with taking notes. Eleanor is a natural advocate and within one year the company believed she was performing as if she had been in the role for double that time. Consequently, I was able to withdraw from regularly accompanying Eleanor and concentrate on a role of 'sounding board'. According to Clutterbuck (1998: 12), I may have strayed into coaching and occasionally counselling during this process, but Eleanor and I continue to view the role as mentoring.

Initially my greater experience of employment law and my very special interest in the subject was a source of guidance for Eleanor, but gradually she has caught up and overtaken and become highly specialist in disability cases, whilst my employment law experiences are more generalist. I need to keep up to date with the law, and do so by regular sittings as a lay member of tribunals in Sheffield, by training provided by the Employment Tribunals Service and by researching for my lecturing role at university. The research is occasionally prompted by specialist queries from Eleanor, which are always interesting and intellectually challenging, and in this manner the two-way relationship aspect of mentoring (Clutterbuck, 1998) is very beneficial to myself as the mentor.

At this point I think it appropriate to inform the reader that Eleanor has a physical disability, arising out of a cerebral haemorrhage that occurred when she was surfboarding off the coast of France when she was 16. I mention this disability last as, although it impairs her mobility in one leg and one hand, it is not something that is relevant to the relationship, other than that it perhaps has brought out enormous courage and determination in Eleanor's personality. The relationship has been totally about her abilities and how to develop them.

Eleanor left Remploy in March 2004 to work for Capital Law as a solicitor, and whilst she specializes in disability discrimination issues and provides training seminars and lectures on the subject she is now enjoying a broader unfair dismissal remit and the sounding board role continues.

I have been asked why I mentor people and it is a very difficult question to answer. The variable inputs that have influenced my belief in carrying out mentoring are:

1. I was brought up to do unto others as I would be done by. My mother, bless her, thought that this was exclusively Christian, but of course it is not and can be found in most religions and probably was first recorded by Confucius.
2. I have had the benefit of support from several mentors myself during my career and there is a 'giving back' element.
3. All of the professional institutions I have belonged to in my career (the Institute of Industrial Managers, the British Institute of Management, the Chartered Institute of Management, and the Chartered Institute of Personnel and Development) have without exception had a strong focus on developing people.
4. I am naturally an effective teacher and take pleasure in seeing others benefit from my experience and ability to relate that experience to situations they find themselves in.

MENTEE'S ACCOUNT

Keith's role for me is a bit like that of a driving instructor. Initially, there were dual controls, and I was only nominally driving. At that stage, Keith had to rev up my interest in driving, as I had grown disgruntled and apathetic about my career. He had to convince me that I could drive, as I and others had lost sight of my ability within my disability. He had to teach me the Highway Code, as he introduced me to employment law. He had to show me how to use the component elements of the car, as he showed me the tactics of employment tribunals – how silence is the most effective advocacy tool and so on. He had to teach me to navigate, as he counselled me to prepare for cases with a thoroughness that I remember finding alarming initially.

But how did I end up in the car with him in the first place? I was quite a fierce 20-something then. No one could teach me anything. In retrospect, the reason I learned so willingly from Keith is that I could see he was a good driver. Additionally, and importantly, he interested me with his manias for wine, gardening and art. So I, arrogantly, could quite understand how he was interested in me, because it was reciprocal.

Certainly many miles have sped past. We already have nearly 10 years on the clock, as it were. We now drive different cars, but I am very conscious of how I need to communicate with Keith on the hands-free set from within my own vehicle on a regular basis. I am amazed when we talk that he has the same calm, methodical, mirror–signal–manoeuvre approach that he always had. It is important not to be fooled by this as it is this that underpins his roll-with-the-punches, think-on-your-feet, trust-your-instincts approach to litigation, when you need to move up a gear as you cross-examine a tricky witness.

The result of this is that I now drive in Keith's style. If there is a single quality in my driving that is most clearly attributable to Keith, it is a degree of boldness. Keith taught me to have confidence in the car I drive and in my driving abilities. When I am on the skid-pan of a tough tribunal case, it is definitely a Metcalf voice I hear inside my head, saying 'Shy bairns get nowt!' and I zoom ahead.

REFERENCES

Clutterbuck, D (1985) *Everyone Needs a Mentor: How to foster talent within the organization*, Institute of Personnel Management, London

Clutterbuck, D (1998) *Learning Alliances*, IPD, London

Clutterbuck, D (2004) *Everyone Needs a Mentor: How to foster talent within the organization*, 4th edn, CIPD, London

Megginson, D and Clutterbuck, D (1995) *Mentoring in Action*, 1st edn, Kogan Page, London

Part 4

What We Know Now

4

Applying the Lessons

INTRODUCTION

In recent decades, all the authors have been responsible for descriptive models of mentoring. We have attempted to analyse the dynamics of the relationship and synthesize practical processes for managing both relationships and programmes to achieve greater effectiveness. In this short review of our cases, however, we have attempted something different and more phenomenological. Our concern has been to extract themes that allow readers to reflect on mentoring in their own way, providing enough context and comment to stimulate them to enrich their own practice and understanding. It is not surprising, perhaps, that this has some elements of a mentoring approach.

In this edition we have integrated the learnings from the organizational cases with those from the individual cases. Organizational cases were considered in Part 2 of this book and individual cases in Part 3.

THEMES EMERGING FROM THE CASES

Themes about mentees

We noticed the following themes about mentees in analysing our cases:

- the need for an issue;
- the value of a network of mentees;
- the importance of mentee safety;
- the mystery of mentoring moments;
- the issue of identity;
- the challenge of difference;
- the opportunity for fun.

The need for an issue

It was in the case with Kirsten Poulsen's women's scheme in Denmark (Part 2.15) that having to have an issue came to our attention. It clearly helps to have things that you want to talk about, but there is also a risk of pathologizing the mentee if we say to them, 'So, what's your problem?' There is also the experience of many mentees that what they value is the *evolution* of their goals as the relationship evolves, almost more than meeting the initial goals (see, for example, Lis Merrick's account in Part 3.8). This point has clear implications for evaluation. Many evaluations just ask about the scheme goals and the extent to which they are achieved. Even if individual goals are taken into account, it is often only those set at the beginning that are used.

Mentee receptivity is highlighted in the Implats case (Part 2.10). Clearly mentees were very much up for personal development. The questionnaire in this case is a useful tool for scheme organizers, and presents a challenging benchmark for their own scheme.

The value of a network of mentees

Those of us who are mentoring nuts (which includes the authors) can find that our individual focus leads us to neglect the benefits of drawing mentees (and indeed mentors) together to review learning and address blockages. These gatherings are often experienced as rich learning experiences and opportunities for networking. If the scheme has a goal to integrate between parts of the organization (as with UBS, Part 2.18), then the gatherings are doubly valuable.

In Judy Morgan's account of mentoring support for victims of domestic abuse (Part 2.2), she raises interesting, and by no means unambiguous, concerns about who should be helped. It would be useful for many senior executive or high-potentials schemes if similar questions were asked. It often seems that those most able to look after themselves also have the benefit of the greatest attention from developers and the easiest access to mentoring.

Perhaps our hero for maintaining a network is Frank Lord (Part 3.7) who has continued to support ex-employees when they have gone to work elsewhere, and who also offers support to those in organizations in which he no longer works!

The importance of mentee safety

The early cases in Part 2 are concerned with mentees who are likely to be vulnerable. It is in these contexts that issues of mentee safety are likely to arise most sharply. In the East of England e-mentoring project for young people (Part 2.4), Colin Hawkins describes how with e-mailed communications there is software available to ensure that unsuitable language is not used and unsuitable topics are not addressed without the knowledge of the scheme organizer.

Later cases in Part 2 also raise safety issues, however. People, howsoever successful, will not address important issues until they have the conditions present that make it safe to do so. From a range of cases in Parts 2 and 3 we have identified the following conditions as valuable precursors of safe exploration of deep or difficult issues:

- assurance that the mentor is 'for' them;
- conviction that the mentor will not disclose confidential information, except in clearly agreed circumstances;
- feeling of closeness, support or even friendship developing;
- not being interrupted or probed unduly – being allowed to develop their own story;
- being shown that they have been listened to actively and that the mentor has heard and understood their issues in their terms.

Once these conditions prevail then it is possible for the relationship to be stretching and challenging without this stressing the mentee.

The mystery of mentoring moments

When and how do mentees learn what they learn? Sometimes it comes from something the mentee has said – see, for example, Lis Merrick's account (Part 3.8) – but often it is in the gaps between contact when the mentee reflects on the exchange (see, for example, Kate Kennett's account of her e-mentoring relationship in Part 3.5). This is vividly described in Kim Langridge's case (Part 3.6). His mentee, Terry, didn't have goals that were articulated on paper, but he found in the mentoring reflective space that he was with someone who:

- didn't judge him;
- never criticized him;
- didn't belittle him;
- gave him time to think through problems;
- believed in him.

These conditions led to him making all sorts of changes spontaneously in his life.

The issue of identity

Mentoring can be about opening up our identities for review. There is nothing like a fixed identity, a firm sense of self, to get in the way of learning to be different. There is an analogy here with strong organizational cultures. Marks and Spencer, the iconic UK retailer, had all the strengths of a strong culture, but when the going got rough these very strengths made it hard for the organization to adapt.

One of the striking cases in this book of identity is the South African one presented by Hilary Geber (Part 2.8). The strong identities of the white academics who were the mentors presented one challenge for the scheme organizer. However, the huge desire on the part of the young black mentees to become academics like their mentors also ran the risk of their giving away too much of the rest of themselves in this quest.

We are cautious when we hear a mentee saying 'That's the kind of person I am' or 'That's just me'. This is the topic that is up for exploration. What is the 'me' that you want to be?

The challenge of difference

Hilary Geber's case alluded to above is only one of many addressing issues of difference. Bridging it is often a challenge – and it is crucial that the mentee has a sense of fairness in the exchange and that there is nothing that the mentor is doing that is going to exploit or take advantage of him or her. Part 2.9 describes Zulfi Hussain's e-mentoring scheme in BT, and gives an account that points to an overall sense of success in the relationships. There is evidence from elsewhere (Bierema and Merriam, 2002) that suggests that e-relationships have benefits where mentees may be feeling disadvantaged. The lack of indicators of status – skin colour, gender differences, voice, size, tendency to interrupt – are all switched off by the medium. Its very stripped-down quality as a communications channel can be an advantage here.

In Kirsten Poulsen's case (Part 2.15), women mentees valued being mentored by men because it gave them a male perspective in a predominantly male-oriented company. A fuller account of these issues is given in Ragins and Scandura (1994), and the research is brought together comprehensively in Clutterbuck and Ragins (2002).

The opportunity for fun

Throughout the individual case studies there is a sense of the joy that comes from collaborative discovery. Mike Allen and Ray Hinchcliffe (Part 3.1) specifically refer to the fun of their relationship and mentoring dialogue. Humour and creativity are very closely aligned processes – both depend on the unexpected juxtaposition of concepts, visions or language. Consider the following quotation from Arthur Koestler (1970): 'The creative act is not an act of creation in the sense of the Old Testament. It does not create something out of nothing; it uncovers, selects, reshuffles, combines, synthesises already existing facts, ideas, faculties, skills. The more familiar the parts, the more striking the new whole.'

The mentoring dialogue picks apart the elements of the mentee's experience and recombines them in similarly insightful ways. It's not surprising, then, that it typically generates good humour and occasional laughter. Seeing oneself and others in new lights is like walking through the hall of mirrors – the strange delight of the incongruous and sometimes grotesque.

Yet humour is much more than a by-product of mentoring. It is also an essential component. It contributes to the building of rapport – it is hard to trust someone you cannot laugh with. It provides a means of giving critical feedback or coaxing the mentee to discuss issues that are otherwise too painful to address. And it enables the mentoring pair to place issues in a wider context.

Among the ways effective mentors bring laughter into their practice are:

- making it part of the contract or expectations for the relationship;
- sharing humorous things that have happened to them recently, to relax the mentee;
- looking for the lighter side in difficult situations;
- exploring incongruities;
- developing visual images that introduce an element of the ridiculous into situations where the mentee experiences fear or anxiety;
- giving mentees permission to access their inner child when it will help them understand their motivations.

Of course, humour needs to be used with a light touch, to ensure that mentor and mentee really do address the important issues in sufficient depth. Yet getting to that depth may sometimes be difficult or impossible to do without the lubricating influence of humour. Effective mentors need the tools to work within the mentee's humour comfort zone – and that takes sensitivity, flexibility and a willingness to let the mentee lead the dialogue into unknown territory.

Themes about mentors

Moving on to mentors, we found a range of issues concerning them in our cases. Those we selected for analysis were:

- style of the mentor;
- the mentor's role;

- mentor development;
- supervision and reflection;
- accreditation.

Style of the mentor

The distinction that we make between developmental and sponsorship mentoring in Part 1 is used in many of the cases in this book (for example Jill Simpson's case of the Youth Justice Board (Part 2.1) raises the issue of whose agenda is being served). See also Colley (2003) for an insightful analysis of this issue in the case of government-funded schemes. In addition to this important issue in the briefing of mentors, the cases also offer other perspectives. Judy Morgan (Part 2.2), with her vulnerable mentees, suggests that a mentoring style is needed that involves listening without probing. This reflects experience we have had in facilitating mentor development, where too much probing can be experienced as interrogation. When we worked with police service groups we found that the CID officers were adept at this approach, and that it had the downside of not letting the mentees know why the questions were being asked or where the conversation was being taken. For those of us who value putting the mentee in charge of the learning, such a non-sharing approach is to be avoided. Judy Morgan's case, on the other hand, also suggests that mentors can sometimes usefully explain and persuade, when the mentee is immobilized and unable to act. Coral Gardiner (in Part 2.3) offers a generalization of the principle being explored here, when she suggests that mentors' styles need to be as diverse as mentees' needs. She notices, with her target population of school pupil mentees, that the stage of development and age of the pupil affect the style that the mentor can usefully employ. Jonathan Gravells's case of mentoring small business leaders (Part 2.13) concludes that greater reflexivity and awareness on the part of mentors can lead to flexibility in how they conduct their role.

Liz Borredon's analysis of learning teams in a French business school (Part 2.7) emphasizes that we cannot simply influence the mentor's style by a simple administrative act or a short session in a training course. There are some styles that are more difficult to deliver than others (in her words, it is easier to make a plumber than a poet). Mentors need to have a capacity for reflexivity – in other words they need to be able to reflect critically on their own behaviour and intentions and to explore the response of the mentee if they are to be able to operate in what Liz Borredon calls a poetic way.

The mentor's role

Several studies point to the value of voluntarism in involving mentors. Tom Riddell's case from HBOS (Part 2.17) is one of these. He argues that voluntarism allows for committed engagement and that it is likely to improve the quality of the mentoring given. On the other hand, Chris Roebuck in his case of very senior mentoring in UBS (Part 2.18) emphasizes the value of having the whole of one level of the bank's management engaged in mentoring the next level. Even here, however, the case is made for voluntarism as the scheme was rolled out down the organization's hierarchy.

There has been much discussion in the past about the value of mentoring being an offline relationship to avoid the problems of hierarchy and mixed agendas on the part of line manager mentors (Megginson and Clutterbuck, 1995: 14). Additional issues of power and mixed motives can arise even when the mentor is not the line manager. This seems to crop up particularly where the mentor has some responsibility for assessment. Part 2.5, Jonathan Wainwright's case of mentoring probationary teachers, is a case in point. It is hard to be helped by someone who holds in his or her hands the power to exclude you from the profession of your choice. This problem seems to be particularly rife in education. Another case, Wits University in South Africa (Part 2.8), has mentors who also supervise the research of the mentees, and the multiple roles involved seem to us to be in danger of precluding the open agenda and generalized helping that are characteristic of much successful mentoring. When these roles tip over into manipulative credit taking on the part of the mentors, then clearly there is a problem.

One final point, from Part 3.1, is Mike Allen's observation, 'if it isn't working, let it stop'. This is important both from the point of view of the scheme organizer, who needs to set the norm of no-blame separation, and on the part of individual mentors, who need the courage to raise the question of whether the relationship needs to be brought to an end with their mentee.

Mentor development

As suggested in the comments about Liz Borredon's scheme (Part 2.7), mentors need to deepen their own personal development if they are going to be able to serve a range of mentees in a flexible and learner-centred way. Nearly all our cases emphasize the importance of initial training and briefing for mentors. Since our first edition, it has also become much more the norm that mentors are supported in a continuing way once their relationships have begun. This CPD focus on developing mentors (Megginson and Whitaker, 2003) is demonstrated in the three networking days in Poulsen's Danish case (Part 2.15), in the mid-point workshop in Imogen Wareing's Weir Warman case in Australia (Part 2.16) and in the follow-up e-briefing in Ruth Garrett-Harris's SME case (Part 2.12). The only exception to this new norm seems to be John Lambert's warning (Part 2.14) where he suggests that paid external mentors should not be over-briefed, as this could jeopardize their dispassionate focus. Even here, he suggests that scheme organizers and senior management can gain a great deal from having collective feedback from external mentors about the lessons from the relationships for the organization as a whole.

Supervision and reflection

Another new area for standard practice is the increasing interest paid to offering supervision to mentors. This is fast becoming the norm for paid mentors, but even with volunteer mentors who have day jobs in their organization and for whom mentoring is only a small part of what they do it is becoming more widely accepted that some form of supervisory support is helpful. This supervision needs to be light-touch, and is there to help them review their practice. Jonathan Wainwright's case from teaching (Part 2.5) makes a strong argument for the need for feedback to mentors, who may otherwise use models from elsewhere in their professional practice and apply them willy-nilly to mentoring with unhappy results. Lis Merrick and Rachel Tobbell's JIVE case (Part 2.6) is another case that offers supervision through network events like those described in the previous section.

Supervision is part of a wider process of reflection, review and recording. These processes have related purposes but they can be distinguished as follows.

Reflection is crucial for:

- remembering what occurred;
- considering one's own and the mentee's actions and reaction;
- highlighting areas for planning and acting for both mentor and mentee.

Review is about:

- making sense of the meeting when out of the bustle of the session itself;
- planning what to do the next time the pair meet;
- opening oneself up to the views of others (the mentee, supervisors or fellow mentors).

Recording is not so universally practised, but what we have found in the schemes that we have been involved with has been that writing down thoughts about the meetings:

- allows for a deep reflection on the process;
- in itself leads to new insights and choices in a way that simply thinking about the relationship does not;
- provides raw material for supervision and for accreditation.

From our cases, schemes to consider this include Garvey's engineering company (Part 2.11), where the pairs did the reviewing; Lambert's scheme referred to above (Part 2.14), where the company found it useful to have review from external mentors as a group; Poulsen's case (Part 2.15), where preparation and logging were an integral part of the scheme; and Kate Kennett's e-mentoring relationship (Part 3.5), where the record of the e-mail exchange forced her to analyse her process of reflection.

Accreditation

Accreditation is still in the air, but it does not seem to have become pervasive in the way that reading the classic text to advocate this process (Parsloe, 1992) would suggest that it might have done. Parsloe and Wray (2000), more recently, make a more considered case for assessment and accreditation, and the European Mentoring and Coaching Council (www.emccouncil.org) has established a benchmarking process for other organizations' accreditation. Many universities have developed postgraduate qualifications at Master's level or below (early Master's programmes were established at Oxford Brookes University and Sheffield Hallam University).

Some of our cases mention it – notably the e-mentoring programme for the NHS by Colin Hawkins (Part 2.4) – but on the evidence of the 18 cases in Part 2 it still remains a minority sport. Perhaps the conflict between the open-endedness, non-judgement and learner-centredness of developmental mentoring clashes with the culture of pre-specified learning outcomes and pass-and-fail routines of traditional assessment.

Themes for scheme organizers

Our analysis of the organizational cases on mentoring has revealed several issues that resonate with, and add to, those scheme organization issues identified in Part 1 of the book. These include:

- e-mentoring: its challenges and opportunities;
- matching;
- definitions;
- models and guiding frameworks;
- range of offerings;
- coordination and management issues.

E-mentoring: its challenges and opportunities

As our case studies and individual relationships on e-mentoring reveal, this mode of mentoring presents us with several challenges and opportunities.

As Kennett's account (Part 3.5) shows, having the help recorded in e-mails allows learners to follow a train of thought and more easily to notice patterns in their own development. Furthermore, as Hawkins (Part 2.4) suggests, e-mentoring can also allow for greater reflection and learning as it removes the need for an immediate response, unlike in a face-to-face interaction. Both Garrett-Harris (Part 2.12) and Hawkins (Part 2.4) are well rounded in terms of their balanced accounts of challenges as well as the opportunities. Garrett-Harris, in particular, provides a rigorous analysis of the MentorsByNet scheme, comparing convenience and ease of access for participants on the one hand with impersonality of the medium on the other.

Matching

As suggested in Part 1, matching can often be messy and difficult. However, our case studies do offer a range of alternatives to managing this process. In Simpson's scheme (Part 2.1), there was very strong evidence of an audit trail and use of assessment tools throughout the process (the Asset programme), which enable mentees to be tracked as well as matched appropriately. Similarly, Hussain (Part 2.9) is very clear that premature matching on the basis of poor information is not an option for his scheme; the EMN scheme has a clear process that matches people against grade, location, shared interests, career aspiration and development needs. Poulsen's process (Part 2.15) was also quite rigorous in terms of gathering strong data for matching purposes; mentees were interviewed face to face whilst mentors (known to the organizers) were interviewed by telephone.

Paying careful attention to the mix of ethnicity, age and gender of mentors is argued for by Gravells (Part 2.13), as this enhances the quality of the matches that can be set up. This can also be enhanced by offering choice to the mentees; in Wareing's (Part 2.16) scheme, mentees were given the opportunity to meet prospective mentors at a joint workshop and then asked to nominate three choices.

Definitions

There has been much debate in the literature on mentoring about how best to define it, with other types of helping, ie counselling, coaching and advising, being compared and contrasted with it. As we point out (Garvey, 2004; Clutterbuck and Megginson, 2005), this has resulted in some deeply held positions on mentoring (and coaching), which becomes unhelpful when this descends into defending one's territory.

Wainwright's case (Part 2.5) argues for an openness of mentoring definitions. He cautions against rigidity in definitions, as a preoccupation with adhering to a given definition can get in the way of making things happen. This is a useful counterbalance to the importance of defining purpose and ensuring that stakeholders are on board; an over-focus on this can be as damaging as a relative lack of purpose, as it also has the potential to disable a scheme.

Models and guiding frameworks

Another interesting contribution has been the use of a guiding model or framework. Merrick and Tobbell's JIVE case study (Part 2.6) provides a useful example of how this can help orient mentors, mentees and scheme organizers so that all stakeholders have an understanding of the overall process that they are engaged in. This is particularly important when the scheme departs from traditional dyadic mentoring, as in Borredon's case (Part 2.7) – her concept of the learning team appears to have helped orientate the participants in terms of their helping conversations. Furthermore, as both Allen and Hinchcliffe's (Part 3.1) and Kennett's (Part 3.5) cases indicate, academic courses can be useful complements to a mentoring scheme, as they also encourage questioning insight. Academic models can also be used retrospectively to make sense of schemes – a good example of this is Garvey's (Part 3.3) use of mentoring dimensions to make sense of a mentoring scheme.

Range of offerings

Some of the schemes we examined had attempted to develop a range of offerings to address a range of clients' needs. Merrick and Tobbell's (Part 2.6) is a very good example of this, offering five different initiatives across a continuum of mentee motivation and engagement. Similarly, in Gravells' scheme (Part 2.13) mentors were offered a range of interventions, including induction, observation and skills development. Furthermore, in both Lambert's (Part 2.14) and Riddell's (Part 2.17) cases, mentoring appears to have been able to address both personal and business development issues. Nevertheless, it is important to recognize that, sometimes, the burden of too much expectation to achieve too many things can be detrimental to mentoring – Garvey (Part 2.11) provides the cautionary tale of Engineering Co where this was the outcome.

Coordination and management issues

There are several additional factors that seem to influence the success of the schemes we looked at. These include:

- the importance of senior management backing (Roebuck, Part 2.18);
- the importance of managing schemes with a light touch (Riddell, Part 2.17);

▓   ensuring that key learning outcomes and key success factors can be distilled out (Garrett-Harris, Part 2.12);

▓   ensuring the appropriate participant checks are made when working with vulnerable mentees (Hawkins, Part 2.4);

▓   the importance of learning for scheme organizers (Borredon, Part 2.7).

These factors are based on strong arguments from our contributors as to why each of these themes should be designed into all mentoring programmes.

Themes about organizations

We also noticed the following organizational issues from our cases:

▓   scheme funding;
▓   evaluation of scheme benefits;
▓   scheme goals;
▓   organizational culture.

Scheme funding

As pointed out in Part 1, scheme purpose and evaluation are critical issues to consider at the start of the scheme. These issues come to a head when decisions need to be made as to whether to continue a scheme or not. Where the scheme is located within a particular organization, there are issues of culture, power and key stakeholders to consider. These issues are also there for community mentoring and public sector mentoring schemes; Langridge's (Part 3.6) account provides a sharp riposte to those who seek to label community mentoring as 'pink and fluffy' but illustrates well the rounds of justification that such scheme organizers have to go through in order to keep their schemes going. Simpson (Part 2.1) argues that this is compounded by the provisional, fixed-term nature of the funding, which fosters an atmosphere of uncertainty and diminishes the value of such schemes. Geber's story of mentoring within higher education (Part 2.8), which decries the lack of support for mentees and mentors at the beginning of her scheme, lends weight to this argument by highlighting the need to support both mentee and mentor development. Furthermore, Lambert's case (Part 2.14) demonstrates what can happen to developmental programmes in the private sector when resources come under pressure.

Evaluation of scheme benefits

Our work at Sheffield Hallam University (Garvey and Garrett-Harris, 2005) has enabled us to identify a range of benefits that come from scheme evaluations. However, there are some useful additions from the cases in this book.

In his study on Nottinghamshire Business Venture, Gravells (Part 2.13) provides some strong data in terms of positive benefits. However, he raises some useful questions about who benefited, ie the mentees' businesses or the mentees themselves, concluding that it is easier to evidence personal benefits than to isolate organizational ones. Wareing (Part 2.16), too, is careful to cite specific benefits such as being able to enhance communications across functional silos – this was also observed in Riddell's (Part 2.17) case at HBOS.

Of course, it is important to celebrate successes and to acknowledge where schemes have worked well – Hussain's (Part 2.9) and Lambert's cases (Part 2.14) do this well and do not seem to report any particular problems or difficulties with the mentoring itself. Furthermore, this is helpful in terms of recruitment and selection of mentors (see Wareing, Part 2.16). However, as Geber (Part 2.8), Garrett-Harris (Part 2.12) and Garvey (Part 2.11), in particular, suggest, it is important to identify and learn from difficulties in order to move closer towards satisfying the needs of the scheme.

Scheme goals

In Part 1, we paid attention to the importance of being clear about scheme purpose and goals. This was also addressed in the section above on scheme funding. In addition to these points, we noticed the following points emerging.

Several of the community-based mentoring schemes referred to, eg Langridge (Part 3.6), Simpson (Part 2.1) and Morgan (Part 2.2), place emphasis on empathizing with the mentee in order to make successful interventions. However, as Colley's (2003) work on community mentoring shows, what mentees want from a scheme is not always easily predicted. Her work shows that it can be easy for scheme organizers (or indeed mentors) within community-based organizations to make assumptions about what mentees want, forgetting that mentees can make their own minds up and can steer a relationship on a different course! This idea of participant agency also applies to other schemes. For example, Garvey's case (Part 2.11) shows how participants can use (and abuse) helping schemes for other purposes. In the education sector, Wainwright (Part 2.5) points out that the need for student teacher mentees to focus on classroom performance can sometimes crowd out the possibility of discussing the student's long-term development goals.

Nevertheless, as pointed out in Part 1, there is still some merit in having a clear statement of goals and intent. Gardiner's (Part 2.3) case contains a clear statement regarding the need for learning mentors, which appears to have contributed to some of the successful outcomes identified in that scheme. This also appeared to be true in the Beck and Van Wyk (Part 2.10) case.

Organizational culture

One of the most striking themes that emerges from all the case studies and contributions is the diversity of organizational cultures of the schemes and relationships. In some organizations, eg HBOS (Riddell, Part 2.17), the culture of the organization seems supportive to the notion of mentoring. However, in others, eg Engineering Co (Garvey, Part 2.11), the odds seem against it. Putting this diversity aside, our contributions have some interesting things in common, which can be best explained by drawing upon a cultural analysis framework.

The well-known cultural researcher Joanne Martin puts forward an interesting framework for analysing organizational culture (Martin, 2002). She argues that culture is mainly written about from one of three perspectives:

- *integration* – emphasis on consensus, consistency and seeing ambiguity as dysfunctional;
- *differentiation* – emphasis on consensus within distinct groups (eg mentors), and differences in understanding, inconsistency and conflict between groups addressed;
- *fragmentation* – emphasis on acknowledging ambiguity, and acknowledgement where there is a lack of consistency and consensus.

The sense we have from our cases is that there is significant emphasis on talking about *the* organization and *the* culture within it. Most cases seem to emphasize the importance of clarity and consistency around scheme objectives (which indeed we have argued for in Part 1). However, this can be disadvantageous as it can encourage a focus on what is agreed *at the expense of* what is disagreed about. As disagreements about scheme purpose, evaluation and so on have the potential to disrupt scheme effectiveness, it is important to be able to understand and acknowledge where those differences come from. That said, some of our contributors do acknowledge difficulties in terms of scheme organization and funding and acknowledge the voices of different stakeholders. However, relatively few explore the ambiguity around identities of those within subgroups; for example, there is relatively little discussion in the cases about overlaps between people who are, at different times, scheme sponsor, mentor, mentee and scheme evaluator!

THE FUTURE OF MENTORING

Fuzzy clarity

Fuzzy clarity may seem to be a contradiction in terms, but it is the best phrase we can come up with (so far) to describe where the debate on *what is mentoring?* is taking us. The past decade and more have seen a transition from a US-centric assumption that everyone knows what mentoring is and what mentors do, to a battle of ideologies and cultures, as different groups from different cultures and disciplines attempt to impose their particular interpretation. Some of us have fuelled this ideological entrenchment by attempting to clarify the distinction between sponsorship mentoring (with its emphasis on power, influence and direct intervention by the mentor in the career of the mentee) and developmental mentoring (with its emphasis on personal development and collaborative enquiry as a route to empowering people to achieve their own career and other goals). At the same time, those adopting a developmental mentoring approach have also expended energy keeping at bay the upstart marauders from the world of developmental coaching.

A much more pragmatic and intellectually challenging dialogue is now emerging, in which the diversity of mentoring and coaching is being embraced as a rich source of knowledge transfer and flexibility. Effective coaches require an eclectic *mélange* of skills drawn from a range of disciplines – strategy, governance, managing, coaching, networking, counselling, psychology, philosophy – and the ability to reflect upon and learn from personal experience, to name but some. Exactly what the mix should look like depends on the circumstances – who the mentoring pair are, what the purpose of the relationship is, the degree and type of change that is intended, the depth of personal insight required and so on.

In other words, our definition of mentoring and its competences is becoming increasingly contextual. Yes, there are common themes. The role is typically seen as holistic, complex, self-aware and charismatic (in the true sense of demonstrating that you care) – but not always! In the future, a great deal of value will, we hope, be extracted by examining the dynamics and influence of approaches used in one context to determine how they might be adapted to others. For example, we have recently had lengthy debates with groups of mentors and mentees in a diversity mentoring programme about the legitimacy of a mentor (or mentee) initiating discussion about a potentially sensitive difference in the other person – for example, an obvious disability or being from a minority ethnic community. Views differed quite vehemently, with people taking one view or another based on personal experience and on discipline. A consensus has gradually emerged that the mentor needs *empathetic curiosity* – the ability to demonstrate interest in the other as a person, while being sensitive to his or her concerns and emotions. No doubt empathetic curiosity will make an appearance in the next edition of *Techniques for Coaching and Mentoring*!

Mentoring and the implications of dialogue

In the completion of a literature review (Garvey and Garrett-Harris, 2005) on mentoring covering an extensive range of both academic and business sources, there seemed to be something missing. There seemed to be a huge opportunity for researchers and practitioners alike to investigate the relationship between mentoring, conversational learning and the importance of dialogue.

We take the following three suppositions to be true:

1. As Boyatzis *et al* (1995) argue, learning requires change but change does not always imply learning. It would be difficult to conceive of learning that does not result in a change of attitude, perspective, motivation or approach to the next situation.
2. As Argyris (1993) suggests, learning is not simply having a new insight or a new idea. Learning occurs when we take effective action, when we detect and correct error and when we can produce what it is we claim to know.
3. As Raelin (2000) contends, learning dialogues are concerned with the surfacing, in the safe presence of trusting peers, of those social, political and emotional reactions that might be blocking operating effectiveness.

If these suggestions have substance, then when looking at what makes mentoring effective we need to explore mentees' journeys from where they are now to where they want to be. To do this we need to investigate how the conversational dialogue between mentor and mentee (and each party's internal dialogue) assists or inhibits the transformative learning process. The European Mentoring and Coaching Council research into mentoring moments, outlined in Part 1, is pursuing this agenda.

Critical analysis

One of the most striking aspects of the contributing case studies was the relative lack of focus on problems, tensions and ambiguities. Perhaps this is understandable in a book that is, in a sense, a celebration of mentoring in action. However, we feel it is important that, in the future, it is possible to talk about mentoring, 'warts and all', so that additional learning and insights might be generated.

Supervision

Supervision is a dominant issue in the mentoring literature at the moment. However, there is relatively little discussion about supervision practice in our contributions, whereas issues such as matching and mentoring skills development were very prominent. As accreditation and professionalization of mentoring continue at a swift pace, we hope to see supervision practices embedded in most mentoring schemes and relationships.

Development networks

More and more, the boundaries between what is called 'mentoring' and what is called 'coaching' are blurring. Perhaps it is more helpful to follow the lead of our US colleague Kathy Kram, who at last year's European Mentoring and Coaching Conference preferred to speak about developmental relationships and networks, rather than getting caught up in debates about definitions.

E-mentoring

E-mentoring now stands in its own right as a different kind of development process from face-to-face mentoring. We envisage that this trend will continue and more schemes will use it, not as a poor relation, but for its advantages:

- time and space independent;
- offering time for reflection;
- removing symbols of domination that get in the way of diversity mentoring;
- retaining a permanent record for subsequent analysis.

Attention on mentoring culture

Mentoring, for the last 15 years, has tended to be locked into a mentality of focusing on the scheme itself. So the key stakeholder has been the scheme organizer. We see this as changing in the future to a wider attention on making a mentoring culture throughout the organization. This will mean that new stakeholders will become crucially engaged in the process – particularly senior management and others concerned about the organization's change agenda. Mentoring will not be seen as just another HR development intervention, but rather as a core contributor to business issues and to managing the process of change.

REFERENCES

Argyris, C (1993) *Knowledge for Action: A guide to overcoming barriers to organizational change*, Jossey-Bass, San Francisco, CA

Bierema, L and Merriam, S (2002) E-mentoring: using computer mediated communication to enhance the mentoring process, *Innovative Higher Education*, **26** (3), pp 211–24

Boyatzis, RE *et al* (1995) *Innovations in Professional Education: Steps in a journey from teaching to learning*, Jossey-Bass, San Francisco, CA

Clutterbuck, D and Megginson, D (2005) *Making Coaching Work: Creating a coaching culture*, CIPD, London

Clutterbuck, D and Ragins, BR (2002) *Mentoring and Diversity: An international perspective*, Butterworth-Heinemann, Oxford

Colley, H (2003) *Mentoring for Social Inclusion: A critical approach to nurturing mentor relationships*, RoutledgeFalmer, London

Garvey, B (2004) Call a rose by any other name and it might be a bramble, *Development and Learning in Organizations*, **18** (2), pp 6–8

Garvey, B and Garrett-Harris, R (2005) *The Benefits of Mentoring: A literature review*, Report for East Mentors Forum, Mentoring and Coaching Research Unit, Sheffield Hallam University, Sheffield

Koestler, A (1970) *The Act of Creation*, Pan, London

Martin, J (2002) *Organizational Culture: Mapping the terrain*, Sage, London

Megginson, D and Clutterbuck, D (1995) *Mentoring in Action*, 1st edn, Kogan Page, London

Megginson, D and Whitaker, V (2003) *Continuous Professional Development*, CIPD, London

Parsloe, E (1992) *Coaching, Mentoring and Assessing*, Kogan Page, London

Parsloe, E and Wray, M (2000) *Coaching and Mentoring: Practical methods to improve learning*, Kogan Page, London

Raelin, J (2000) *Work Based Learning: The new frontiers of management development*, Prentice Hall, New Jersey

Ragins, BR and Scandura, TA (1994) Gender differences in expected outcomes of mentoring relationships, *Academy of Management Journal*, **37** (4), pp 957–71

References

Adair, J (1983) *Effective Leadership*, Pan, London

Alred, G and Garvey, B (2000) Learning to produce knowledge: the contribution of mentoring, *Mentoring and Tutoring*, **8** (3), pp 261–72

Alred, G, Garvey, B and Smith, R (1998) *The Mentoring Pocket Book*, Management Pocket Books, Alresford, Hampshire

Argyris, C (1993) *Knowledge for Action: A guide to overcoming barriers to organizational change*, Jossey-Bass, San Francisco, CA

Baker, A, Jensen, PJ and Kolb, DA (2002) *Conversational Learning: An experiential approach to knowledge creation*, Greenwood, Westport, CT

Barrett, R (2002) Mentor supervision and development: exploration of lived experience, *Career Development International*, **7** (5), pp 279–83

Benioff, S (1997) *A Second Chance*, Belmont Press, London

Bianco, RS and Bianco, J (2002) *Small Business Scoping Study: E-mentoring for SMEs*, South East England Development Agency, Guildford

Bierema, L and Merriam, S (2002) E-mentoring: using computer mediated communication to enhance the mentoring process, *Innovative Higher Education*, **26** (3), pp 211–24

Boyatzis, RE *et al* (1995) *Innovation in Professional Education*, Jossey-Bass, San Francisco, CA

Bruner, J (1990) *Acts of Meaning*, Harvard University Press, Boston, MA

Bullis, C and Bach, BW (1989) Are mentoring relationships helping organizations? An exploration of developing mentee–mentor–organizational identification using turning point analysis, *Communication Quarterly*, **37**, pp 199–213

Clutterbuck, D (1985) *Everyone Needs a Mentor: How to foster talent within the organization*, Institute of Personnel Management, London

Clutterbuck, D (1992) *Everyone Needs a Mentor: How to foster talent within the organization*, 2nd edn, Institute of Personnel Management, London

Clutterbuck, D (1998) *Learning Alliances*, IPD, London

Clutterbuck, D (2004) *Everyone Needs a Mentor*, 4th edn, CIPD, London

Clutterbuck, D and Lane, G (eds) (2004) *The Situational Mentor: An international review of competences and capabilities in mentoring*, Gower, Aldershot

Clutterbuck, D and Megginson, D (1999) *Mentoring Executives and Directors*, Butterworth-Heinemann, Oxford

Clutterbuck, D and Megginson, D (2001) Winding up or winding down? Proceedings of the 8th European Mentoring Centre Conference, Cambridge (UK), November

Clutterbuck, D and Megginson, D (2004) All good things must come to an end: winding up and winding down a mentoring relationship, Chapter 15 in *The Situational Mentor: An international review of competences and capabilities in mentoring*, ed D Clutterbuck and G Lane, pp 178–93, Gower, Aldershot

Clutterbuck, D and Megginson, D (2005) *Making Coaching Work: Creating a coaching culture*, CIPD, London

Clutterbuck, D and Ragins, BR (2002) *Mentoring and Diversity: An international perspective*, Butterworth–Heinemann, Oxford

Colley, H (2003) *Mentoring for Social Inclusion: A critical approach to nurturing mentor relationships*, RoutledgeFalmer, London

DfEE (1997) *Excellence in Schools*, White Paper, DfEE, London

DfEE (1998) *The Learning Age*, Green Paper, DfEE, London

DfEE (1999) *Learning to Succeed*, White Paper, DfEE, London

DFEE (1999) *Planning Guidance for LEAs on Learning Mentors*, CircularEiC (G) 0/99–8/99, DfEE, London

Egan, G (1993) *Adding Value: A systematic guide to business-driven management and leadership*, Jossey-Bass, San Francisco, CA

Egan, G (1994) *The Skilled Helper: A problem management approach to helping*, Brooks & Cole, Pacific Grove, CA

Emler, N and Heather, N (1980) Intelligence: an ideological bias of conventional psychology, in *Coming to Know*, ed P Salmon, Routledge and Kegan Paul, London

Engstrom, T (1997) Personality factors' impact on success in the mentor–protégé relationship, MSc thesis to Norwegian School of Hotel Management

Erikson, E (1995) *Childhood and Society*, Vintage, WW Norton, Reading, first published by Imago Publishing in 1951

Fagenson-Eland, E and Yan Lu, R (2004) Virtual mentoring, Chapter 13 in *The Situational Mentor: An international review of competencies and capabilities in mentoring*, ed D Clutterbuck and G Lane, Gower, Aldershot

Furlong, J and Maynard, T (1995) *Mentoring Student Teachers*, Routledge, London

Gardiner, C (1998) Mentoring: towards a professional friendship, *Mentoring and Tutoring Journal*, **6** (1/2), Summer, Trentham Books, Stoke-on-Trent

Gardiner, C (1999) Community justice mentoring: a congruent mentoring network, Unpublished, Presented to the 6th European Mentoring Conference, Robinson College, Cambridge

Garvey, B (1994) Ancient Greece, MBAs, the Health Service and Georg, *Education and Training*, **36** (2)

Garvey, B (1994) A dose of mentoring, *Education and Training*, **36** (4), pp 18–26

Garvey, B (1995) Healthy signs for mentoring, *Education and Training*, **37** (5), pp 12–19

Garvey, B (1999) Mentoring and the changing paradigm, *Mentoring and Tutoring*, **7** (1), pp 41–54

Garvey, B (2004) Call a rose by any other name and it might be a bramble, *Development and Learning in Organizations*, **18** (2), pp 6–8

Garvey, B and Alred, G (2000) Developing mentors, *Career Development International*, 5 (4/5), pp 216–22

Garvey, B and Alred, G (2001) Mentoring and the tolerance of complexity, *Futures*, **33**, pp 519–30

Garvey, B and Galloway, K (2002) Mentoring at the Halifax plc (HBOS): a small beginning in a large organisation, *Career Development International*, **7** (5), pp 271–78

Garvey, B and Garrett-Harris, R (2005) *The Benefits of Mentoring: A literature review*, Report for East Mentors Forum, Mentoring and Coaching Research Unit, Sheffield Hallam University, Sheffield

Garvey, B and Williamson, B (2002) *Beyond Knowledge Management: Dialogue, creativity and the corporate curriculum*, Pearson Education, Harlow

Gibb, S and Megginson, D (1993) Inside corporate mentoring schemes: a new agenda of concerns, *Personnel Review*, **22** (1), pp 40–54

Gladstone, MS (1988) Mentoring: a strategy for learning in a rapidly changing society, *Research Document CEGEP*, John Abbott College, Quebec

Goleman, D (1995) *Emotional Intelligence: Why it can matter more than IQ*, Bantam, New York

Habermas, J (1979) *Communication and the Evolution of Society*, trans T McCarthy, Heinemann, London

Hale, R (2000) To match or mismatch? The dynamics of mentoring as a route to personal and organisational learning, *Career Development International*, **5** (4/5), pp 223–34

Hansford, B, Tennent, L and Ehrich, LC (2002) Business mentoring: help or hindrance?, *Mentoring and Tutoring*, **10** (2), pp 101–15

Hawkins, P and Shohet, R (2002) *Supervision in the Helping Professions*, Open University Press, Buckingham

Honey, P and Mumford, A (1986) *The Manual of Learning Styles*, 2nd edn, Peter Honey, Maidenhead

Inglis, S (1994) *Making the Most of Action Learning*, Gower, Aldershot

Isaacs, W (1999) *Dialogue and the Art of Thinking Together*, Doubleday, New York

Jekielek, M *et al* (eds) (2002) *Child Trends, Research Brief*, Washington, DC, http://wwwchildtrends.org

Kessels, J (1996) *The Corporate Curriculum*, Inaugural lecture, Leiden University, Netherlands

Koestler, A (1970) *The Act of Creation*, Pan, London

Kolb, D (1984) *Experiential Learning: Experiencing as the source of learning and development*, Prentice Hall, New Jersey

Kram, KE (1985) Improving the mentoring process, *Training and Development Journal*, April, pp 40–42

Kram, KE (1985) *Mentoring at Work: Developmental relationships in organisational life*, Scott, Foresman, Glenview, IL

Lave, J and Wenger, E (1991) *Situated Learning: Legitimate peripheral participation*, Cambridge University Press, Cambridge

Lee, G (2003) *Leadership Coaching: From personal insight to organisational performance*, CIPD, London

Levinson, DL (1979) *The Seasons of a Man's Life*, Alfred A Knopf, New York

Long, J (1997) The dark side of mentoring, *Australian Educational Research*, **24** (2), pp 115–23

March, JG and Weil, T (2003) *Le Leadership dans les Organisations* (Un cours de James March, rédigé et annoté par T Weil), Les Presses de l'École des Mines, Paris

Martin, J (2002) *Organizational Culture: Mapping the terrain*, Sage, London

Megginson, D and Clutterbuck, D (1995) *Mentoring in Action*, 1st edn, Kogan Page, London

Megginson, D and Clutterbuck, D (2005) *Techniques for Coaching and Mentoring*, Elsevier Butterworth-Heinemann, Oxford

Megginson, D and Garvey, B (2004) Odysseus, Telemachus and Mentor: stumbling into, searching for and signposting the road to desire, *International Journal of Mentoring and Coaching*, **2** (1) (online journal, www.emccouncil.org)

Megginson, D and Stokes, P (2000) Mentoring for export success, 7th European Mentoring Conference, Sheffield Hallam University, Sheffield

Megginson, D and Stokes, P (2004) Development and supervision for mentors, Chapter 8 in *The Situational Mentor: An international review of competences and capabilities in mentoring*, ed D Clutterbuck and G Lane, pp 94–107, Gower, Aldershot

Megginson, D and Whitaker, V (2003) *Continuous Professional Development*, CIPD, London

Merrick, L and Stokes, P (2003) Mentor development and supervision: a passionate joint enquiry, *International Journal of Mentoring and Coaching*, **1** (1) (electronic journal of the European Mentoring and Coaching Council, www.emccouncil.org)

Neilson, T and Eisenbach, R (2003) Not all relationships are created equal: critical factors of high-quality mentoring relationships, *International Journal of Mentoring and Coaching*, **1** (1) (electronic journal of the European Mentoring and Coaching Council, www.emccouncil.org)

Ofsted (2003) *Excellence in Cities and Education Action Zones: Management and impact*, Ofsted, London

Parsloe, E (1992) *Coaching, Mentoring and Assessing*, Kogan Page, London

Parsloe, E and Wray, M (2000) *Coaching and Mentoring: Practical methods to improve learning*, Kogan Page, London

Raelin, J (2000) *Work Based Learning: The new frontiers of management development*, Prentice Hall, New Jersey

Ragins, BR and Scandura, TA (1994) Gender differences in expected outcomes of mentoring relationships, *Academy of Management Journal*, **37** (4), pp 957–71

Ragins, BR, Cotton, JL and Miller, JS (2000) Marginal mentoring: the effects of type of mentor, quality of relationship and program design on work and career attitudes, *Academy of Management Journal*, **43** (6), pp 1117–94

Realm Magazine (2002) Realm mentorship: electronic mentoring, http://realm.net/mentor/howment/ement.html

Rosinski, P (2003) *Coaching across Cultures: New tools for leveraging national, corporate and professional differences*, Nicholas Brealey, London

Rushdie, S (1998) in B Williamson, *Lifeworlds and Learning: Essays in the theory, philosophy and practice of lifelong learning*, National Institute of Adult and Continuing Education (NIACE), Leicester

Scandura, TA et al (1996) Perspectives on mentoring, *Leadership and Organization Development Journal*, **17** (3), pp 50–56

SEEDA Fund (2002) *Management Development Proposal*, Business Link, Surrey

Sheehy, G (1974) *Passages: Predictable crises of adult life*, Dutton, New York

Shiner, M et al (2004) *Mentoring Disaffected Young People: An evaluation of 'Mentoring Plus'*, Joseph Rowntree Foundation, York

Single, PG and Muller, CB (1999) *Electronic Mentoring: Issues to advance research and practice*

Tierney, JP and Grossman, JB with Resch, NL (1995) *Making a Difference: An impact study of big brothers/big sisters*, Public/Private Ventures, Philadelphia, PA

Whitmore, J (2003) *Coaching for Performance: GROWing people, performance and purpose*, 3rd edn, Nicholas Brealey, London

Wilson, JA and Elman, NS (1990) Organisational benefits of mentoring, *Academy of Management Executive*, **4** (4), pp 88–94

Zachery, L (2000) *The Mentor's Guide*, Jossey-Bass, San Francisco, CA

Index

(*Italics* indicate figures or tables in the text)

Further reading
from Kogan Page

Coaching and Mentoring: Practical Methods to Improve Learning, Eric Parsloe, 2000

Coaching for Change: Practical Strategies for Transforming Performance, Kaye Thorne, 2004

The Coaching Handbook: An Action Kit for Trainers and Managers, Sara Thorpe, 2003

Coaching Made Easy: Step-by-step Techniques That Get Results, Mike Leibling, 2003

Facilitation Made Easy: Practical Tips to Improve Meetings and Workshops, 3rd edn, Esther Cameron, 2005

Performance Management: Key Strategies and Practical Guidelines, 3rd edn, Michael Armstrong, 2005

Practical Facilitation: A Toolkit of Techniques, Christine Frances Hogan, 2003

Tales for Coaching: Using Stories and Metaphors with Individuals and Small Groups, Margaret Parkin, 2001

Understanding Facilitation: Theory and Principle, Christine Frances Hogan, 2002

The above titles are available from all good bookshops or direct from the publishers. To obtain more information, please contact the publisher at the address below:

Kogan Page
120 Pentonville Road
London N1 9JN
Tel: 020 7278 0433
Fax: 020 7837 6348

www.kogan-page.co.uk

ALSO AVAILABLE FROM KOGAN PAGE

0 7494 4293 X   Hardback   2005

Kogan Page is Europe's largest independent publisher of business books

For further information, and to order, visit our website

www.kogan-page.co.uk

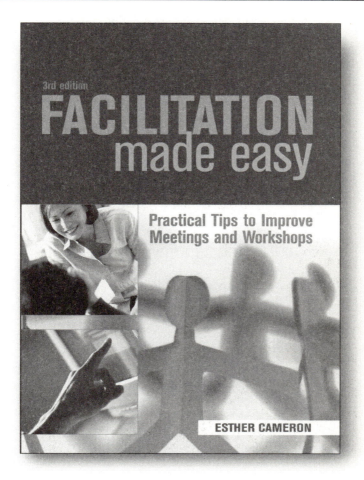